Children in Culture, Revisited

Also by Karín Lesnik-Oberstein

CHILDREN IN CULTURE: Approaches to Childhood (*editor*)

'CHILDREN IN LITERATURE', Volume 32 of the *Yearbook of English Studies* (*editor*)

CHILDREN'S LITERATURE: Criticism and the Fictional Child

CHILDREN'S LITERATURE: New Approaches (*editor*)

THE LAST TABOO: Women and Body Hair (*editor*)

ON HAVING AN OWN CHILD: Reproductive Technologies and the Cultural Construction of Childhood

Children in Culture, Revisited

Further Approaches to Childhood

Edited by

Karín Lesnik-Oberstein

palgrave
macmillan

First published 2011 by
PALGRAVE MACMILLAN

Palgrave Macmillan in the UK is an imprint of Macmillan Publishers Limited,
registered in England, company number 785998, of Houndmills, Basingstoke,
Hampshire RG21 6XS.

Palgrave Macmillan in the US is a division of St Martin's Press LLC,
175 Fifth Avenue, New York, NY 10010.

Palgrave Macmillan is the global academic imprint of the above companies
and has companies and representatives throughout the world.

Palgrave® and Macmillan® are registered trademarks in the United States,
the United Kingdom, Europe and other countries.

ISBN: 978–0–230–27554–6

This book is printed on paper suitable for recycling and made from fully
managed and sustained forest sources. Logging, pulping and manufacturing
processes are expected to conform to the environmental regulations of the
country of origin.

A catalogue record for this book is available from the British Library.

Library of Congress Cataloging-in-Publication Data

Children in culture, revisited : further approaches to childhood /
edited by Karín Lesnik-Oberstein.
    p. cm.
Includes index.
ISBN 978–0–230–27554–6 (hardback)
    1. Children in literature. 2. Identity (Psychology) in children.
I. Lesnik-Oberstein, Karín.

PN56.5.C48C48 2011
305.23—dc22   2011012057

10 9 8 7 6 5 4 3 2 1
20 19 18 17 16 15 14 13 12 11

Printed and bound in Great Britain by
CPI Antony Rowe, Chippenham and Eastbourne

Contents

Illustrations

Acknowledgements

This volume owes a great deal to the invaluable support of Paula Kennedy at Palgrave Macmillan and the kind and efficient help of Ben Doyle, also at the publishers. The contributors to this book have been fantastic. I cannot thank them enough for their hard work, generosity and deep engagement. Special thanks are due to Simon Flynn and Sarah Spooner for their crucial help in the final stages. My colleagues, friends and students at the Graduate Centre for International Research in Childhood: Literature, Culture, Media (CIRCL) both within and outside the University of Reading are always at the heart of my work on childhood. Above all, no one could wish for better friends or more inspiring and supportive colleagues than Sue Walsh and Neil Cocks. Love, always, to all my wonderful friends and family, and love and thanks every day to my partner, Hoyte. This book is dedicated with great love to my nephews and niece: Zev, Ayal, Elah and Avi.

KARÍN LESNIK-OBERSTEIN

Contributors

Helen Ainslie heads her own dance school in Reading. She completed her PhD in 2009 at the University of Reading on constructions of autism, titled 'Why Autism? Perspectives, Communication, Community'. Helen has a continuing interest in constructions of 'the autistic' as an identity, particularly in relation to 'the child', and is currently working on issues relating to autobiography and autism.

Hannah Anglin-Jaffe is Lecturer in Special Educational Needs at the University of Exeter. Previously, she lectured at the University of Plymouth after completing her doctorate on constructions of D/deafness, orality and sign. Hannah's main areas of research and teaching are disability studies and inclusive education. She also has an interest in cultural approaches to difference and diversity in the study of childhood. She has published on the relationship between deaf culture and inclusive education and is currently completing a book exploring attitudes to sign language and D/deafness.

Jenny Bavidge is Senior Lecturer in English at the University of Greenwich. She has written on the representation of children in urban spaces, urban ecocriticism and the role of London in children's literature. She is the author of *Theorists of the City: Lefebvre, De Certeau and Benjamin* (2011) and co-edited (with Robert Bond) *City Visions: The Work of Iain Sinclair* (2007).

Jonathan Bignell is Professor of Television and Film at the University of Reading and a member of the board of the Graduate Centre for International Research in Childhood: Literature, Culture, Media (CIRCL). His books include *Beckett on Screen* (2009), *Postmodern Media Culture* (2000) and his co-edited collections includes *A European Television History* (2008), *Popular Television Drama: Critical Perspectives* (2005) and *British Television Drama: Past, Present and Future* (2000). His work on children's television and toys includes articles on *Doctor Who*, Action Man and the *Teletubbies*.

Erica Burman is Professor of Psychology and Women's Studies at Manchester Metropolitan University. Her work addresses intersections between gender, culture and models of subjectivity, including attending to the role of representations of childhood and memory within these. Her most recent books include *Deconstructing Developmental Psychology* (2nd edition, 2008) and *Developments: Child, Image, Nation* (2008), and she is co-editor of *Gender and Migration* (2010) and of the special issue of *Feminist Theory* on 'Feminisms and Childhood' (2010). She is also a group analyst.

Neil Cocks is Lecturer in English, American and Children's Literature at the University of Reading. His publications on childhood include his monograph *Student Centred: Education, Freedom and the Idea of Audience* (2009) and articles and chapters on childhood, reading, sexuality and death.

Eleanor Conlin Casella is Senior Lecturer in Archaeology at the University of Manchester. She has directed fieldwork projects in the UK, Australia and North America. Her recent books include *The Alderley Sandhills Project: An Archaeology of Community Life in (Post-)Industrial England* (2010) and *The Archaeology of Institutional Confinement* (2007). She is a co-editor of *The Archaeology of Plural and Changing Identities* (2005) and *Industrial Archaeology: Future Directions* (2005). Her current work focuses on the materiality of gender, sexuality and childhood, household archaeology, incarceration and places of confinement, and British colonialism.

Simon Flynn is training as a child and adolescent psychotherapist at the Tavistock Clinic and working clinically in the NHS. Before this, he completed a doctorate on contemporary fiction and children's literature at Cardiff University and was a lecturer in English and children's literature at several universities. Simon has published a series of articles on the BBC *Children's Hour* broadcasts, in particular looking at the programme's construction of evacuees and evacuation during the Second World War and the celebrated adaptations of John Masefield's novel *The Box of Delights*. He is interested in the way Kleinian and post-Kleinian psychotherapeutic writings use literary texts and also in the relationships between psychoanalysis and science fiction.

Karín Lesnik-Oberstein is Reader in Critical Theory at the University of Reading and the director of the Graduate Centre for International Research in Childhood: Literature, Culture, Media (CIRCL). Her research engages with transdisciplinary critical theory, particularly as it relates to issues of identity. Karín's publications on childhood include the monographs *Children's Literature: Criticism and the Fictional Child* (1994) and *On Having an Own Child: Reproductive Technologies and the Cultural*

Construction of Childhood (2008); the edited volumes *Children in Culture: Approaches to Childhood* (1998), 'Children in Literature' (a special issue of the *Yearbook of English Studies*, 2002) and *Children's Literature: New Approaches* (2004); and numerous chapters and articles.

Daniel Monk is Senior Lecturer in Law at Birkbeck College, University of London. His research engages critically with a wide range of issues relating to children's rights and attempts to create a dialogue between child law and the sociology of childhood. His publications include *The Family, Law and Society* (co-author, 2009), '(Re)constructing the Head Teacher: Legal Narratives and the Politics of School Exclusions' (*Journal of Law and Society*, 2005), 'Children's Rights in Education: Making Sense of Contradictions' (*Child and Family Law Quarterly*, 2002), 'Theorizing Education Law and Childhood: Constructing the Ideal Pupil' (*British Journal of Sociology of Education*, 2000), *Feminist Perspectives on Child Law* (co-editor, 2000), and *Legal Queeries* (co-author, 1998).

Sarah Spooner works in legal publishing. In 2006 she completed her PhD, titled 'Knowing Its Place? Language and Landscape in Arthur Ransome', and she has published on ideas of the 'exotic' and 'foreign' in children's literature. Sarah continues to be interested in theoretical issues concerning landscape, heritage, mapping and childhood.

Sue Walsh is Lecturer in English, American and Children's Literature at the University of Reading. Her publications in the field include her monograph *Kipling's Children's Literature: Language, Identity and Constructions of Childhood* (2010) and chapters and articles on constructions of the animal and the child, irony and childhood, the Gothic and the child, and childhood, children's literature and (auto)biography. Sue is pursuing research into childhood and irony.

Introduction: Voice, Agency and the Child

Karín Lesnik-Oberstein

Over ten years ago, the first volume of *Children in Culture: Approaches to Childhood* appeared.[1] It was one of the first,[2] and remains to date the most multi- and interdisciplinary volume on childhood to be published, engaging with constructivist approaches to childhood[3] across a range of disciplines, from psychology to film studies, from literature to history. All the chapters in the book took as their starting point the idea that childhood (but also any identity) is a historically and culturally contingent construction, not an essential, transhistorical or transcultural continuity, predetermined by inherent biological or physiological factors. As discussed in the introduction to *Children in Culture*,[4] the approach that definitions and perceptions of childhood change through time and from place to place, and within times and places, has been widely attributed to the French historian Philippe Ariès's famous, and still controversial, book *Centuries of Childhood: A Social History of Family Life*, where Ariès famously argued that:

> But have we any right to talk of a history of the family? Is the family a phenomenon any more subject to history than instinct is? It is possible to argue that it is not, and to maintain that the family partakes of the immobility of the species. It is no doubt true that since the beginning of the human race men have built homes and begot children, and it can be argued that within the great family types, monogamous and polygamous, historical differences are of little importance in comparison with the huge mass of what remains unchanged. On the other hand, the great demographic revolution in the West, from the eighteenth to the twentieth century, has revealed to us considerable possibilities of change in structures hitherto believed to be invariable because they were biological. ... I accordingly looked back

1

into our past, to find out whether the idea of the family had not been born comparatively recently, at a time when the family had freed itself from both biology and law to become a value, a theme of expression, an occasion of emotion.[5]

Children in Culture drew on elaborations of this idea in critical psychology, in the work of Valerie Walkerdine,[6] Rex and Wendy Stainton Rogers,[7] and Erica Burman,[8] and in cultural studies and literary and critical theory, in the work of Jacqueline Rose,[9] James Kincaid[10] and Carolyn Steedman[11] (Valerie Walkerdine, Erica Burman and Rex and Wendy Stainton Rogers contributed to *Children in Culture*, and Erica Burman contributes to this volume also, considering the child in discourses of gender and capitalism).

Since *Children in Culture*, there have been further changes in approaches to childhood, most significantly perhaps in the development and consolidation of what are now called 'childhood studies', an interdisciplinary field emerging from the early 1990s, largely developed from the sociology of childhood, and taking much of its theoretical bases from that area, notably the work of eminent sociologists Jens Qvortrup, Chris Jenks, Allison James and Alan Prout.[12] It should be noted, however, that Qvortrup's work can be defined (as he too defines it) as being from a 'structural perspective',[13] while Jenks, James and Prout introduced a constructivist approach in to the sociology of childhood and childhood studies.

This second volume, *Children in Culture, Revisited: Further Approaches to Childhood*, is prompted by two considerations: first, however interdisciplinary childhood studies may strive to be, it still defines itself broadly in terms of a division between the social sciences (especially sociology, psychology and education with to a lesser extent anthropology) and the humanities, not the wider multi- and interdisciplinarity (in fact, it might be justly described as 'transdisciplinarity') that the first *Children in Culture* embraced. As Jens Qvortrup, William Corsaro and Michael Sebastian Honig write in their introduction to *The Palgrave Handbook of Childhood Studies*:

The formulation [of the title] is not intended to monopolize the concept of childhood, as some might object – in particular since not all disciplines preoccupied with children are equally well represented. We are well aware of this fact and we do not seek to disguise that the volume is primarily about children and childhood in a broader social scientific context.[14]

The interdisciplinarity of both volumes of *Children in Culture* is, importantly, not simply a case of including as many fields as possible for their own sake or for the sake of some principle of inclusivity, but is specifically argued to have theoretically and methodologically important effects and implications. Although much has changed with respect to approaches to childhood, this is one aspect which, in our view, remains under-explored, and it is the aim of this volume to demonstrate further what this kind of 'interdisciplinarity' (or transdisciplinarity) is exactly about. As with the first volume, it is important to stress that although many fields are included in this volume in terms of their engagement with childhood, this is not a random bundling together of otherwise separate and self-contained disciplines, but that the underlying constructivist approaches shared by all unite these chapters, even where the forms of constructivism used may differ and vary somewhat in turn across the volume. It is the way that certain understandings of constructivism, however, enable the analyses of assumptions and perspectives across what are usually held to be disparate fields that enables otherwise unanticipated links between these fields to be made. What are deemed to be quite different problems and issues turn out to have unexpected similarities, or even to be about the same issue after all. The chapters in this volume are, therefore, deliberately not clustered or put in to sections according to disciplinary overlaps or specific disciplinary links as the issues that come together around considerations of childhood thread their way through all the chapters; moreover, it is precisely this that the volume sets out to demonstrate.

Considering further precisely how and why the child is argued to be constructed in any field is the second reason, then, for this *Further Approaches to Childhood*. This second reason is closely interlinked with the first reason described, to do with ongoing tendencies to focus separately on social sciences' and humanities' childhood studies. For where research on childhood may have continued to change further in the past 15 years or so, there are also things which can be argued to have changed less, or not to have changed at all. In the first *Children in Culture* I argued that childhood was claimed as essential most of all in the humanities (literature, children's literature, history and philosophy). In these fields, claims and assertions about what real children are like underpin many of the studies. I analysed this to be the case because of an underpinning liberal humanist investment in the humanities in particular ideas of the family and emotion, where the child is the guarantee for a transcendent human emotion. This emotion in turn produces a transcendent family necessary to certain cultural

and historical conceptions of moral and emotional humanity. Such a
family functions as a realm of privacy in opposition to a public realm
of a consumerist market which is itself upheld by its opposition to that
family. Furthermore, I argued, approaches to the child as constructed
were more prevalent in the social sciences, especially critical psychology
and sociology. This situation, I argue, has not fundamentally changed.
Although (de)constructivist approaches to the child in the humanities
have been widely discussed, written about, and even much advocated,
I have continued to argue both before and since the first *Children in
Culture* that even in such works childhood often continues after all to
be retrieved as 'real' in the end.[15] In other words, understandings of
what constructivist approaches to childhood are and do, and what their
consequences are, have a tendency to differ between the humanities
and social sciences. This volume is interested in considering again how
and why this is the case.

Susan Honeyman, for instance, herself writing about childhood studies from an interdisciplinary literary and cultural studies perspective in
her book *Elusive Childhood: Impossible Representations in Modern Fiction*,[16]
raises the issue of a difference between social sciences' and humanities'
childhood studies in terms of children's literature critic Karen Coats's
concern that 'social scientists are too likely to essentialize children, and
literary critics are too likely to completely dissociate their studies from
real children.'[17] Honeyman, however, in turn critiques Coats's position
by arguing that

> Real children rarely enter the academy,...and even if their voices
> do, they are eventually mediated by adults in dissemination. Coats
> would understandably characterize my approach as limited, but any
> literary study of childhood is limited to the *idea* of childhood accord-
> ing to the discursive nature of our specialisation.[18]

Honeyman adds in the light of this that 'confusing the concept of
childhood with that of the (albeit undefinable) subject position as it
may truly exist in the experiences of certain youth, many critics have
glossed over the distinction between studying discourse and studying
its subjects.'[19] She concludes, therefore, that in order for literary critics to avoid the accusation of 'trying to get away with amateur social
science in our otherwise text-based analyses,...we must be careful to
recognise the discursive level of our expertise and respect the discursive limitations of our study.'[20] For Honeyman, this approach is not
'restrictive', but instead 'levels literary, historical and scientific sources,

opening up the possibility for them all to be read as discourse, provided that we approach them as texts, not testimonies that provide us with authoritative access to "real children." '[21]

It may be noted that although Honeyman here importantly critiques certain assumptions about 'real children', nevertheless a certain 'real' still underpins her arguments. For 'real children' and their 'voices' *are* known to exist in her formulations. Honeyman's argument that these are always 'eventually mediated' in dissemination makes this point further, for something has to be there in order to be 'mediated' in turn. In the same way, the child as 'idea' splits an aspect of the child away from a real which underpins, by opposing, the realm of ideas, just as 'discourse' is split off from 'its subjects' and from 'experience'. Honeyman's arguments constitute discourse or text as a level or layer on top of an underlying subject, experience, or 'true' existence, however difficult the knowing of them is argued to be. Even where the knowing of such existence or experience is claimed to be impossible by Honeyman, it is still nevertheless simultaneously claimed to be *there*, known as unknowable. This very existence is not 'neutral', but itself already presupposes and involves further consequences. Honeyman, in this sense, does not disagree with arguments such as those of Karen Coats in terms of the premises of their approach to the child, but in terms of how difficult they each judge the access to any knowledge of those 'real children' to be (as Honeyman's title puts it, 'elusive'). This is, therefore, a disagreement of degrees of attenuation of the real child, rather than a disagreement about definitions of reality and discourse, or the child as real or discourse.

Sociology of childhood and childhood studies especially have incorporated constructivist approaches to childhood more widely, and often more pervasively, than in the humanities. But this volume is interested in the fact that even where constructivism is accepted and forms the main approach to childhood, issues and questions remain within certain understandings of constructivism and its implications. We argue here that this is also the case for 'childhood studies' and the further social sciences studies of childhood. It is, therefore, the aim of this volume to continue with the project of the first *Children in Culture* in examining closely, through the juxtaposing of constructivist work in a range of fields, the workings and consequences of constructivist approaches to childhood. The main drive for this project, moreover, is a conviction shared by all the contributors that research on childhood has benefitted, and can continue to benefit in crucial ways, from such explorations and analyses. Precisely because, as Jacqueline Rose argued in her seminal

1984 book for all work on childhood (not only children's literature, its ostensible focus) *The Case of Peter Pan or the Impossibility of Children's Fiction*, essentialist views of childhood assume childhood as being *anti-theoretical* by its very nature, as not requiring investigation or theorization, theoretical explorations have often been seen (and still are in some arenas) as inappropriate, or even hostile, to the child. Despite the wide acceptance of challenges to commonly held Romantic views – both academic and popular – which see the child as innocent, transparent and simple (if not simplistic), certain theoretical approaches nevertheless remain seen persistently as inappropriately complex, abstract or even obfuscating: a step too far in theorizing the child.

As the contributors of this volume explore, then, even where theoretical investigations have been welcomed, the question of the child remains a thorny issue. In our own research, the child continues to throw up unanticipated and unacknowledged questions and challenges. Not all can be ultimately resolved or addressed, and indeed, the very desire for resolution and answer may itself precisely be implicated in the questions and challenges. As Jacqueline Rose warns, '[a]nd yet for all the apparent shifts in the way that childhood is discussed, what always seems to return in the analysis, in one form or another, is this idea of mastery'.[22] Nevertheless, it remains the overarching conviction of this volume that the continued mobilization of analyses of the constitutive discourses of childhood reaps many rewards; that the ongoing process of analysis itself challenges the embedding and ossification of assumptions. The benefits, moreover, and very importantly, are not seen as being profitable only for an isolated realm of theory or some academic abstraction, in opposition to some realm of 'real life' 'out there', a muddy and messy realm of everyday endeavour, left to one side by the navel-gazing theorists. Indeed, this volume questions again, from a variety of angles, this claimed opposition between 'theory' and 'experience' itself. As in my discussion of Susan Honeyman's work above, it can be said that this is an opposition that rests on the child: the 'real' or 'actual' child claimed even in much constructivist work, sometimes overtly and sometimes indirectly, to be the ultimate beneficiary of investigations of an 'ideal' or 'stereotypical' child. In such views, an 'unreal' child is to be identified by a theoretical penetration which allows precisely for the 'real' child to be seen, and heard, finally, for what it is: in this sense, constructivism is understood in such arguments as pertaining only to a layer of 'incorrectly' created or constructed childhood which rests 'on top of' an unconstructed, spontaneous, self-constituted, 'real' or 'actual' child (even when, as in Honeyman's discussion, that child is known only as existing as the unknown). In relation to this lack of working through of the implications of certain theoretical arguments, David Rudd and Anthony Pavlik argue in relation to children's literature studies in the special issue of *Children's Literature Association Quarterly* devoted to Jacqueline Rose's 1984 work, that 'references to Rose's work are, more often than not, *en passant*, and once made, the critic then proceeds as though it were "business as usual".'[23]

These discussions of differing forms, definitions, and uses of (de)constructivist approaches circulate also in other identity-studies concerning, for instance, gender, ethnicity, nationality, disability and sexual identities. As critic Daniela Caselli writes in relation to gender:

> Constructivist approaches have had a rather sad fate of late, being reduced, as both [queer theorists] Judith Butler and Eve Kosofsky Sedgwick have often lamented, to an idea of a socially imposed (and thus dispensable and disposable) structure over something real or already there. But there would be no need for constructivism if this were the case; a plethora of political arguments in favour of social change have historically played that role.[24]

It is in relation to ideas of children being able to be 'seen' or 'heard' that I wish to raise here two ongoing central issues for approaches to childhood in all fields: 'voice' and 'agency'. Both these terms relate centrally to the concerns of this volume: on the one hand to demonstrate how 'agency' and 'voice' occur and are used across a range of fields' engagements with childhood, and, on the other hand, to explore further how both these terms have a range of consequences and continue to raise a number of difficulties. Although I am focusing here specifically on 'voice' and 'agency' because of their prominent currency and purchase across a wide range of disciplines (in relation to childhood, but not just childhood), it is important also to note that what it means to 'see' the child raises theoretically parallel questions. This is demonstrated extensively in this volume in the chapters by Neil Cocks (on 'picturing' the child in art history and photography), by Jonathan Bignell (on children's television and globalization) and Jenny Bavidge (on the child and the urban, in both (children's) literature and film).

Qvortrup, Corsaro and Honig explain how and why 'agency' and 'voice' are seen by them to be central to childhood studies:

> Agency and voice for children: Among those who embarked on the study of children within the framework of the new paradigm of

childhood it was a common observation that children were largely appreciated as people who were on the receiving end in terms of provision and knowledge. Children were reduced to vulnerable people to be protected without being seen also as participants – in any case, not participants in the larger social fabric, which was an adult privilege and prerogative. Therefore it became imperative for social studies of childhood to look into these charges or prejudices. Was it 'naturally' or necessarily the case that children lacked qualities and capacities for participation? If this proved not to be so, were these qualities and capacities merely useful or applicable in a childhood context – because nobody would deny, of course, that children did possess resources, creativity and inventiveness. ... Social studies of childhood have made available numerous studies about children's agency in circumstances and surroundings far beyond the more narrow vicinities in which children have so far been seen as victims conceptually and empirically.[25]

The opposition Qvortrup, Corsaro and Honig note here between the child as agent and the child as victim is used widely. Marah Gubar, for instance, in relation to her consideration of 'the golden age of children's literature', formulates what she sees as her disagreement with Jacqueline Rose's view of childhood as follows:

> Rose's ... unfortunate tendency to characterize young people as artless beings devoid of agency ... her provocative and persistent use of such rhetoric ... suggests that children are invariably exploited and oppressed by adult attention. ... the generalizations [Rose] makes about children's fiction, repeatedly characterize children as helpless pawns in the hands of all-powerful adults. As a result, the critics who adhere most closely to her argument routinely represent young people as voiceless victims. ... I believe it is too reductive to view 'representations of children as unproblematic socialization narratives which "Other", smother, and colonize the child subject'.[26]

Two issues can be seen to be at stake in this argument: first, the idea that to be an agent or a participant, and to have a voice, are seen, as Qvortrup, Corsaro and Honig put it, as a privilege and prerogative, or, as Gubar and many others see it, as part of children's 'resources, creativity and inventiveness'. The contributors to *Further Approaches to Childhood*, however, continue to explore the question of what 'agency' and 'voice' *are*. Are they, necessarily, the liberation from adult exploitation and oppression that critics such as Gubar would claim? And, moreover, what are precisely the 'voice' and 'agency' of *childhood*? What allows them to be seen as such? Qvortrup, Corsaro and Honig describe the resources of childhood being seen as something 'nobody would deny, of course', but for some of the contributors to their volume as well as for the contributors to this volume the question remains what these resources are in fact seen to be, by whom, and why. As Steedman, Urwin and Walkerdine explain in their 1985 volume *Language, Gender and Childhood* in relation to their writing on both childhood and gender:

> [our] approach requires a form of analysis which does not simply point to the existence of either alternative forms of language or lacunae of silence as expressions of social inequality. Rather, it demands that we understand the possibilities for change by examining how forms of speaking and forms of truth have been produced, and how these regulate and circumscribe what can be said about what, when and where. In this process, we are also forced to re-analyse what constitutes subversion and resistance, and how the subjective and the political intersect.[27]

Using this perspective allows us to ask, for instance, when a child is seen to speak, how and why is it seen to be speaking *its own voice*? This issue is fundamental to difficulties surrounding both the study and the care of the child in any context, including in legal, educational or social welfare situations, where the question is often asked whether the child is not speaking the words it has been told to speak, and in this volume Simon Flynn, in considering radio productions of 'children's voices', engages closely with this complex area. Similarly, Hannah Anglin-Jaffe and Daniel Monk's chapters on children in discourses of education, specifically in relation to emotional wellbeing in the classroom and the problem of homophobic bullying respectively, raise questions of who is speaking for whom and how and why. 'Voice' is also analysed in Helen Ainslie's chapter in terms of childhood and disability as she extends the question of whether a child 'voice' can speak its 'self' into the question of whether autistic (child) narratives can speak 'autism' itself. Sarah Spooner's chapter on the work of children's writer Arthur Ransome engages with related issues in examining ideas of language for and of the child in terms of what is often still assumed to be its single outstanding characteristic: simplicity, while Sue Walsh's chapter tackles the same issue from the other side of the coin, as it were, exploring how childhood and ethnic identity are constructed in relation to the complexities of reading irony.

In all these investigations it remains crucial to stress again that there is no final 'answer' that the contributors to this volume believe they can deliver. That is to say, none of the chapters in this volume claim to be accurately able to diagnose an incorrect or artificial child 'voice' to be separated out from a correct and authentic child voice to be heard and acted upon. It is the argument of this volume, as was the case with the first *Children in Culture*, that there is no such 'voice', neither for the child nor for any other identity. But neither does this position, this particular understanding of (de)constructivism, claim as answer that, therefore, voice and agency are themselves the 'wrong' terms, which ought to be replaced with other, more correct or true, or more efficacious terms. As Pam Alldred and Erica Burman argue with respect to 'Analysing Children's Accounts Using Discourse Analysis':

> First and foremost, discursive approaches highlight the interpretive nature of any research, not only that with children. As a consequence, they challenge the conventional distinction between data collection and analysis, question the status of research accounts and encourage us to question taken-for-granted assumptions about distinctions between adults and children. Hence our emphasis here will be on the active and subjective involvement of researchers in hearing, interpreting and representing children's 'voices'. The case has already been made for listening to children. ... however, we want to highlight processes involved in (to follow the aural metaphor) *hearing* what children say.[28]

In this sense this volume continues the engagement of the first volume with what sociologist Chris Jenks formulated in his founding collection of essays on *The Sociology of Childhood* as the asking of 'the basic ontological questions, "What is a child?", "How is a child possible as such?".[29] These 'ontological questions' arise both with respect to 'voice' and 'vision' ('seeing') and in the use of 'agency' in relation to the child, and continue to be central to methodological debates within childhood studies. Henriques, Hollway, Urwin, Venn and Walkerdine explain in the 1998 'Foreword' to the re-issuing of their seminal 1984 critical psychology volume *Changing the Subject: Psychology, Social Regulation and Subjectivity* that it is psychoanalysis and post-structuralism that are at the heart of the questioning of the 'subject' which in turn allows the explorations of voice and agency that both volumes of *Children in*

Culture pursue, following in the footsteps of this argument in Henriques *et al*, in Jacqueline Rose's *The Case of Peter Pan* and in Steedman, Urwin and Walkerdine's *Language, Gender and Childhood*:

> Discourses rooted in the notion of a unitary, rational subject still predominate in the social sciences in spite of critiques which have shown such a concept to be untenable. ... [It] survives not so much in explicit defences of the model as in the implicit assumptions of various dualisms: social and cognitive, content and process, the intentionality of agents and determination by structures, the subject as constituted or constitutive. ... we utilized post-structuralist theories and psychoanalysis to show up the limitations that cognitivism imposes for those, who, like us, wanted to break with the tendency of psychology's research to reproduce and naturalize the particular rationalist notion of the subject.[30]

As Henriques *et al.* state, what is central here is the implication of psychoanalysis in terms of the 'splitting' of the rationalist, unitary subject not just in terms of a questioning of assumptions about the 'content' of such a rational subject, but also in terms of the perspectives of researchers themselves (as Alldred and Burman also refer to in the quote above). For the researchers too can no longer assume their own rational, unitary subjectivity in terms of a dualistic split from their object of research. The question of how and why and when researchers 'see' or 'hear' the child come to the forefront in this kind of work. Literary critic and theorist Shoshana Felman makes the same argument with respect to her account of the implications (rather than 'applications') of psychoanalysis for reading. Felman includes as an epigram a quote from the French psychoanalyst and theorist Jacques Lacan at the start of her volume *Literature and Psychoanalysis. The Question of Reading Otherwise*:

> This is what analytical discourse is all about: what can be read. What can be read beyond what the subject has been incited to say. [...] In analytical discourse, the signifying utterance is given another reading than what it means.[31]

Lacan here disrupts at once a unitary, intentional author and reader, as well as text as a separate object of study. As Felman further elaborates:

> Literature, by virtue of its ironic force, fundamentally deconstructs the fantasy of authority ... and, for the same reasons, ... psychoanalysis

deconstructs the authority of the fantasy – its claim to belief and to power as the sole window through which we behold and perceive reality, as the sole window through which reality can indeed reach our grasp, enter into our consciousness. Psychoanalysis tells us that the fantasy is a fiction, and that consciousness is itself, in a sense, a fantasy-effect.[32]

Taking Henriques *et al.* and Felman together, psychoanalysis is here the disruption of the dualities of object and subject, of viewer and viewed, of the real and fantasy, of, as Rose draws out, child and adult. These disruptions also lead to Felman articulating precisely how the issue of 'interdisciplinarity' may be thought in relation to psychoanalysis and literature, as I have also thought it above more widely with respect to the interdisciplinarities of these volumes of *Children in Culture*:

Since literature and psychoanalysis are *different* from each other, but, at the same time, they are also 'enfolded within' each other, since they are, as it were, at the same time outside and inside each other, we might say that they compromise, each in its turn, the interiority of the other. The cultural division, in other words, of scholarly 'dis-ciplines' of research is by no means a natural geography: there are no *natural* boundaries between literature and psychoanalysis, which clearly define and distinguish them; the border between them is undecidable since they are really *traversed* by each other.[33]

Although Felman is considering 'enfoldings' specific to psychoanalysis and literature, the child too, we are arguing here, traverses fields with its accompanying and underpinning structures.

It is precisely this kind of understanding of, and engagement with, psychoanalysis and post-structuralism which also marks differences with views of childhood agency such as those of Allison James, even though she herself, as I mentioned above, is one of the sociologists who introduced constructivist approaches to the sociology of childhood. James, like Qvortrup, Corsaro and Honig in the quote I discuss above, diagnoses 'the agentic child [as] the radically different model of "the child" that was to become a key feature of the "emergent paradigm" within the new sociology of childhood.' James traces this new paradigm as having two main principles. On the one hand, it draws from ideas such as Charlotte Hardman's that 'children, too, might inhabit a "self-regulating, autonomous world which does not necessarily reflect early development of adult culture" in which they could be seen as social actors'.[34] On the other hand, it relies on Anthony Giddens's suggestion that 'every act which contributes to the reproduction of a structure is also an act of production and as such may initiate change by altering the structure at the same time as it reproduces it.'[35] James, Giddens and Hardman allocate to children both the possibility of a self-contained culture which is not merely a retrospectively defined developmental phase in the service of adulthood as the final end-point, but an ability to be 'active participants in society... as much contributors to its shape and form, as well as being "socialized" by it.'[36]

The difference here with the (de)constructivism of Henriques *et al.* or Rose, however, is that these views of child agency and child culture in turn continue to rely on both an ability to 'see' what is appropriately 'child' about those particular actions and cultures, and, paradoxically, to take those actions and cultures away from adult vision altogether. As James and Prout write in their important 1990 book *Constructing and Reconstructing Childhood*, 'children are *and must be seen* as active in the construction of their own lives',[37] and 'children's social relationships and cultures are worthy of study in their own right, independent of the perspective and concerns of adults.'[38] As with Honeyman, children's social relationships and cultures are known in these statements to be there, to exist, even without adults seeing them or having concerns in relation to them. Yet in order to make the claim that these exist at all, they must have been seen and have resulted in being of concern, even if in terms of being kept 'independent'. Together with this, James relies on 'choice', by definition in her formulations *conscious* choice, as the correlate of agency: 'agency, in the end, is an attribute of individual children. It is something which they may or may not choose to exercise'.[39]

The dualities of subject and object, of adult and child, of viewer and viewed and of passivity and activity, are finally after all upheld then, in writings such as those of James and Prout, Giddens and Hardman in ways which the implications of psychoanalysis, as understood by Felman, Rose, and Henriques *et al.* do not allow as possible. For James's constructivism, the child can nevertheless still be *read* and known *as such* by a vision not of the child. (In this volume, archaeologist Eleanor Casella's considerations in her chapter, for instance, of how and when and why archaeologists allocate objects or site evidence to childhood engages with these difficulties of attributing agency and autonomy to the child.) 'Individuality' too does not dissolve childhood, but instead introduces specific variation *within* it, both maintaining the all-encompassing category of childhood for all the 'individual[s]' within it, while also assuming individuality as necessarily the smallest unit for culture and society. Jacqueline Rose writes in relation to these issues in *The Case of Peter Pan* that

> Childhood is not an object, any more than the unconscious, although that is often how they are both understood. The idea that childhood is something separate which can be scrutinised and assessed is the other side of the illusion which makes of childhood something that has simply ceased to be. In most discussions of children's fiction which make their appeal to Freud, childhood is part of a strict developmental sequence at the end of which stands the cohered and rational consciousness of the adult mind. ... this is the most reductive, even if it is the most prevalent, reading of Freud. ... it holds off the challenge, which is present in Freud's own work, to the very notions of identity, development and subjective cohesion which this conception of childhood is so often used to sustain.[40]

It is this understanding of psychoanalysis and the child of and as psychoanalysis that this volume wishes to explore further.

Notes

1. K. Lesnik-Oberstein (ed.), *Children in Culture: Approaches to Childhood* (Houndmills: Palgrave Macmillan, 1998).
2. For probably the most significant prior interdisciplinary volume on childhood see C. Steedman, C. Urwin and V. Walkerdine (eds), *Language, Gender and Childhood* (London: Routledge & Kegan Paul, 1985).
3. In all chapters bar one, that by Kim Reynolds and Paul Yates on 'Too Soon: Representations of Childhood Death in Literature for Children' (in K. Lesnik-Oberstein [ed.], *Children in Culture: Approaches to Childhood*, pp. 151–78) which formulates an essentialist approach to childhood and children's literature.
4. K. Lesnik-Oberstein, 'Childhood and Textuality: Culture, History, Literature', in K. Lesnik-Oberstein (ed.), *Children in Culture: Approaches to Childhood*, pp. 1–29.
5. P. Ariès, *Centuries of Childhood: A Social History of Family Life*, trans. R. Baldick (New York: Vintage Books, 1962, first published in French in 1959), pp. 9–10.
6. See, for instance, V. Walkerdine, *Schoolgirl Fictions* (London: Verso, 1990) and *Daddy's Girl: Young Girls and Popular Culture* (London: Palgrave Macmillan, 1997).
7. See, for instance, R. and W. Stainton Rogers, *Stories of Childhood: Shifting Agendas of Child Concern* (Hemel Hempstead: Harvester Wheatsheaf, 1992).
8. See, for instance, E. Burman, *Deconstructing Developmental Psychology* (London: Routledge: 1994, 2nd edn, 2008) and *Developments: Child, Image, Nation* (London: Routledge, 2008).

9. J. Rose, *The Case of Peter Pan or the Impossibility of Children's Fiction*, series: Language, Discourse, Society, (eds), S. Heath and C. MacCabe (London: Palgrave Macmillan, 1984, 2nd edn, with new introductory essay, Philadelphia: University of Pennsylvania Press, 1992).

10. J. Kincaid, *Child-Loving: The Erotic Child and Victorian Culture* (London: Routledge, 1992); J. Kincaid, *Erotic Innocence: The Culture of Child Molesting* (Durham, NC: Duke University Press, 1998).

11. See, for instance, C. Steedman, *The Tidy House: Little Girls Writing* (London: Virago, 1983) and C. Steedman, *Strange Dislocations: Childhood and the Idea of Human Interiority, 1780–1930* (Cambridge, MA: Harvard University Press, 1995).

12. J. Qvortrup, *Childhood Matters: Social Theory, Practice and Politics* (Aldershot: Avebury, 1994); J. Qvortrup (ed.), *Studies in Modern Childhood: Society, Agency, Culture* (Houndmills: Palgrave Macmillan, 2005); C. Jenks (ed.), *The Sociology of Childhood: Essential Readings* (London: Batsford Academic and Educational, 1982); C. Jenks, *Childhood* (series: Key Ideas, series ed. Peter Hamilton) (London: Routledge, 1996); A. James and A. Prout (eds), *Constructing and Reconstructing Childhood: Contemporary Issues in the Sociological Study of Childhood* (London: Falmer Press, 1990, 2nd edn 1997); A. James, C. Jenks and A. Prout, *Theorizing Childhood* (Cambridge: Polity Press, 1998). See also, as mentioned in *Children in Culture*, J. Pilcher and S. Wagg (eds), *Thatcher's Children? Politics, Childhood and Society in the 1980s and 1990s* (London: Falmer Press, 1996). For an important early example of this kind of thinking see V. A. Zelizer, *Pricing the Priceless Child: The Changing Social Value of Children* (New York: Basic Books, 1985, republished with a new preface by Princeton University Press, 1994).

13. J. Qvortrup, W. A. Corsaro and M.-S. Honig, 'Why Social Studies of Childhood? An Introduction to the Handbook', in J. Qvortrup, W. A. Corsaro and M.-S. Honig (eds), *The Palgrave Handbook of Childhood Studies* (Houndmills: Palgrave Macmillan, 2009), pp. 1–19, p. 17, n. 4.

14. J. Qvortrup *et al.*, 'Why Social Studies of Childhood?', p. 2.

15. See for further examples of where I argue this to be the case for a variety of specific fields: K. Lesnik-Oberstein, '*Oliver Twist*: The Narrator's Tale', *Textual Practice*, 15: 1, 2001, 87–100; 'The Psychopathology of Everyday Children's Literature Criticism', *Cultural Critique*, 45: Spring, 2000, 222–42; K. Lesnik-Oberstein and S. Thomson, 'What is Queer Theory Doing with the Child?', *Parallax*, 8: 1, 2002, 35–46; K. Lesnik-Oberstein, '*Holiday House*: Grist to *The Mill on the Floss*, or: Childhood as Text', in K. Lesnik-Oberstein (ed.), *The Yearbook of English Studies*, Special Section on 'Children in Literature', vol. 32 (Maney Publishing for the Modern Humanities Research Association: Leeds, 2002), pp. 77–94; 'The *Philosophical Investigations*' Children', *'Educational Philosophy and Theory'*, 35: 4, 2003, 381–94; 'Children's Literature: New Approaches' in K. Lesnik-Oberstein (ed.), *Children's Literature: New Approaches* (Houndmills: Palgrave Macmillan, 2004), pp. 1–25; *On Having an Own Child: Reproductive Technologies and the Cultural Construction of Childhood* (London: Karnac, 2008); 'Childhood, Queer Theory and Feminism', *Feminist Theory*, 11: 3, 2010, 309–21.

16. S. Honeyman, *Elusive Childhood: Impossible Representations in Modern Fiction* (Columbus, OH: Ohio State University Press, 2005).
17. Honeyman, *Elusive Childhood*, p. 13.
18. Honeyman, *Elusive Childhood*, p. 14.
19. Honeyman, *Elusive Childhood*, p. 14.
20. Honeyman, *Elusive Childhood*, p. 14.
21. Honeyman, *Elusive Childhood*, p. 14.
22. Rose, *The Case of Peter Pan*, p. 10.
23. D. Rudd and A. Pavlik, 'The (Im)Possibility of Children's Fiction: Rose Twenty-Five Years On', *Children's Literature Association Quarterly*, 35: 3, Fall, 2010, 223–9, 225.
    It should be noted, however, that this issue of *CLAQ* itself claims to 'emerg[e] from different theoretical traditions' to Rose and cites the 'social realities' (p. 226) of its cause as the root of this difference.
24. D. Caselli, ' "Wives of Geniuses I Have Sat With": Body Hair, Genius and Modernity', in K. Lesnik-Oberstein (ed.) *The Last Taboo: Women and Body Hair* (Manchester: Manchester University Press, 2006), pp. 18–48, p. 19.
25. J. Qvortrup *et al.*, 'Why Social Studies of Childhood?', p. 5.
26. M. Gubar, *Artful Dodgers: Reconceiving the Golden Age of Children's Literature* (New York: Oxford University Press, 2009), p. 32, quoting from M. Myers, 'Reading Children and Homeopathic Romanticism: Paradigm Lost, Revisionary Gleam, or "Plus Ça Change, Plus C'est la Même Chose"?', in J. McGavran, *Romanticism and Children's Literature in Nineteenth-Century England* (Athens, GA: University of Georgia Press, 1991), pp. 44–84, p. 50.
27. C. Steedman, C. Urwin and V. Walkerdine, 'Introduction', in C. Steedman, C. Urwin and V. Walkerdine (eds), *Language, Gender and Childhood* (London: Routledge & Kegan Paul, 1985), pp. 1–10, p. 2.
28. P. Alldred and E. Burman, 'Analysing Children's Accounts Using Discourse Analysis', in S. Greene and D. Hogan (eds), *Researching Children's Experience: Methods and Approaches* (London: Sage, 2005), pp. 175–98, p. 175.
29. Jenks (ed.), *The Sociology of Childhood*, p. 10.
30. J. Henriques, W. Hollway, C. Urwin, C. Venn and V. Walkerdine (eds), 'Foreword', in J. Henriques, W. Hollway, C. Urwin, C. Venn and V.Walkerdine, (eds), *Changing the Subject: Psychology, Social Regulation and Subjectivity* (London: Routledge, 1998), pp. ix–xx, pp. ix–x.
31. S. Felman (ed.), *Literature and Psychoanalysis. The Question of Reading: Otherwise* (Baltimore, MD: Johns Hopkins University Press, 1982 [1977]), no page number.
32. S. Felman, 'To Open the Question', in S. Felman (ed.), *Literature and Psychoanalysis. The Question of Reading: Otherwise* (Baltimore, MD: Johns Hopkins University Press, 1982 [1977]), pp. 5-11, p. 8.
33. Felman, 'To Open the Question', pp. 9–10 (emphases Felman).
34. A. James, 'Agency', in J. Qvortrup *et al.* (eds), *The Palgrave Handbook of Childhood Studies* (Houndmills: Palgrave, 2009), pp. 34–45, p. 38, referring to C. Hardman, 'Can There Be an Anthropology of Children?', *Journal of the Anthropological Society of Oxford*, 4: 2, 1973, 85–99, 87.
35. A. Giddens, *The Central Problems of Social Theory* (Cambridge, MA: Polity Press, 1973), p. 69, as quoted by James, 'Agency', p. 39.

36. James, 'Agency', p. 39.
37. A. James and A. Prout (eds), *Constructing and Reconstructing Childhood* (Basingstoke: Falmer Press, 1990), p. 8 (my emphasis).
38. James and Prout, *Constructing and Reconstructing Childhood*, p. 8.
39. James, 'Agency', p. 44.
40. Rose, *The Case of Peter Pan*, p. 13.

1
Gender and Childhood in Neoliberal Times: Contemporary Tropes of the Boychild in Psychological Culture

Erica Burman

This chapter addresses political ambiguities surrounding recent recon-figurations of gendered childhood, both as markers of 'old' and 'new', and as key effects of a contemporary political economy that is increas-ingly governed by modes of psychologization and feminization. While also central to prevailing modes of affect and subjectivity, the motif of childhood has long been a forum for the articulation of cultural con-cerns around nature, technology and sociocultural change – including around gender and familial relations.

Drawing on exploration of three popular cultural texts that explicitly focus on boys, I explore how prevailing discourses of knowledge and expertise are mobilized in relation to specific modalities of identifica-tion and temporality surrounding childhood. These modalities imply particular, and gendered, orientations to the doubled perspective on technology and temporality (as topic and process). The appeal to the past functions in two ways: first, to install a normative developmen-tal trajectory while, second, the motif of technology signals a marked 'break' with the past, invoking a new (post)modern, flexible subject – but one which, I argue here, nevertheless reiterates significant features of the old.

I argue that affective consequences of the temporalities mobilized by such mainstream cultural representations of childhood are constitu-tive of, but also resist, contemporary political-economic imperatives, in part by recalling older varieties. Whether conceived as technologically-savvy or as post-natural romantic, the (male) child persists as a key counterpart to the (currently economically displaced and emotionally de-skilled) adult male. Memorial identifications (facilitated by gendered continuities, within a particularly conservative rendering of identification) may offer possibilities of a redemptive position, as well as new sites of regulation (and market exploitation). This, however, is at the cost of limiting utopian subjective possibilities to traditional narratives of gender (hetero)normativity.

This chapter takes some mainstream cultural texts of childhood to reflect upon the preoccupations and agendas they fulfil. I am using the term 'trope' in Judith Butler's[1] sense of a repetition or reiteration that is also a potential turning point; instituting a revisionary moment that anticipates the possibility of change. At a rather mundane level, the topic of this chapter represents something of a turning point for me in focusing on 'the boychild'. I should explain that, like other feminists, I attempted to critique and disrupt the focus on the boychild as prototypical, normative developing subject, as part of the project of challenging the culturally masculine developmental trajectory towards detachment, autonomy and mastery. This child, we said, was not only a fiction (since it was an ideal-typical model) but it instituted exclusionary regimes around who was deemed to be the better or proper kind of child. Hence Valerie Walkerdine's study *Counting Girls Out*[2] documented how even women teachers regarded their girl pupils as being less able at Mathematics and less clever than the boys because they did not show this ineffable quality of 'flair' even when they gained higher marks than their male peers.

All this seems a long time ago now, with current widespread public concern now focusing on girls 'overtaking' boys at school (although whether this is a gender or a 'race' and class issue remains an open question) – and interestingly we did not hear in those days concern about boys' overachievement... But, just to complete my brief thumbnail sketch of the earlier state of play, the corollary of the normative masculine developing child was the feminized childvictim, the girlchild as the quintessential deserving object of help and support, with all the additional political problems of associations of dependency, feminization and infantalization when mobilized in the context of international humanitarian aid. Obviously I do not want to overstate this point (which is pretty obvious anyway) especially as aid organizations are probably among the most responsible and aware of the politics of representation around images of childhood. But nevertheless the child remains a key motif legitimating, and often mandating, intervention. My interest in this chapter is to reflect on how broader socio-political changes are reflected in the meanings and modes of expression of gendered childhood, in this era of high technology, democracy by mobile phone and individualization. My starting point is to see subjectivity as both shaped by and reshaped through technological and other changes that demand careful scrutiny and evaluation. This means that it is also – as in Foucauldian analyses – a technology of (self) regulation in which the 'psy' sciences of psychology and psychotherapy are implicated, and via their popularization (under the 'psy complex'[3]) these technologies of subjectivity surround us in everyday culture.

There are three, related key frames for this analysis, which I (have space only to) briefly outline before moving on to explore how these are realized and reworked in relation to the representation of childhood, gender and (as we shall see) memory. The three frames are:

1. The psychosocial turn;
2. Emotions, feminization and masculine deficits; and
3. Childhood as the polysemic domain of enduring and flexible subjects.

The psychosocial turn

Emotions, or 'affects', feature significantly in current political and academic agendas. Whether as critique of scientistic objectivity,[4] or as a reflexive grounding practice in social science analysis, they are increasingly being mobilized, textualized and discussed.[5] Practices of psychologization and individualization exemplify the neoliberal project of instrumentalization and maximization of hitherto untapped human resources,[6] so that we are both explicitly incited (and also coerced) into subscribing to these practices. Whether concerned with home-working (good for the middle class professionals of the global north, exploitative for poorly paid, casual labourers of the south), with programmes of 'emotional intelligence' to sanitize conflict from the protests of disaffected young schoolchildren,[7] or with state policies of continuing professional development/lifelong learning policies,[8] we are rendered – in significantly different ways – flexible and precarious subjects under mounting state and transnational scrutiny.

To illustrate, these themes are displayed across the 'appointment pages' of any recent issue of *The Psychologist* (the magazine all members of the British Psychological Society receive as part of their subscription to the national professional organization of psychologists). Here a circle is traced from trauma and counselling to lifelong learning, to empowerment and finally back to protection and security (also illustrating the State structure behind university and local authority funding, and even private practice). For example the British security services (MI5) advertise for recruits, focusing on the need for experts on both 'psychological screening' and the 'development of security cultures', such that the unit of analysis is not only the individual.

Emotions, feminization and masculine deficits

Contemporary practices of (what might be called) psychological culture or emotionalization range from the psychic flexibility to deal with insecure conditions and the injunction to keep working on one's development to fit the shifting demands of the labour market.[9] As the World Bank and IMF turn to women and children's work as a final untapped economic resource,[10] it is stereotypically feminine relational skills that are acquiring new value in post-industrial, service-sector-based economies,[11] such that, unsurprisingly, some women emerge as beneficiaries of this new feminized economic regime. But, as many feminists have asserted, this is nothing to do with any kind of feminism. Middle class women managers may have been allowed through the glass ceiling but this is to do the work of capital better, just as varieties of femininity are mobilized within contemporary army recruitment and arms publicity campaigns.[12]

Under neoliberalism, traditional masculine physical labour with its values of hard work, physical strength and reliability is now displaced and de-skilled. Within social policy, the incitement to intervention has correspondingly shifted to problematize men's physical and mental health in the UK, with men's physical and psychological vulnerability (with countless undiagnosed medical and mental health difficulties – from diabetes to depression) now the focus. Perhaps, therefore, it is no accident that it is now men's problematic emotions that are the subject of concern. From knife crime to road rage, the gendered expression of anger wrought of dispossession and alienation can now be cast as an individual skills deficit.

Childhood as the polysemic domain of enduring and flexible subjects

According to dominant conventions that, although local in origin, have become global (through historical and current relations of economic and cultural domination), childhood has come to be invested as the originary/alternative site of authentic (non-alienated, whole, happy...) subjectivity. Notwithstanding the many oppressions this trope supports, as (for example) fundraising for aid and development campaigns illustrate in complex ways, this and other imaginary resources can be mobilized in a range of ways to challenge as well as sustain prevailing inequalities. Yet any politics of solidarity relies on some kind of identificatory connection, even if its basis has to be interrogated and understood as misrecognition (compare Judith Butler's point that identification precisely relies upon its opposite – disidentification[13]). A feature of the texts I focus on below is that they rely upon an unproblematic invocation of an interpellated, remembered childhood, whose normative current arrangements escape critical evaluation through the presumed generality of address mobilized by the trope of the child.

Such new forms of naturalism, or revivals of 'old' kinds, abound. CAT scans, and other images of the shiny new technological scientific world, merely complement rather than replace the older romantic views of childhood in circulation. Given the fragility of prevailing contemporary models of political subjectivity,[14] the nostalgias that these mobilize are far from innocent. Some of these nostalgias take the form of invoking a kind of breathless engagement with technology that re-invent traditional gendered and childhood positions even as they apparently transcend them. Others reclaim a lost world of nature that apparently predates this, which insists on expression and emancipation. Although apparently contrary, the texts I discuss below all rely upon affectively engaged temporalities mobilized by a similar trope of the child.

Having outlined these frames, I now move on to discuss how they apply to and inform current configurations of childhood, technology and memory.

The child as other

A 2006 newspaper story reports how a 3-year-old Lincolnshire[15] boy used his parents' computer password to purchase a 'vintage' car on the Internet shopping site eBay. The fact that this story was published in the 'funny slot', at the bottom of the front page of a British 'quality' newspaper, already cues us into the prescribed interpretive frame. So, significantly, this purchase was presented as an action whose contractual obligations could be discounted precisely because it was entered into by a child. Indeed the child's own intentionality, while clearly documented ('The following morning Jack woke up and told his parents "I've bought a car"'), is dismissed: 'She [his mother] said: "Jack's a whizz on the PC and just pressed all the right buttons"'. The story is not only marked as 'non-serious' by virtue of its spatial location in the newspaper, but this is also reinforced by the child status of the protagonist. In accounting for how he did not pursue the purchase of the 'Barbie-pink' 1.0 litre Nissan Figaro,[16] the 'owner and co-director of Worcester Road

Motors, Stourport-on-Severn, Worcestershire' fell back onto clichés about children:

> as soon as I heard it was a young boy who had done it by mistake I cancelled the bid. ... He must have good taste in cars. We've all got children and they do silly things at times, so it was no problem.[17]

The predication of indulgence on assumptions of incompetence (but appropriate aspiration – 'he must have good taste in cars') is, of course, what marks this story as originating from the global north. Elsewhere such notions of triviality and irresponsibility might not have been so easily deployed, while the responsibilities typically assumed by the poorer children of the south become part of what stigmatizes and pathologizes them. Among many other matters, therefore, this story is a small document of the shaping of consumer desires, minimized and naturalized by this account of childlike rehearsal for a future role. The triviality connoted by the actions of a child situates it within a class-coded child-centred discourse (that does not panic at the thought of the child having spent £9,000 that the parents are unlikely to have) while at the same time it is rendered outside more general moral evaluation attending such consumer desires.[18]

This story rehearses a familiar version of the oedipal narrative as played out in relation to the Internet. It contains the anxiety about technologically proficient children outstripping and literally ruining their parents. Yet it renders this theme safely 'entertaining' only at the cost of simultaneously trivializing both the child's actions (as fortuitous rather than skilled) and intentions (as not malign), along with disclaiming responsibility for his actions (as performed by a minor and safely sanctioning them as subject to adult control). (Here it also may be relevant to note that 'Jack' has remained the most popular boy's name in the UK for many years, so confirming the 'everyboychild/everyman' status of the story.)

Significantly, despite the cultural status of the child as synonymous to interiority/selfhood,[19] this is not a child-centred story – the reader is not told of 'Jack's' disappointment at not getting the car he bought, nor how his parents explain to him why he cannot have the car. It is a story about the child as an (endearing, irritating, dangerous?) other, the kind of other we are harbouring and indeed moulding within our very own homes, as new technologically sophisticated subjects. Indeed although within a different genre, the erasure of the child's subjectivity represented here is reminiscent of that noted by Karen Lury[20] within the genre of 'expert taming of naughty children' characterizing contemporary TV family makeover series such as *Supernanny* or *House of Tiny Tearaways.*

My second example (which will also inform a later example) moves us from printnews trivia to TV advertising, in this case for the 2008/9 promotional campaign for the washing powder, Persil. (My justification for staying with this earlier campaign is because it remains the brand's primary campaign, up to the time of writing in August 2010.)

Roboboy: child as self

Persil's TV advertisement campaign in 2008/9 portrayed a robot leaving a house to enter a garden, in which playful activity accompanies his transformation into a boy. In the product advertising website's description:

> A small robot in a hall cupboard is splashed with dirt by a dog shaking itself after coming in from the garden, and starts to move slowly outdoors. Walking through the fallen leaves its mechanical feet become human, as do its hands when picking up a worm. Rain falls, and splashing around in a muddy pool the robot evolves into a young boy, as the narrator says that every child has a right to get dirty and the right to be a child – 'Dirt is Good' she concludes.[21]

A key feature to note in this text is that the tensions and uncertainties of the figure of the cyborg, even of the delusional temporalities and uncertainties of the films like *Robocop*, are mobilized but demoted to a safe story of roboboy, where a 'genuine', intact child subjectivity is portrayed as hidden within a mechanical exterior. No cyborg hybridization is depicted here that might offer some more creative mutual engagement with changing technologies – but instead it is (almost) a straightforward (technophiliac) story of the imprisonment and liberation of a pre-existing subjectivity. Interestingly, in contrast to what is perhaps the dominant reading of the TV ad, the verbal description above however offers a slightly different riff to this narrative with its claim that the 'robot *evolves* into a young boy' (my emphasis), thus suggesting an equation between embodiment and (masculine) gender as indices of developmental advance (rather than a return to a pre-technological natural past). Much could be made of this linkage between human and specifically gendered positioning (not least in terms of the history of artificial intelligence and the Turing test[22]).

For now though, two points demand comment. First, given the address to mothers coded by the product – washing powder – there is doubtless also some misogyny to consider, along with the devaluation of the feminized domestic space as a developmental arena. The boy as robot is thus doubly estranged from his supposedly intrinsic ('right to') childhood, with the robot polysemically also invoking scenarios of authoritarian subjection (as automaton), implicitly via maternal domination. Second, naturalizations of childhood typically evoke calls to a past that necessarily rationalizes the present, including colonial and gendered legacies, with evocations of play in sunny, fertile, well-tended gardens a key trope.

Whether evolution (installing a progressive narrative) or nostalgic recovery, what is offered here is a redemptively restorative narrative, reassuring the possibility of a return to a natural, good childhood, guaranteed by developmentally appropriate parental (read: maternal[23]) practice (here secured by the purchase of the 'right' washing powder). It also marks a new moment of brand confidence (and of course classed 'good taste') that subordinates the explicit marketing of a product to the evocation of some other, higher moral, 'good' (child development) – in a move reminiscent of Walkerdine and Lucey's[24] classic analysis, rendering mothers' household labour invisible to focus on providing 'free play' activities for their children. We might also consider the role of the dog as awakening the desire to go outside, and the embodied (phallic?) link with the writhing worm; tempting also to develop an analysis connecting up with Kathryn Bond Stockton's discussion of the queer child.[25] Yet even despite, or precisely because of, this there is nevertheless a definitely normative masculinity being evoked here.

In the case of this campaign, Persil's 'Dirt Is Good!' (D.I.G.!) engages in deliberate strategies of reversal, 'embracing the nemesis' (as one marketing commentator put it[26]) to celebrate 'dirt' as something to promote, so elaborately addressing the subjectivity of the good parent who cares more about their child's curiosity and creativity (guaranteed) through play than (the class coded through its implication for domestic labour) concern with merely keeping clean. Although launched in 2006, the 'D.I.G.!' campaign gained new impetus in the context also of a burgeoning moral panic about obesity, with activity and exercise also (marketed as) a feature of outdoor play and alongside documentation of the escalation of child allergies which in turn have generated the claim that these may occur because of bringing our children up in too-sanitized environments.[27] But overall, of course this campaign recapitulates a long-standing, implicitly psychodynamically-informed narrative[28] of play as children's work, such that this is interfered with only at the risk of inciting designation as (psychologically) neglectful or overcontrolling parents who are distorting the 'natural' course of development.

Key intertextual relations to consider include how the shift from physical to moral hygiene has worked as a longstanding mode of regulation and evaluation of the poor. 'Persil' – made by Unilever – extends this by a step further from merely inciting (middle class) mothers to clean their children's clothes, to recruiting them into a particular identity as good mothers. There are further material connections between the children whose clothes are cleaned by 'Persil' and those whose labour makes the material for the clothes in which they exercise their correct childhood by getting dirty.[29] Moreover, discourses of child-educating, soap-washing parents are reminiscent also of such international development initiatives such as Global Handwashing Day, an event designed to promote hygiene and reduce infection which both obscures and yet fosters the interests of the multinational corporations that manufacture soap, and overlooks the much more pressing problem of access to adequate and safe water supplies.[30]

If 'Jack' gets his expertise by being 'a whizz', rather than being trained or acquiring the label of a child prodigy, then 'Roboboy' is noteworthy for invoking implicit technical knowledges about child development along with moral exhortations associated with child rights. While the 'D.I.G!'' campaign is subtitled 'every child has the right', mixing up rights claims with developmental concepts in ways that, arguably, could be seen as destabilizing or else banalizing both,[31] it explicitly lays claim to consultations with child development experts – unsurprisingly from the US. Note here how the narrator of 'Roboboy' is marked as female, so installing a superior, feminized authority over the mothers addressed by the campaign. The campaign has received favourable British government attention, being cited in policy documentation as promoting activity and exercise in the countryside. As a history of the present, therefore, its technical claims have attained the position of being evidentiary 'truths'. Notwithstanding its rhetoric, 'D.I.G.' is no more child-centred than the 'Jack' story, but is much more explicitly pedagogical in its address to parents/ mothers. The expertise lies firmly with the professionals.

Childhood as memory

While my analysis so far has been concerned to tease out implicit appeals to memory and other more tortuous temporalities covertly invoked within representations of childhood, my final text for analysis mobilizes these explicitly. This text requires a return to Persil's 'D.I.G.!', but in its particular incarnation in the *What's [Not] On TV* campaign of August 2008 (i.e. during prime time summer holidays), when the mass circulation TV listing magazine *What's On TV* included a free eight page leaflet launching Persil's 'Every child has the right' campaign called *What's [Not] On TV*. Here memory operates as the trope that not only links the child of the present with that of the future, but also with the past of the adult who cares for them. The 'right to be a child' collaboration (between *What's [Not] On TV* and 'Persil') deploys all of these and more, indicating the ways that memory may foster the too easy shifts made between rights and developmental claims.

First, the adult past is evoked: 'Remember when you were a child? Plenty of scraped knees climbing trees and muddy hands from making mud pies' (*What's [Not] On TV*) that is mobilized to warrant the more 'serious' and 'abstract' voice of the expert in the sentence that follows: 'Today experts are worried that our kids' childhoods are being lost. ...'. The wider associations of simplicity and proximity to nature which are prompted via this invitation for biographical recollection affords not only claims of being natural (in the conflation of biography and chronology), but via such contrasts also grants the warrant of authenticity. The effect is a mutual strengthening of each claim, with such links both conferring and being conferred greater legitimacy by the 'expert' opinion.

Second, there is an address to the adult that the child will become. Here the desire of the parent/mother is central to this transition between past and present, as in, for example: 'We understand mothers want their children to grow up having a variety of stimulating experiences' (*What's [Not] On TV*). A hybrid representation of childhood is at play – as both lifestage and futurity. That such combinations readily coexist, usually without comment, is precisely why they are worthy of reflection. As I discuss elsewhere,[32] 'Persil' invokes, via its conflation of children's rights with developmental statements, a model of that childhood presented as both (privileged) state and stepping point, with such statements as: 'There's nothing more precious than childhood: it's a time of wonder, discovery and exploration ...' along with a sense of its proper (natural) temporality that, precisely because of its transience, confers greater poignant value upon it: 'children today seem to grow up faster' (Persil.com). Yet there is a trace of the viewing, desiring adult in this 'seem', that could perhaps offer some resources for warding off the naturalized developmental imperative. For example, we might draw attention to the implied relational character of the comparative term and ask who it is that children grow up 'faster' than? When posed so starkly, the answer is of course clear; they grow up faster than 'us', we who 'remember' ourselves as children, and so reminds us instead of the ways the physical and symbolic are always intertwined, with meanings unstable and proliferating, especially in relation to 'the child':

> If the child-figure's embodiment is so often utterly material, its materiality is also always the (im)materiality of a sign, with its endless chain of significations. Interest, desire, and knowledge are part of what constitutes – realizes – bodies, and part of what bodies realize in turn.[33]

Thus a further layer of meaning emerges: childhood as memory. In this sense Carolyn Steedman's[34] discussion of the mode of 'personification' warranted by the figure of the child is both useful and merits further development. For the child becomes the disembodied and abstracted emblem of memory, and by such means facilitates the mobilization of memory detached from who it is who is doing the remembering (with all the cultural-historical specifications of such locations). Subtle exchanges and substitutions of identification complicate this process even more,[35] for while the childhood invoked may be one remembered, or wished as remembered, by the parent, a second focuses on shaping the childhood that 'you'/ the reader, as your child's parent, would want her to be able to remember: 'helping you give your children a childhood to remember', 'to encourage Mums and kids to keep a record of summer play time', 'get out there, have fun and make some fantastic memories' (Persil.com and *What's [Not] On TV*). Significantly, this presumes that (unlike most remembered childhoods) these memories are positive, precisely through the frame equating childhood with nostalgia. This – within prevailing discourses of memory – thereby excludes or marginalizes traumatic memories which do not lend themselves to such narrative encoding, in part perhaps precisely by virtue of their departure from these conventional stories of 'happy childhoods'.

But there is a further move which returns the discourse to the pedagogical/developmental mode. Persil.com clearly builds on and bolsters a widespread desire, the desire for the parent to confirm they are being a good parent, and it invites confirmation of this not only through the cleaning of clothes from your child's worthwhile childlike activities but through the generation of (good) memories of childhood. The website advice proposes the activity with your child of recording such memories in a 'virtual scrapbook': 'To start things off we've made a virtual scrapbook to encourage Mums and kids to keep a record of summer play time, whatever shape or form it takes!' An inescapable irony is that the exhortation to active, outdoors play has now mutated into inside, desk-based work and, more tellingly, of precisely the (adult-directed) variety that the figure of the promotional TV campaign, 'Roboboy' (discussed earlier) was supposed to be being liberated from. Alongside this, via the claim to be 'helping' 'mums' with the demanding work of helping their children develop, it also addresses them as developmental subjects; for while their children have incontestable developmental needs, mothers are positioned as in need of education (to become child-centred parents) lacking in 'inspiration', 'ideas', to 'help' secure their own Roboboy's transformation into a 'real' (human) through his own activity and contact with 'nature'.

So in circular fashion the childhood memories of adults are tidied up and, albeit perhaps reparatively, pinned onto the anticipation and manipulation of children's remembered childhoods. Such childhood 'souvenirs', like the travel variety discussed by John Hutnyk,[36] function performatively. He highlights how visual representations of children work in two ways: representations of children as 'trinkets' or 'souvenirs' reify children from their cultural-political contexts and so, in turn, they abstract attention away from questions of culture and politics such that they become trivialized traces of them. In this sense, such evocations of children simultaneously acknowledge, but in that very process fix, the various instabilities and ambiguities set in play by representations of childhood as a (non-developmental) state associated with times past while also occluding such (developmental) questions as what this childhood is for. What fills in these yawning gaps (around *whose* childhood is at issue, and *whose* development, for that matter) and enables such fixing, is rendered (as psychotherapists would say) concrete or material in the 'scrapbook' 'Persil' exhorts 'Mums' to make with their children. Here the very term 'scrapbook' could be explored for its associations, semiotically blending the boysie activity of 'scrapping' with the dog outside and other outside activity (but rendered much more benign than, say, 'fighting' – which would also produce significant amounts of washing, if not bodily injury) alongside the worthy (femininely thrifty) and (educationally) creative craftwork of using up scraps; all linguistically united by putting the 'scraps' into a 'book' which can then be looked back at. This 'record' or 'scrapbook' of incited and prescribed fantasy rendered into a material reality not only highlights how the memorialization, the backward-looking reach into the past, is shaped by present demands; it also underscores how memory and childhood mobilize complex identifications formed of adults' projections (even if, given their widespread currency, children also actively subscribe to these).

The reinvention via retroactive installation of hegemonic masculinity

I have dealt with several texts of childhood, each depicting the engagement with a specific form of technology. The first text (about 'Jack') was explicitly concerned with modes of communication and consumption afforded through technologies such as the Internet. Here the (child's) expertise qualifies a precocious neoliberal subject, albeit one rendered invalid via parental interdiction. In the second text ('Roboboy') the technology is rendered more abstract with expert knowledge evoked, rather than specified, but which nevertheless assumes superiority status and so displaces parental authority. Finally, with the related *What's [Not] on TV* text, the technical expertise shifts from the manufacture and properties of the soap powder to the emotional domain concerned with the regulation of feelings (in terms of the generation and management of – parental – anxiety as good-enough parents) as well as of bodies (in terms of exercise and hygiene). Here, in particular, psychological knowledge (about child development) is mobilized, presented as commonsense but covertly authorized by the manufacturer's claims to have consulted with appropriate (developmental psychology) experts.

But there is one more point to note about all this. All the texts of childhood I have discussed evoke oedipal anxieties in the sense of exploring cultural themes of generational rivalry and the threat of children outstripping or displacing parental authority. But while 3-year-old, 'Jack's ambitions are curbed even as they are acknowledged, 'Roboboy' gains his freedom – albeit at the expense of attaining a particular kind of isolated masculinity. If this analysis holds then two further, related, areas of inquiry arise. The first of these concerns the significance of the return to the boy as the prototypical subject, and the second to interrogate or trouble the mode of identification that this relies upon.

To take these in turn, clearly there are consequences of such gendered depictions of subjectivity – especially of developmental subjects. Of course there are various ways of reading this, but the culturally masculine (if immature) subject of development is now portrayed as a potential casualty, as well as beneficiary, of a new feminized economic regime. Such representations of fragile or damaged (as well as immature) masculinity could be seen as working both to separate and to exonerate this new subject from past legacies of privilege to which it would otherwise be seen as heir. Hence rather than depicting alternative developmental subjects (girls, women or cyborgs for that matter as in other recent – cultural or policy – narratives), the texts could perhaps be read as marking a nostalgic return to, or desire for re-inscription of, an older gender order.

This brings me to the second issue, concerning the significance of the intersection of gender and age in these texts, and in particular the suppression of overt sexuality secured (accordingly to conventional mythology) by the youth of the boys. Current theoretical debates – within and beyond discussions of childhood – emphasize the need to trouble the dynamic of identification that the humanist narrative relies upon. In particular the reiteration of prevailing understandings of (hetero)sexed/gendered relations in these texts foreclose potentially transformative modes of relationship. In the 'Jack' text, the boy's desire could be said to be portrayed within the heteropatriarchal order, as addressed to but limited by his mother and confirmed by her subordinate position within the symbolic economic order (represented by the garage owner). Alternatively, 'Roboboy' achieves his freedom (notwithstanding any queering we might discern) via a conventional narrative of heroic masculine development, in the appropriately gendered and sexed separation from maternal attachment. This gender narrative retains its traditional cultural legacies. For, given the prevailing unequal distribution of these qualities of western childhood, the motif of 'play' seems to specify a reading in terms of 'race' and colonial privilege, while his 'freedom' is sanctioned by invisible authorities (child development experts). Further, (within prevailing conditions of human reproduction) subscription to the child as a token of futurity covertly presumes its status as the offspring of a heterosexual coupling, so maintaining this heterosexed as well as multinational order.[37] So even as gender mainstreaming threatens to co-opt feminist interventions at the moment of their institutionalization,[38] a reconstructed masculine boychild as subject of development seems likely only to maintain this order. Gender and childhood narratives must remain a key arena for suspicion in reconstructing the political, as well as psychic, formations of the past.

The texts I have discussed mark a shift from the exploration of subjective relations to technologies of subjectivity. I have indicated how both the appeal to and normalization of particular notions of childhood involved the shaping of memorial practices that confirm the reproductions of existing inequalities, including gendered and sexed relations. Together – unless actively contested – these contribute to prevailing strategies of impoverishing and instrumentalizing subjectivity into mere individualization. As Jennifer Croissant noted, in a prescient treatment:

> With evolutionary narratives naturalizing the emergence of cyborgs as anthropomorphized robotic systems, and cybernetic metaphors playing an increasingly important role in describing and normalizing development, flexible bodies and unhappy decentred subjectivities are part of the erosion of collectivities for refashioning politics and the public sphere.[39]

Notes

1. J. Butler, *The Psychic Life of Power* (New York and London: Routledge, 1997).
2. V. Walkerdine, *Counting Girls Out: Girls and Mathematics* (Abingdon: FalmerRoutledge, 2nd edn, 1998).
3. See: N. Rose, *The Psychological Complex: Psychology, Politics and Society in England 1869–1939* (London: Routledge, 1985) and D. Ingleby, 'Ideology and the Human Sciences: Some Comments on the Role of Reification in Psychology and Psychiatry', in T. Pateman (ed.), *Countercourse: A Handbook for Course Criticism* (Harmondsworth: Penguin, 1972) pp. 51–81.
4. W. Hollway, *Subjectivity and Method in Psychology* (London: Sage, 1989).
5. See for instance, P. Ticineto Clough with J. Halley (eds), *The Affective Turn: Theorizing the Social* (Durham, NC: Duke University Press, 2007) and M. Tamboukou, *Women, Education and the Self* (London: Palgrave Macmillan, 2003); M. Tamboukou, 'Interrogating the "Emotional Turn": Making Connections with Foucault and Deleuze', *European Journal of Psychotherapy, Counselling and Health*, 6: 3, 2003, 209–24.
6. N. Rose, *Inventing Our Selves: Psychology, Power, and Personhood* (Cambridge: Cambridge University Press, 1998); [J. De Vos first reference is still 'in press']; J. de Vos and A. Gordo Lopez, *Annual Review of Psychology (Special Issue on 'Psychologisation')*, 8, 2010.
7. M. Boler, *Feeling Power: Emotions and Education* (New York and London: Routledge, 1999).
8. L. Fendler, 'Educating Flexible Souls: The Construction of Subjectivity through Developmentality and Interaction', in K. Hultqvist and G. Dahlberg (eds), *Governing the Child in the New Millennium* (New York and London: RoutledgeFalmer, 2001), pp. 119–42; E. Burman, 'Beyond Emotional Literacy in Feminist and Educational Research', *British Education Research Journal*, 35: 1, 2009, 137–56.
9. Fendler, 'Educating Flexible Souls'; C. Morini, 'The Feminisation of Labour in Cognitive Capitalism', *Feminist Review*, 88, 2007, 40–59.
10. O. Nieuwenhuys, 'Embedding the Global Womb: Global Child Labour and the New Policy Agenda', *Children's Geographies*, 5: 1–2, 2007, 149–63.

11. A. Gordo Lopez and E. Burman, 'Emotional Capital and Information Technologies in the Changing Rhetorics around Children and Childhoods', *New Directions in Child and Adolescent Development*, 105, 2004, 63–80.
12. E. Burman, 'Taking Women's Voices: The Psychological Politics of Feminisation', *Psychology of Women Section Review*, 6: 1, 2004, 3–21; E. Burman, 'Feminism(s) or Feminisation? Between Autonomous Triumphalism and Victimhood', keynote talk at 'The Frailty of Social Relations' conference, Circulo de Bellas Artes, Madrid, March, 2006; E. Burman, 'Emotions, Reflexivity and Feminised Action Research', *Educational Action Research*, 14: 3, 2006, 315–32.
13. J. Butler, *Precarious Lives* (London: Verso, 2004).
14. V. Pupavac, 'The International Children's Rights Regime', in D. Chandler (ed.), *Re-thinking Human Rights: Critical Approaches to International Politics* (London: Palgrave Macmillan, 2002), pp. 57–75.
15. Lincolnshire is a rural county in the east of England, which, at the level of cultural stereotyping, connotes parochiality.
16. The 'Barbie-pink' designation works to emphasize how young the boy is, and so also his feminized status, since he is portrayed as oblivious to the 'obvious' gender-coding that would typically generate antipathy in older boys.
17. 'Boy aged three buys £9,000 car on internet', *The Guardian*, 26 September 2006, at: http://www.guardian.co.uk/technology/2006/sep/26/news.consumernews (accessed 10 August 2010).
18. Outside capital's 'centres' this also includes generating intra-familial divisions through efforts to embed the generalized gesture of humanitarian assistance within a specified local context, 'individualizing' relationships of care and support through interventions such as child sponsorship – see E. Bornstein, 'Child Sponsorship, Evangelism and Belonging in the Work of World Vision Zimbabwe', *American Ethnologist*, 28: 3, 2001, 595–622.
19. C. Steedman, *Strange Dislocations: Childhood and the Idea of Human Interiority 1780–1930* (London: Virago, 1995).
20. K. Lury, ' "For Crying Out Loud": The Repression of the Child's Subjectivity in *The House of Tiny Tearaways*', unpublished ms, 2006.
21. http://www.visit4info.com/advert/Persil-Dirt-is-Good-Persil-Range/61597 (accessed 28 September 2008)
22. A. Gordo Lopez and R. Cleminson, *Techno-Sexual Landscapes: Changing Relations between Technology and Sexuality* (London: Free Association Books, 2004).
23. It is fair to assume this, since after two mentions early on of 'family' the remainder of the entire 'D.I.G.!'/'Every Child Has the Right...' website explicitly discusses and addresses mothers (usually as 'Mums'), while 'Dads' gain no mention whatsoever.
24. V. Walkerdine and H. Lucey, *Democracy in the Kitchen: Regulating Mothers and Socialising Daughters* (London: Virago, 1989).
25. K. Bond Stockton, *The Queer Child, or Growing Sideways in the Twentieth Century* (Durham, NC: Duke University Press, 2009).
26. H. Ganczakowski, 'ITV 50 Years of Fame: Private View – Persil', http://www.brandrepublic.com/Campaign/News/518811/ (accessed 28 September 2008).

27. See: http://immunology.suite101.com/article.cfm/a_little_dirt_may_be_good_ for_your_immune_system (accessed 10 August 2010).
28. See: V. Walkerdine, 'Sex, Power and Pedagogy', *Screen Education*, 38, 1981, 14–21.
29. 'Persil' is manufactured by Unilever, whose Indian subsidiary Unilever Hindustan Ltd has been implicated in exploitative child labour practices concerned with cotton picking (see my review in E. Burman, *Developments: Child, Image, Nation* [London and New York: BrunnerRoutledge, 2008] and http://www.crocodyl.org/wiki/unilever, and http://www.powerset.com/ explore/semhtml/Child_Labour_Issues_of_Unilever_in_India).
30. A. Plyushteva, 'This Benevolent Hand Gives You Soap: Reflections on Global Handwashing Day from an International Development Perspective', *Journal of Health Management*, 11: 2, 2009, 419–30; E. Burman, 'Un/thinking Children in Development: A Contribution from Northern Antidevelopmental Psychology', in G. Canella and L. Soto (eds), *Childhoods: A Handbook* (New York: Peter Lang, 2010), pp. 9–26.
31. E. Burman, 'Un/thinking Children in Development: A Contribution from Northern Antidevelopmental Psychology'.
32. E. Burman, 'Desiring Development: Psychoanalytic Approaches to Antidevelopmental Psychology' (submitted for publication).
33. C. Castañeda, *Figurations: Child, Bodies, Worlds* (Durham, NC: Duke University Press, 2002), p. 81.
34. Steedman, *Strange Dislocations*.
35. E. Burman, 'False Memories, True Hopes: Revenge of the Postmodern on Therapy', *New Formations*, 30, 1997, 122–34; E. Burman, 'Pedagogics of Post/ modernity: The Address to the Child in Walter Benjamin and Jean-Francois Lyotard', in K. Lesnik-Oberstein (ed.), *Children in Culture: Approaches to Childhood* (New York and London: Palgrave Macmillan, 1998) pp. 55–88; E. Burman, *Deconstructing Developmental Psychology* (Hove: Routledge, 2nd edn, 2007).
36. J. Hutnyk, 'Photogenic Poverty: Souvenirs and Infantilism', *Journal of Visual Culture*, 3: 1, 2004, 77–94.
37. L. Edelman, *No Future: Queer Theory and the Death Drive* (Durham, NC and London: Duke University Press, 2004).
38. A. Cornwall, E. Harrison and A Whitehead (eds), *Feminisms in Development: Contradictions, Contestations and Challenges* (London: Zed Press, 2007).
39. J. L. Croissant, 'Growing Up Cyborg. Development Stories for Postmodern Children', in R. Davis-Floyd and J. Dumit (eds), *Cyborg Babies. From Techno-Sex to Techno-Tots* (New York and London: Routledge, 1998), pp. 285–301, p. 296.

2
Playthings: Archaeology and the Material Ambiguities of Childhood

Eleanor Conlin Casella

The method by which Hotavila (Hopi) girls build play houses is quite ingenious. First, house walls are modelled from wet mud and then they are filled with dry sand with a wet earthen roof applied to the top of the structure. ... These houses are furnished with all manner of items that the girls scavenge from the village. A small piece of mirror is used as the dressing mirror, a piece of linoleum is the rug, and a small can becomes the stove, while an empty spool of thread stands in for the sewing machine. Sticks with clothing tied onto them become the Hopi child's dolls and also the inhabitants of these villages. ... Gardens, cornfields, and fruit orchards are often built around these houses by sticking twigs and leaves into the ground.[1]

Towards a materiality of childhood

Despite a growing enthusiasm for research on the material aspects of social identities and subjectivities in the discipline of archaeology, relatively few publications have considered the age-related dimensions of human life. And yet, we know logically that children were not only frequently present within our study sites, but often played a significant role in the actual deposition of the material remains we recover, analyse and interpret. This chapter will explore the constructivist approach to childhood in archaeology by both tracing emerging scholarship within the discipline, and by considering the implications of this work in relation to the material assemblages recovered from two historic sites I have excavated.

Over the past decade, a small – if vibrant – literature base has begun to emerge within archaeology to identify past cultural constructions of childhood and explore the everyday lived experiences of children in both the remote and recent past.[2] As in other fields in the arts and social sciences, these publications helped create a conceptual shift away from biologically-determinist and passive enculturation studies that previously dominated research based on childhood development and childhood communication. Instead, the constructivist approach offered a means for considering 'childhood' as a changing social experience situated within its own historical trajectory and cultural context.

In seeking to explore the materiality of childhood from recent historic periods to the remote prehistoric past, archaeologists have contributed to this wider body of constructivist scholarship by explicitly emphasizing the material dimensions of children and childhood in past human societies. Their research can be seen to coalesce into two dominant themes: the study of children as a topic itself (children's material culture, spatial distributions, use patterns) and study of childhood as a time of preparation or apprenticeship for adulthood. However, when we examine these archaeological case studies in greater detail, far from offering discrete intellectual pathways, these scholarly themes immediately entangle.

This chapter will question whether the experiences of childhood can be somehow associated with a distinct, 'unique', or 'child-specific' materiality. Is it possible to discern, as some recent publications have attempted, "the material culture of childhood"?[3] How does such a concept rely implicitly not only upon familiar models of social agency, but also particular social contexts for the experience of childhood itself? And ultimately, what critical understandings of childhood can be offered by archaeological perspectives on both the remote and recent past?

Where were the children?

One crucial paradox emerges throughout the archaeological literature. Children are both *necessary* components for understanding past human societies, and simultaneously *invisible* in our traditional scholarly interpretations of these material worlds. As can be all-too-easily found in the public reconstructions of archaeological sites that illuminate student textbooks, newspapers, and natural history museums, childhood is popularly understood as a 'natural', biologically-based, universal experience – one associated with 'common-sense' understandings of security, nurture and control, and significantly shaped by 'well-known' stages of cognitive development and physiological growth. And yet, while specific biological changes occur as individual *Homo sapiens* mature, the diverse meanings, understandings, ideals and rituals that surround these shared phenomena are not only arbitrary correlations within any culture group, but also vary dramatically across both cultures and (pre) historical periods.[4]

But more importantly, the discipline has tended to exclude children from scholarly interpretations because of a generally perceived invisibility within the material record. Characterized as an undifferentiated cohort of non-adults, 'children' have become traditionally associated with unpredictable, distorted or randomized artefact distribution patterns, and with miniature object forms (defined uncritically as 'toys'). Further, they are generally assumed to use a highly restricted range of both artefacts and cultural spaces, despite extensive evidence to the contrary in both ethnographic and historical scholarship.[5] And regardless of whatever minimal contributions children might possibly have added to the physical residue of a past cultural site, their material presence would be ultimately obscured by the anonymity of the archaeological record, as specific artefact clusters could never be linked to them with any degree of objective certainty.

Responding to this perception of invisibility, a growing range of archaeologists have turned to explore mortuary (burial) and domestic (household) contexts as prime opportunities for exploring the unique materiality of childhood. Adopting an explicitly constructivist approach to the concept of childhood, mortuary archaeologists have used excavated sites, particularly their material intersections of biological and cultural data, to interpret contextually age-related social identities on both individual and community-based scales. This work has explored, for example, how the post-mortem treatment and placement of non-adult skeletons may themselves illuminate past structures of identity, social organization, status or ritual,[6] and how the spatial relationships of individual graves within cemeteries may reflect variations in the identification of 'child' as a relevant social category, changing patterns of religious and iconographic practice, or even broader mobilizations of political ideology, ethnicity and citizenship.[7] Much attention has been paid to the 'grave goods' (artefacts intentionally placed in association with skeletons within burials), with scholars variously linking their material nature and/or spatial position within the grave to aspects of magic and social ritual, age-identity categories, or even relative wealth or status within the past community.[8]

On the domestication of childhood

Other scholars have attempted to rectify the absence of children from archaeological research by focusing upon household sites and domestic landscapes. Particularly in non-western and prehistoric contexts, this scholarship has illuminated the active role of children in traditional crafts, either in a position of learning apprenticeship or as direct producers in their own right. Children have thus been linked to the creation of material goods including both stone and bone tools, terracotta ceramics, and woven textiles.[9] Other archaeologists have questioned the social use of space, considering both the influence of children on distributions of artefacts throughout household sites,[10] and the physical organizations of domestic landscapes that reflect an investment into childcare and play activities.[11]

Archaeological research based within historic and contemporary periods typically relies upon the presence of excavated artefacts that can be functionally associated with children, often identified under generic categories such as 'educational' (slate or graphite pencils, transfer-printed ceramics inscribed with alphabets or moral messages), 'child-rearing' (glass feeding bottles, small-sized leather shoes, infant and juvenile clothing) or 'toys' (bisque porcelain doll parts, glass or ceramic marbles, miniature ceramic or plastic-moulded figurines, wooden dominoes, bone dice). Such assemblages have been interpreted to illuminate broader material ideologies of domesticity, class and labour, ethnicity, respectability and inter-generational kinship relations.[12]

While this literature has primarily focused on a combination of family households in a combination of urban and rural contexts, other work has extended 'the domestic' to encompass less-familiar or marginal spaces – including frontier mining settlements, boarding-house brothels, and even officer's quarters within maximum-security penitentiaries – that also provided homes for children.[13] Archaeological techniques of analysing material deposits have also been applied in the contemporary domestic context of a recently abandoned British council house to explore the poignant materiality of a late-twentieth century dysfunctional or 'failed' household.[14] Recording the spatial distributions of abandoned everyday items of clothing, foodstuff, soft toys, children's books, family photos, toiletries, Christmas decorations and methadone supplies discarded throughout a rapidly vacated two-bedroomed house managed by the local housing authority, Victor Buchli and Gavin Lucas offered a stark archaeological model of domestic 'alienation' as an all-too-common characteristic of modern urban childhoods. Interpreting the distribution of abandoned artefacts across the various rooms as evidence of a relationship breakdown between the mother and non-resident father of two children (known from council records as a boy of 4 years, and girl of 6 years), this study examined the material residue of a dystopic household to trace the disintegration of familial relations created by the toxic mix of heroin addiction, unemployment and poverty.

Given the growing diversity of these regional and period-specific case studies, one particularly compelling model for exploring a comparative materiality of children has been recently developed by Jane Eva Baxter.[15] In this study, she compared the landscape distribution of child-related artefact assemblages across five separate domestic sites from nineteenth-century North America, observing that in all cases 'children's material culture does not simply mirror the overall density patterns [of household artefacts] ... and instead represents the remains of children's behaviour.'[16] Particularly high-density clusters of children's artefacts (defined by the author as 'toys' and 'child-rearing devices') were discovered through distribution analysis of excavated collections, suggesting material patterns of habitual play activities situated within the overall domestic landscape.

While the majority of these child-specific artefacts were recovered in areas that could easily be seen from the house sites – suggesting both direct and indirect forms of adult supervision and attention – a few small concentration zones were discovered in locations well away from areas of habitual use, and out of sight from the house itself. Implicitly influenced by sociological concepts of 'agency', Baxter interpreted these artefact clusters as evidence of 'secret or special place[s] of childhood where children went to play away from adult supervision'.[17] As locations used to 'create and shape their own experiences with the environment through peer interaction and child-structured play', these autonomous play-worlds served as 'the sole domain of children'.[18]

But how 'unique' is this materiality? From a methodological perspective, Baxter has argued:

> The association of children and adults with particular objects may be used to identify not only distinctions of age and gender but also the objects used and activities pursued by members of certain groups. Establishing the material culture used and identifying the activities undertaken by members of different groups may aid [with] interpreting artefacts encountered in archaeological deposits.[19]

And yet, we must ask whether this process of material identification can be substantiated.

Turning to consider similar domestic sites outside of this North American context, her approach would initially appear to hold a certain interpretive resonance. Funded by English Heritage from 2003, the Alderley Sandhills Project was developed as the first European-based archaeological study of the revolutionary domestic transformations created through both early-modern industrialization and the subsequent shift to a consumer-based economy.[20] Excavations revealed the structural foundations of two workers' cottages based in Alderley Edge, a north-west rural village located in Cheshire, approximately 25 km away from central Manchester. Although elements of the site could be traced back to the seventeenth century,[21] the vast majority of recovered artefacts dated to the inter-war period of the twentieth century, when the two houses had been internally subdivided into four households, and accommodated four local families: the Perrins, Barbers, Barrows and Ellams.

In addition to the historic perspectives gained through research at the Cheshire County Archives, our recovered household assemblages were interpreted through a combination of memories and family photographs shared by three oral history participants – Mrs Edna Younger (*née* Barrow), Mrs Molly Pitcher (*née* Barber), and her older brother Mr Roy Barber, who visited the excavation site to see their childhood homes emerge from the soil. Through this complex array of the documented, the remembered, and the material, we discovered a lived experience of rural English childhood over the inter-war decades that at first appeared to resonate with Jane Baxter's North American model of children's materiality.

A range of objects were recovered from inside the excavated house structures that represented manufactured goods related specifically to children. These included child-rearing objects – such as a double-ended, clear glass baby bottle, banana-shaped to help prevent the baby swallowing air during feedings (Figure 2.1).[22] The majority of this assemblage consisted of objects associated with play activities, predominantly doll fragments and body parts that had been moulded from unglazed or 'bisque' porcelain.[23] The earliest of the six recovered doll's heads dated to the nineteenth century, and displayed a moulded quiff of hair at the front with the faint residue of an original dark pigment. The other five heads (dated from the late nineteenth through early twentieth centuries) were all simply decorated with some combination of hand-painted eyebrows and eyelashes (Figure 2.2), wavy hair, and coloured lips, eyes

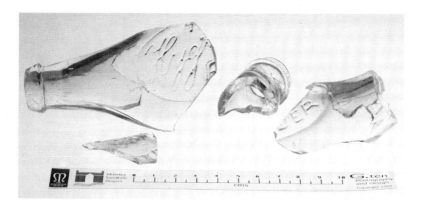

Figure 2.1   Clear glass baby bottle, Alderley Sandhills Project, 2003

or cheeks. One represented a Continental import, displaying a maker's stamp that read: 'Germany/275.19/0/**oppers**'.

Other artefacts traditionally categorized as 'play-related' were distributed around the immediate households, including a small bone doll's brush, a metal-alloy mouth organ and a metal table-tennis net clamp. Evidence of bicycle ownership consisted of a metal pedal, the upper components of a bike bell, and rusted ferrous fragments of gears. From the early twentieth century, rubber and plastic toys began to appear in archaeological deposits, with four small rubber balls and a larger tennis ball recovered from the Barber household, a plastic moulded male figure stamped (in English) 'Made in Germany' from the Barber household, and several cream-coloured plastic 'tiddly-wink disks' recovered from both areas.[24]

In an echo of Jane Baxter's domestic distribution model, oral histories demonstrated a strong pattern of child-led play *outside* the immediate household domain. The most vivid memories of all three oral history participants detailed the surrounding landscape as their childhood playground (Figure 2.3). Favoured games included winter tobogganing down the hill to the southeast of the excavated cottages – identified as a 'belting spot' for this sport. The sledges used for this activity were all homemade from tea trays recycled by their fathers. During summer months the Sandhills (a unique landscape feature that characterized this region of Alderley Edge) provided an additional arena for unsupervised play. The children would ride down the Sandhills on a tray. Mrs Younger explained 'and you'd go Whoosh! Right down to the bottom!

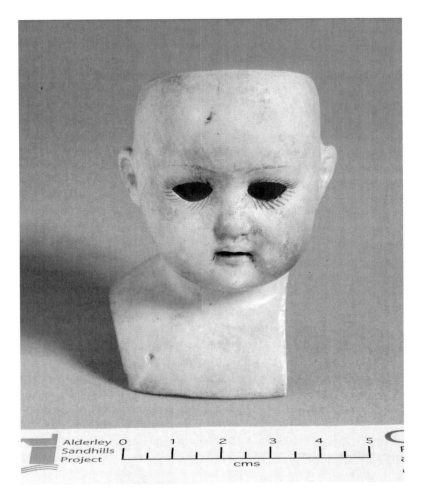

Figure 2.2 Bisque porcelain doll's head, Alderley Sandhills Project, 2003

It was very good.'[25] Although the Sandhills had originated as contaminated waste material dumped by the neighbouring industrial mines, in the geography of children's play they were only associated with fun, games and family events.

Nevertheless, Mrs Younger's memories simultaneously challenge any simple categorization of these play-related artefacts. Her sledding tea trays (selected and modified by their fathers) formed part of a wider repertoire of shared domestic objects requisitioned by the children for their

Figure 2.3 Children of the Hagg at play, 1920s. Photograph courtesy of E. Younger

play activities. Like the Hopi children described in the opening quote of this chapter, our project participants described a creative recycling and co-option of everyday household objects for play activities. Mrs Edna Younger, for example, recalled how all three of the children had played in the base of a hollowed-out tree in the neighbouring woods. Unsupervised by adults, they would borrow a frying pan, some lard and potatoes from their respective homes, and fry chips in their secret den as part of their games. Even when prompted by specific artefacts such as the mouth organ or dolls' heads, it was the outdoor play, the fields, tree houses and Sandhills that figured most prominently in the recollections of childhood at Alderley Edge. But could this distribution of material practices be specifically associated with an archaeology of childhood?

Further, additional oral histories shared by our former residents demonstrated that objects typically identified as 'toys' could hold far more baroque social meanings. One single undecorated white-glazed ceramic plate from a doll's tea set was recovered during the Alderley excavations. When this artefact was shown to former resident Mrs Molly Pitcher, she remembered the object in terms of her family history, and recounted her special link with Mrs Lena Perrin, her Great-Aunt who occupied the adjoining cottage at our Alderley site:

> MP: ... when she got to the church, my mother had decided what they decided to call me and told her [Mrs. Perrin], told my father, and she [Mrs. Perrin] took over when I was being christened and gave me this Lena Mary for *her* daughter. So I've been lumbered with that ever since. So as soon as I came back, my mother said 'I'm not having that!' so they called me Molly. But I mean ... I mean that's just a family thing, you know ... .
>
> ... .
>
> MP: ... and of course when Mrs. Perrin died I got left everything because she'd given her daughter's name, who'd died at 21 you see.
>
> ... .
>
> MP: So I've got some of her treasures. I've still got them. Kind of she'd got them for her daughter. I've got a 30-piece, little baby's, well I don't know whether ... coffee set or tea service, the whole lot. And a fender with LMB on it, which was Lena Mary Barber. And *she* took me to be christened because my mother was ill ... I know this isn't relevant, I don't know ... .[26]

These memories demonstrated the intricate bonds of family kinship and materiality that forged a rich experience of childhood within this rural working community. More importantly, they invested these excavated artefacts with complex social meanings that ultimately questioned the traditional archaeological process of object categorization or functional interpretation. Indeed, as Baxter herself recognizes:

> The object does not have to be a toy or a child-specific tool to be an important part of a child's experience or to represent something

about that child to members of her family and community. ...These material objects were not the isolated possessions of one type of individual but rather the tangible links that helped forge and maintain social relationships.[27]

The ambiguous object holds multiple, intimate and often contradictory meanings. A 'toy', in other words, is not always a toy.

Twelve little girls in two straight lines[28]

Thus, archaeological research on childhood has embraced the household context as the primary arena of examination. Through their detailed interpretations of artefact assemblages and discard patterns associated with household sites, this work has exposed crucial questions over the idea of a 'unique' materiality created by and for children themselves. It has significantly expanded our appreciation of children as active social agents, rather than passive recipients of psycho-social and cultural norms.

But *was* this domesticity a universal experience of childhood? Particularly in the historic past, childhood also frequently unfolded as a far more institutionalized experience than commonly acknowledged by the childhood archaeology literature, with field studies published on sites that have ranged from wealthy residential schools to single-room schoolhouses, from juvenile detention camps and charitable orphanages to Aboriginal Missions and Indian Industrial Schools.[29] Historic examples of institutionally-based childhoods can be found not only cross-culturally, but across various socio-economic classes, with the elite boarding schools of the trans-Atlantic world offering both a stark contrast and curious resonance with the various institutional missions and orphanages established across the colonial frontiers.

Perhaps, within these austere contexts, 'childhood' exists as an ideal (or idealized) concept, rather than a household-based experience.[30] Indeed, archaeological research has recorded an inherent material tension between the domestic versus institutional nature of these sites, and struggled to locate 'childhood' through both 'the search for domestic artefacts and the behavioural patterns that those objects represent' but also 'the architecture...and associated structures such as fuel storage sheds and coal bins, privies, fences, walls, and other special use buildings (e.g. dormitories, chapels, and gymnasia).'[31]

I developed the Ross Factory Archaeology Project to examine the archaeological remains of a mid-nineteenth century prison established to accommodate female felons sentenced to criminal transportation from Great Britain to the Australian penal colonies. Many of the 12,000 women exiled to the Van Diemen's Land colony (renamed Tasmania in 1854, in an effort to cleanse its 'convict stain') were accompanied by their dependant children – infants and toddlers who had either accompanied their convict mothers in imperial exile, or represented the result of an unsanctioned sexual encounter within the penal colony. The Ross Female Factory, its name a contraction of the word 'Manufactory,' was established in 1846 as a special purpose depôt for pregnant and nursing convict women. It operated until the cessation of British criminal transportation in 1853. Never substantially re-occupied, the archaeological site is now managed by the Parks Service as a state historic reserve.[32]

Located in the rural district of the Northern Midlands, this inland prison was originally intended to supply female convict domestic labour to local pastoral properties, and provide a healthy bucolic atmosphere for the convict children, thereby alleviating overcrowding in the two contemporary urban Female Factories within the penal colony. In accordance with regulations of the Convict Department, infants at Ross Factory were accommodated with their convict mothers for nutritional purposes, until weaning was enforced at approximately 9 months of age. Following transfer of their mothers to the main prison compound, their children were separated from them and accommodated within the Nursery Ward until the age of 3, when they were transferred to the Queen's Orphan School in Hobart Town, located approximately 69 miles to the south of Ross.[33] By the 31 December 1848, muster counts reported that Ross Female Factory incarcerated 62 women, 22 girls and 20 boys.[34]

Funded through the British Academy, I directed archaeological excavations during January 2007, with local support provided by the Parks and Wildlife Service, Heritage Tasmania, and the Queen Victoria Museum and Art Gallery. Consisting of an open-area trench of 4x8 square metres, the excavations revealed structural remains of the Nursery Ward and adjoining Work Room (Figure 2.4). Artefact assemblages were also recovered from soil deposits that had accumulated in underfloor spaces associated with the Female Factory occupation of the site,[35] and therefore represented social activities undertaken within the Nursery Ward.

Despite extensive archival and archaeological evidence identifying this region of the Ross Factory as the Nursery Ward, a general absence of obvious child-specific materials (toys, feeding bottles, clothing, etc.) characterized the recovered artefact assemblage. Although initially surprising, particularly in comparison with the Alderley Sandhills Project

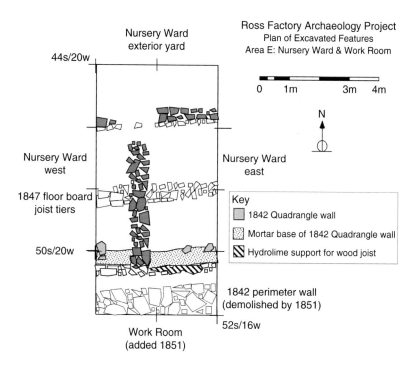

Figure 2.4 Plan of Nursery Wards, Ross Female Factory, Tasmania, Australia. Ross Factory Archaeology Project, 2007

household site discussed above, the general absence itself begged an immediate question: what would constitute a material signature of childhood within this particular archaeological context, a Nursery Ward within a British colonial female prison?

What would be the material implications of a childhood dominated by the experience of penal confinement? Recent archaeological studies of *non-carceral* historic institutions dedicated to the care of children, places such as orphanages or schools,[36] demonstrated the frequent presence of toy dolls, marbles, rubber balls, writing slates and pencils, toothbrushes, and combs – all objects explicitly related to a process of childhood socialization, and as previously detailed, objects commonly recovered from domestic households including the working-cottages of the Alderley Sandhills Project. Why were cognate artefacts missing from this penal site?

Perhaps the absence of such items from the Nursery Ward at the Ross Female Factory was not accidental. While the absence of obvious formal 'toys' could be related to the general scarcity of personal belongings within this carceral site, previous archaeological research has critiqued simplistic interpretations of this special category of artefact.[37] Indeed, in her influential cross-cultural ethnographic study of childhood play, Helen Schwartzman observed Hopi children (introduced at the start of this paper) creating extended play-families from 'bone dolls', with different elements of the carpal/tarsal (ankle) bones collected from sheep or calves used to impersonate various family characters.[38]

Perhaps a 'toy' ultimately resides in the eye (or grasping little hands) of the beholder. An estimated count of six large ferrous serving spoons were recovered from the Ross Factory Nursery-related under-floor deposits (Figure 2.5), although no archival evidence suggested the preparation of meals within these special dormitories. Were they used for apportioning and distributing foods to the Nursery children? As objects that could be bounced, banged, sucked – but crucially, *not* swallowed – perhaps these kitchen implements served as 'toys' for the infant and toddler residents of the Nurseries? Perhaps, like the poly-valent 'toys' of our Hopi children, they held both capacities? Or as Jane Baxter observed, 'The activities and material culture of childhood,

Figure 2.5   Ferrous serving spoon, detail *in-situ*. January 2007

however, extend beyond the small or often absent category of child-specific artifacts.'[39]

Regardless of these functional ambiguities, given the specifically *carceral* context of the Nursery Ward, the absence of child-specific arte-facts might further suggest an intentional form of delayed socialization, a negation of the materiality of the 'child' within this place of (adult) punishment.[40] By addressing the biological survival of these new colo-nial subjects, while simultaneously limiting both maternal and material contacts, perhaps the colonial administrators were linking the moment at which the convict child became a social being to their institutional transfer to the Royal Orphan School? Within the Female Factory, their segregated Nursery Wards ultimately provided a useful means for ideo-logical displacement. Separated from the general penal compound, these unique dormitories offered an effective architectural means for avoid-ing all direct reference to the transgressive generative practices behind the creation of these children, for as observed by Michel Foucault:

> sex must not be named imprudently, but its aspects, its correla-tions, and its effects must be pursued down to their slenderest ramifications.[41]

Perhaps the intentional unravelling of emotional bonds between the incarcerated mothers and children additionally provided a significant affective component of the colonial socialization process – the stark act of separation *itself* generating a story of removal, neglect and alien-ated familial ties that became the painful experience of non-domestic childhood shared amongst these institutionally-raised 'convict babies'? Ultimately, the invisibility of children within this excavated assem-blage raises questions on the nature of a *carceral* childhood, where the absences themselves created a unique spatial cartography of power. As the embodied products of their convict mother's unsanctioned liaison, these children were, unlike their domestic counterparts, necessarily made to be materially invisible.

Children as material paradox

By way of conclusion, a few issues have emerged from this brief con-sideration of the archaeology of children. While the transition away from both biologically-determined and passive enculturation mod-els has opened an intellectual pathway towards more theoretically-sophisticated constructivist approaches, a disciplinary tendency to focus on household sites has resulted in a model of childhood socialization derived from sociological theories of 'agency'. This growing body of literature has certainly encouraged us to acknowledge materially the existence of self-determining, creative, decision-making children within the familiar domestic context. The artefact distribution models, in particular, have illuminated the archaeological significance of child-related playthings and private outdoor play-spaces in the creation of children's own material worlds.

But how universal is this domestic experience? And to what degree do children have the ability to exercise their social agency? At the risk of invoking the spectre of biological-determinism, it seems important also to recognize the different material possibilities and limitations that accompany separate stages in ontological and cognitive development. An infant will conceptualize an object differently than an adolescent; a child typically enjoys a far less restricted spatial range than a toddler. How would these developmental changes in the shifting nature of 'childhood' produce different forms of 'agency'? How would they produce changing forms of materiality?

Further, by expanding our framework of inquiry to encompass non-domestic places of childhood, we must acknowledge that the institutional arena provided (and continues to provide) the dominant childhood experience for many confined within Aboriginal Missions, juvenile detention centres, charitable orphanages and elite boarding schools. These non-domestic environments typically restricted landscapes of potential action, with children's social lives characterized by disciplinary routines of access and movement, and regulated expressions of familial support and parental affection. How would this less bucolic, less comforting version of childhood challenge agency-based models of children's materiality?

And more significantly, despite the worthy attempts of scholars not to only 'find' children in past human societies, but to understand a material world created by children themselves, we are ultimately confronted by more uncertainties than understandings. We are left to contemplate the impossibility of a 'toy' – a special category of play object that can potentially encompass *anything*, and therefore *everything*, and therefore *nothing*. But this necessary disruption of a direct link between the form and the function of an artefact holds tremendous disciplinary implications for the practice of archaeological interpretation. How can we reconstruct past human activities, past social identities, past lifeways, without relying upon the certainty of the form/function correlation? The concept of 'children', therefore, forces us to acknowledge a fundamental, if rather distressing, material paradox: we know they were present, and yet their materiality remains ambiguous, at best. Like their 'playthings', children exist as an archaeological conundrum: simultaneously necessary and impossible.

Acknowledgements

Funding for the Alderley Sandhills Project was provided by English Heritage through the Aggregates Levy Sustainability Fund. The Ross Factory Archaeology Project (2007) was funded through the British Academy, and supported by the Tasmanian Parks and Wildlife Service, and the Queen Victoria Museum and Art Gallery of Launceston. Many generous volunteers, colleagues and students participated in these excavations and laboratory stages over the years, and deserve my full recognition and gratitude. Acknowledgements are due to Karín Lesnik-Oberstein for providing me with the opportunity to develop my comparative work on this difficult subject. Particular thanks are due to Alison Oram for her helpful advice, perspectives and intellectual support throughout the creation of this study.

Notes

1. H. Schwartzman, *Transformations: The Anthropology of Children's Play* (New York: Plenum Press, 1978), p. 158.
2. J. Baxter (ed.), 'Children in Action: Perspectives on the Archaeology of Childhood', *Archaeological Papers of the American Anthropological Association*, 15 (Berkeley: University of California Press, 2006); K. Kamp (ed.), *Children in the Prehistoric Puebloan Southwest* (Salt Lake City: University of Utah Press, 2002); J. Moore and E. Scott (eds), *Invisible People and Processes: Writing Gender and Childhood into European Archaeology* (London: Leicester University Press, 1997).
3. M. Gutman and N. de Coninck-Smith (eds), *Designing Modern Childhoods: History, Space, and the Material Culture of Childhood* (New Brunswick, NJ: Rutgers University Press, 2008).
4. K. Kamp, 'Where Have All the Children Gone? The Archaeology of Childhood', *Journal of Archaeological Method and Theory*, 8: 1, 2001, 1–34.
5. Kamp, 'Where Have All the Children Gone?'; see also J. Baxter (ed.), 'Children in Action: Perspectives on the Archaeology of Childhood'; J. Sofaer Derevenski (ed.), *Archaeological Review from Cambridge: Perspectives on Children and Childhood*, 13: 2 (1994); Schwartzman, *Transformations*; E. Ross, *Love and Toil: Motherhood in Outcast London, 1870–1918* (Oxford: Oxford University Press, 1993); A. Davin, *Growing Up Poor: Home, School and Street in London, 1870–1914* (London: Rivers Oram Press, 1996).

6. N. Rothchild, *Prehistoric Dimensions of Status: Gender and Age in Eastern North America* (New York: Garland, 1990); E. Scott, *The Archaeology of Infancy and Infant Death*, British Archaeological Reports International Series 819 (Oxford: Archaeopress, 1999); M. Perry, 'Redefining Childhood through Bioarchaeology', in J. Baxter, 'Children in Action', pp. 89–114; J. Sofaer, *The Body as Material Culture: A Theoretical Osteoarchaeology* (Cambridge: Cambridge University Press, 2006).

7. S. Lucy, 'Children in Early Medieval Cemeteries', *Archaeological Review from Cambridge*, 13: 2, 1994, 21–34; J. Sofaer Derevenski, 'Age and Gender at the Site of Tiszapolgar-Basatanya, Hungary', *Antiquity*, 71: 274, 1997, 875–89; H. McKillop, 'Recognizing Children's Graves in Nineteenth-Century Cemeteries: Excavations in St. Thomas Anglican Churchyard, Belleville, Ontario, Canada', *Historical Archaeology*, 29: 2, 1995, 77–99; S. Houby-Nielsen, 'Child Burials in Ancient Athens', in J. Sofaer Derevenski (ed), *Children and Material Culture* (London: Routledge, 2000), pp. 151–66.

8. S. Crawford 'Children, Grave Goods and Social Status in Early Anglo-Saxon England', in J. Sofaer Derevenski, *Children and Material Culture*, pp. 169–79; G. McCafferty and S. McCafferty, 'Boys and Girls Interrupted: Mortuary Evidence of Children from Postclassic Cholula, Puebla', in T. Ardren and S. Hutson (eds), *The Social Experience of Childhood in Ancient Mesoamerica* (Boulder: University Press of Colorado, 2006), pp. 25–52; R. Storey and P. McAnany, 'Children of K'axob: Premature Death in a Formative Maya Village', in T. Ardren and S. Hutson, *The Social Experience of Childhood in Ancient Mesoamerica*, pp. 53–72.

9. J. Spector, *What This Awl Means: Feminist Archaeology at a Wahpeton Dakota Village* (Minneapolis: Minnesota Historical Society Press, 1993); N. Finlay, 'Kid Knapping: The Missing Children in Lithic Analysis', in J. Moore and E. Scott, *Invisible People and Processes*, pp. 203–12; B. Bagwell, 'Ceramic Form and Skill: Attempting to Identify Child Producers at Pecos Pueblo, New Mexico', in K. Kamp, *Children in the Prehistoric Puebloan Southwest*, pp. 90–107; K. Kamp, 'Prehistoric Children Working and Playing: A Southwest Case Study in Learning Ceramics', *Journal of Anthropological Research*, 57, 2001, 427–50; P. Crown, 'Learning to Make Pottery in the Prehispanic American Southwest', *Journal of Anthropological Research*, 57, 2001, 451–69; P. Greenfield, 'Children, Material Culture and Weaving: Historical Change and Developmental Change', in J. Sofaer Derevenski, *Children and Material Culture*, pp. 72–86.

10. R. Bonnichsen, 'Millie's Camp: An Experiment in Archaeology', *World Archaeology*, 4: 3, 1973, 277–91; G. Hammond and N. Hammond, 'Child's Play: A Distorting Factor in Archaeological Distribution', *American Antiquity*, 46: 3, 1981, 634–6.

11. S. Hutson, 'Children Not at Chunchcmil: A Relational Approach to Young Subjects,' in T. Ardren and S. Hutson, *The Social Experience of Childhood in Ancient Mesoamerica*, pp. 103–32; B. Clark, 'Lived Ethnicity: Archaeology and Identity in *Mexicano* Colorado', *World Archaeology*, 37: 3, 2005, 440–52; J. Baxter, *The Archaeology of Childhood* (Walnut Creek: AltaMira Press, 2005), pp. 67–80.

12. A. Praetzellis and M. Praetzellis 'Faces and Façades: Victorian Ideology in Early Sacramento', in E. Yentsch and M. Beaudry (eds), *The Art and Mystery*

of Historical Archaeology (Boca Raton: CRC Press, 1992), pp. 75–99; L. Wilkie, 'Not Merely Child's Play: Creating a Historical Archaeology of Children and Childhood', in J. Sofaer Derevenski, *Children and Material Culture*, pp. 100–14; C. LaRoche and G. McGowan, 'Material Culture: Conservation and Analysis of Textiles Recovered from Five Points', *Historical Archaeology* 35: 3, 2001, 65–75; S. Lampard, 'The Ideology of Domesticity and the Working-Class Women and Children of Port Adelaide, 1840–1890', *Historical Archaeology*, 43: 3, 2009, 50–64.

13. J. Prangnell and K. Quirk, 'Children in Paradise: Growing Up on the Australian Goldfields', *Historical Archaeology*, 43: 3, 2009, 38–49; D. Seifert (ed.), 'Sin City', *Historical Archaeology*, 39: 1, 2005; C. Nobles, 'Gazing Upon the Invisible: Women and Children at the Old Baton Rouge Penitentiary', *American Antiquity*, 65: 1, 2000, 5–14.

14. V. Buchli and G. Lucas, 'The Archaeology of Alienation: A Late Twentieth-Century British Council House', in V. Buchli and G. Lucas (eds), *Archaeologies of the Contemporary Past* (London: Routledge, 2001), pp. 158–67; V. Buchli and G. Lucas, 'Children, Gender and the Material Culture of Domestic Abandonment in the Late Twentieth Century', in J. Sofaer Derevenski, *Children and Material Culture*, pp. 131–8.

15. Baxter, *The Archaeology of Childhood*.

16. Baxter, *The Archaeology of Childhood*, p. 75.

17. Baxter, *The Archaeology of Childhood*, p. 78.

18. Baxter, *The Archaeology of Childhood*, p. 79.

19. Baxter, *The Archaeology of Childhood*. p. 87.

20. E. C. Casella and S. Croucher, *The Alderley Sandhills Project: An Archaeology of Community Life in (Post)-Industrial England* (Manchester: Manchester University Press, 2010); E. C. Casella ' "You Knew Where You Were": An Archaeology of Working Households in Turn-of-Century Cheshire', in A. Horning and M. Palmer (eds), *Crossing Paths or Sharing Tracks* (Woodbridge: Boydell and Brewer, 2009), pp. 365–80.

21. E. C. Casella, 'The Excavation of Industrial Era Settlements in North West England', *Industrial Archaeology Review*, 27: 1, 2005, 77–86.

22. Casella and Croucher, *The Alderley Sandhills Project*, pp. 64–6.

23. Casella and Croucher, *The Alderley Sandhills Project*, p. 171.

24. Casella and Croucher, *The Alderley Sandhills Project*, p. 172.

25. Casella and Croucher, *The Alderley Sandhills Project.*, p. 175.

26. Mrs Molly Pitcher, Oral History Interview. Alderley Sandhills Project, August 2003.

27. Baxter, *The Archaeology of Childhood*, p. 114.

28. L. Bemelmans, *Madeline* (New York: Simon & Schuster, 1939).

29. T. Markus, *Buildings and Power: Freedom and Control in the Origin of Modern Building Types.* (London: Routledge, 1993); S. Tarlow, *The Archaeology of Improvement in Britain, 1750–1850* (Cambridge: Cambridge University Press, 2007); A. Beisaw, 'Constructing Institution-Specific Site Formation Models', in A. Beisaw and J. Gibb (eds), *The Archaeology of Institutional Life* (Tuscaloosa: University of Alabama Press, 2009), pp. 49–66; D. Rotman, 'Rural Education and Community Social Relations: Historical Archaeology of the Wea View Schoolhouse No.8, Wabash Township, Tippecanoe County, Indiana', in A. Beisaw and J. Gibb, *The Archaeology of Institutional Life*, pp. 69–85; G. Jackman,

'Get Thee to Church: Hard Work, Godliness and Tourism at Australia's First Rural Reformatory', *Australasian Historical Archaeology*, 19, 2001, 6–13; L. Feister, 'The Orphange at Schulyer Mansion', in A. Beisaw and J. Gibb, *The Archaeology of Institutional Life*, pp. 105–116; O. Lindauer, *Not for School, but for Life: Lessons from the Historical Archaeology of the Phoenix Indian School* (Tempe: Office of Cultural Resource Management, Arizona State University, 1997); J. Lydon, 'Imagining the Moravian Mission: Space and Surveillance at the Former Ebenezer Mission, Victoria, Southeastern Australia', *Historical Archaeology*, 43: 3, 2009, 5–19.

30. See Davin, *Growing Up Poor*, pp. 23–5, 39–41 on institutional childhoods in pre-war London.

31. J. Gibb and A. Beisaw, 'Learning Cast up from the Mire: Archaeological Investigations of Schoolhouses in the Northeastern United States', *Northeastern Historical Archaeology*, 29, 2000, 107–29, 125.

32. E. C. Casella, *Archaeology of the Ross Female Factory: Female Incarceration in Van Diemen's Land, Australia*, Records of the Queen Victoria Museum, 108 (Launceston: QVMAG Publications, 2002).

33. L. Scripps and J. Clark, 'The Ross Female Factory', unpublished report for the Tasmanian Parks and Wildlife Service, Department of Parks, Wildlife and Heritage, Hobart, Australia, 1991; J. Brown, *Poverty Is Not a Crime: Social Services in Tasmania, 1803–1900* (Hobart: Blubber Head Press, 1972).

34. T. Rayner, 'Historical Survey of the Ross Female Factory Site, Tasmania', unpublished report prepared for the Tasmanian Parks and Wildlife Service, Department of Environment and Land Management, Hobart, Australia, 1980, pp. 30–1.

35. Casella, *Archaeology of the Ross Female Factory*, p. 32 & Figure 10.

36. See Beisaw and Gibb, *The Archaeology of Institutional Life* for numerous case studies.

37. Baxter, *The Archaeology of Childhood*, pp. 41–53; L. Feister, 'The Orphanage at Schulyer Mansion' in A. Beisaw & J. Gibb, *The Archaeology of Institutional Life*; Schwartzman, *Transformations*, pp. 187–9, 302–8.

38. Schwartzman, *Transformations*, p. 158 and Figure 12.

39. Baxter, *The Archaeology of Childhood*, p. 114.

40. Casella 'Little Bastard Felons: Childhood, Affect, and Labour in the Penal Colonies of 19th Century Australia', in B. Voss and E. C. Casella (eds), *Sexual Effects: The Archaeology of Imperial Intimacies and Colonial Entanglements* (Cambridge, Cambridge University Press, 2011, in press).

41. M. Foucault, *The History of Sexuality, Volume 1* (New York, Vintage Books, 1990 [1978]), p. 19.

3
Homophobic Bullying: A Queer Tale of Childhood Politics

Daniel Monk

Homophobic bullying in schools is an issue that in recent years has attracted considerable attention in the UK and internationally. It has been identified as an issue of concern by academic[1] and governmental sources;[2] but also by the Conservative Party while it was in opposition and some religious bodies – organizations with little (or ambivalent) history of sympathy to LGBT issues.[3] Consequently it is possible to argue that it is now a legitimate and *depoliticized* object of social concern across civil society.

To a certain extent the mainstreaming of the issue is an unproblematic 'good'. The coupling of 'childhood' and '(homo)sexuality' in political discourses has a long history and one that has been dominated by narratives of 'lost innocence', seduction and abuse. So, the apparent legitimacy of speaking about homophobic bullying can be read as a fearless break from a misguided and prejudiced past and a challenge to cultural resistance to the acknowledgement of child sexuality. Within this progressive narrative children, and especially LGBT children, are both saved and liberated.

Questioning this liberal progressive account does not deny the existence of the harm experienced in schools but is an attempt to take seriously the injunction from feminist legal scholars Diduck and Kaganas that:

> While giving a voice to any previously disempowered or marginalized constituency is important, and listening to children is long overdue, we must be alert to the discourses through which that voice is heard and interpreted.[4]

A key premise here is that 'homophobic bullying' is not a neutral descriptive label but a more complex and *productive* narrative. The aim

55

here is to examine the discursive means by which the issue has become perceived as a legitimate subject of concern, to identify the 'conditions of possibility' that have *enabled* it to become a harm that can be spoken of, and, in doing so, to demonstrate the extent to which this speak-ability is contingent on contemporary understandings of childhood(s) located at the interface of sexuality and education.

A number of discourses and narratives are examined here: 'abuse', child and gay 'victims'; (queer) developmentalism; and the criminal gaze. These varied ways through which homophobic bullying is made speakable attest to the cultural malleability of 'the child' as an object of concern and renders visible the extent to which agendas of child wel-fare are always politically embedded projects which mask more com-plex understandings of (child) liberation.

A form of child abuse

Homophobic bullying, however defined, is not new. Consequently the recent concern represents a 'discovery' that parallels earlier 'discoveries' such as domestic violence and child abuse more generally. These com-parisons give rise to two themes: the contingency of the 'discovery' of harms and the contingency of the notion of harm itself.

The discovery of domestic violence and child abuse both effectively challenged the ideal image and patriarchal myth of the family as the 'haven in the heartless world'. In a similar fashion homophobic bully-ing challenges the idea that 'school years are the best years of your life'. In both cases theses truisms represented political investments in the home and family and compulsory schooling.

The introduction of compulsory education late in the nineteenth century required an immense and complex spatial and cultural shift in understandings of childhood. As Walkerdine comments, 'it was gener-ally agreed' that it 'brought about the idea of childhood as something separate'.[5] But the silence and collective amnesia about this attests to the extent to which the school has become perceived, like the family, in universal ahistorical terms as an almost 'natural' *a priori* institution. This is particularly evident in the work of the influential child psycholo-gists Winnicott and Bowlby for whom the child's initial journey to 'the school' is invested with the *a priori* naturalness akin to a child's journey to 'the mother' or 'the father'.[6] Here the rendering of the school as a 'natural' institution is complicit with the silencing of speaking of the harms within the school. Bowlby for example, commented confidently in 1973 that, bullying was 'little more than' a rationalization for school phobia.[7] The current speakability of homophobic bullying represents a significant departure from this view but it also attest to the spatial contingency of the speakability; for the impact of *parental* homophobia on children remains an issue that is *not* addressed by organizations like Stonewall and children's rights organizations. In other words, in seeking to explain why homophobia in the school space has become open to widespread political criticism it is necessary to look beyond simple concern about the well being of children.

Taking a long view here is informative. For whereas the dominant post-war child psychologists' masking of child harms within schools cohered with political and social shifts unrelated to children's needs, so too does the new found ability to do otherwise. While it is important to avoid simplistic causal explanations, it is possible to see the new concern if not enabled at least not unconnected to broader political and socio-economic shifts in the perception of schooling. In particular, the increased questioning of the public interest in education and its reinscription as a private rather than a public good; the political construction of parents no longer as passive recipients but as consumers supported by the rhetoric of choice; increases in home education as a legitimate option and, more broadly, the impact of the phenomenon of school shootings, have all in different ways rendered the school potentially dangerous, open to question and at odds with the earlier constructions of it as an unquestionable natural good.[8] Significantly, they serve too to explain the dichotomy referred to above between the speakability of homophobia within the school and within the home for these broader shifts in many respects have served to *reinscribe* the home and parental child relations as *safer* places.

Extent and definition are key issues in the literature about homophobic bullying and here too important parallels can be drawn with domestic violence and child abuse. Archard asks 'Can Child Abuse be Defined?', and while he acknowledges concerns that questioning the meaning of abuse risks suggesting that it does not exist he concludes that:

> the increasing versatility of the concept of child abuse – its ability to pick out more and more types of wrong done to children – has only been purchased at the cost of its increasing vacuity, its lack of any distinctive content possessing clear evaluative connotations.[9]

This concern is critical when reading the literature about homophobic bullying. The campaigns by Stonewall (The leading LGBT rights lobby) refer to homophobic bullying as being 'endemic in schools' and cite statistics that 75 to 80 per cent of pupils experience it one time or another.[10] Yet these statistics are based on an extremely broad definition of homophobic bullying. One that stretches from, at one end of the spectrum, extreme repeated systematic violence, to, at the other end, overhearing the word 'gay' being used in a pejorative way and to experiencing a sense of being different. Moreover the empirical literature cited to support these statistics, while not down playing the significance of homophobic bullying, cites comparative studies with very different results and is much more cautious about causal claims made as to the effect of homophobic bullying.[11]

This selective statistical representation coheres with and appeals to the broader cultural shifts within which schooling itself is increasingly perceived as a dangerous space. More particularly it attests to the extent to which the homophobic bullying agenda here utilizes and is spoken of through the dominant image of childhood as vulnerable and one premised on the status of victim.

The child as victim

Empirical research about homophobic bullying frequently identifies causal links between homophobic bullying and alcoholism, suicide, low school attendance and a variety of emotional disorders.[12] Mirroring in this way the literature on child abuse, it enables homophobic bullying to be included discursively within this ever expanding category. This is strategically important, for under the label of child abuse, homophobic bullying is represented as an unquestioned wrong, a legitimate and, crucially, a *depoliticized* harm and one, therefore, able to garner widespread sympathy.

One of the reasons why this discursive categorizing of homophobic bullying achieves this status is because images of the child as victim reassure as much as they appal. As Patricia Holland has argued:

> *Without an image of an unhappy child the concept of childhood would be incomplete.* Real children suffer in many different ways and for many different reasons, but pictures of sorrowing children reinforce the defining characteristics of childhood – dependence and powerlessness. *Pathetic images of children create a desired image in which childhood is no longer a threat and adults are back in control.*[13]

This perspective – a provocative challenge to aspects of children's rights agendas – is important because it reveals the extent to which enabling the speakability of homophobic bullying through the imagery of the child as victim renders silent other concerns.

The most notable silence is about sex. Indeed one of the most striking aspects of the homophobic bullying agenda is the extent to which it speaks of LGBT youth through a desexualized discourse. For example the Stonewall website page that addresses school issues is dominated by homophobic bullying but has no mention of young people's needs for information about safer sex and education about HIV.[14] Similarly, the Conservative Party 2009 report noted above *More Ball Games* (no pun intended) supports tackling homophobic bullying, but in the broader context of a nostalgic support for children to play more sports. As Ellis argues the approach adopted here is 'a plea for tolerance that doesn't speak about what is to be tolerated'.[15] While challenging homophobia in schools and providing information about HIV are arguably distinct this does not explain the silence. Information on bullying and HIV education can both be understood as essential rights. Indeed the harm suffered by the absence of the latter is arguably as, if not more, significant than the former. Statistics about HIV infections indicate that gay teenagers are increasingly the most at risk group. The argument here consequently is that the distinction between challenging bullying and providing information about HIV is not an obvious or neutral one but rather one that is indicative of the extent to which the homophobic bullying agenda coheres with and is contingent on the reassuring image of the brutalized child. To speak of safer sex would require speaking of sexual agency, pleasure, choice and in doing so would challenge the ideal of the child as non-sexual. This silencing is not new, as Piper has observed, in tracing the origins of the dominant norm of childhood sexual innocence and its relationship with the development of welfare policies:

> There is a sense in which the price paid by children over the last 150 years for the presumed benefits of child welfare legislation and provision has been their 'de-sexing'.[16]

The gay victim

While the child as victim resonates with dominant constructions of childhood in this context there is a double victimhood. For what is striking from the literature is the extent to which the image of the queer child in the homophobic bullying discourse mirrors the contemporary discursive representations of the homosexual in the years pre-liberation: depressed, lonely, isolated, suicidal. While critical engagements with the discourse of the child as victim demonstrate how that image *reassures* and reinscribes a social and cultural binary, in that case between adult and child; so too can the gay as victim. Reinforcing the portrayal of gay life as one of tragedy as a key part of the demand for tolerance implicitly can reassure the heteronormative[17] hegemony. At the very least it begs the question: how significant a shift is the recognition of homophobic bullying by conservative groups when it is presented through the portrayal of homosexual lives as one experienced by a majority (according to the statistics) as one of tragedy? It is important to emphasize here that the point is not that real suffering does not exist but the extent to which the dominance of this image is a *condition of possibility* for the speakability of homophobic bullying and in doing so reduces the experience of homophobic bullying to one of passive victimhood.

Alternatives narratives about homophobic bullying do however exist. Ian Rivers, the leading empirical UK researcher in the area whose work is used by Stonewall and campaigning groups, recently argued that: 'despite the nature and severity of bullying participants experienced at school, many overcame it successfully.'[18] The productive role of shame in forming identities is one example where future research could provide alternative narratives. Munt argues that a proud defiant sexuality is 'premised on an uncomfortable historically discursive shame' and that:

> In any personal trajectory, the growing consciousness of same-sex desire must, in a Western context, give rise to feelings of difference and exclusion…The presence of shame has been repressed in the discourse of homosexual rights in an unhelpful way, *in order to gain greater agency, we must learn to revisit its ambivalent effects*.[19]

The argument here is that attempts to remove, outlaw, or silence shame-inducing practices through expansive definitions of homophobic bullying is an example of rights discourse overlooking the *productive* role of shame. The focus here is on the lower end of forms of homophobic bullying: name calling, being identified as different, identifying oneself and experiencing difference such as exclusion as uncomfortable. These practices share much with the emotion of shame: the blush of recognition as different (whether or not self-identified as 'gay' or 'lesbian') might sometimes be a painful sensation but one that may be constituted as having a role in identity formation.

Enabling the speakability of this experience of shame as anything other than a harm that must be prohibited coheres with both the notion of child-as-innocent-victim and with a particular construction of post-homophobic gay identity, explored below. It mirrors broader fears and attempts to reinscribe childhood spaces as harm free, pain free spaces.[20] This utopian desire is not surprising; as queer theorists Bruhm and Hurley argue, 'Utopianism follows the child around like a family pet.'[21] But in the context of 'shame', by way of stark contrast, the playground represents here a paradise, an Eden, pre-The Fall, pre-Shame; a space premised on welfarist understandings of protection but within which children are denied productive individuation, denied self-consciousness and one that reinforces homogeneity.

That alternative stories remain unexplored attests to an investment within contemporary LGBT politics in the predominant *reassuring* image of the queer child as victim. Braveman, in developing a critical queer historiography that disrupts a linear progressive narrative, quotes D'Emilio's assertion that gay liberationists of the 1960s and 1970s constructed a mythology that 'until gay liberation, gay men and lesbians were always the victims of systematic, undifferentiated, terrible oppression'.[22] Coupled in this context with the reassuring image of the child as innocent victim, this has a particular resonance and discursive power in the context of queer children.

Queer developmentalism – beyond homophobia?

The current acknowledgment of homophobic bullying undoubtedly represents a significant and important shift away from the explicit political and juridical homophobia of the past. It is now homophobia that is identified as the problem, not homosexuality, and this shift represents a vindication of a liberal progressive narrative. It also represents a challenge to a certain queer critique. For example, Edelman argues how the queer, and queerness, is subtly but continually represented and understood as antithetical to childhood in ways that ensure that, 'the cult of the child permits no shrines to the queerness of boys or girls.'[23] The acknowledgment of homophobic bullying could suggest that there *is* a space for including LGBT youth within the category of legitimate childhood. But it is important to explore the conditions of this inclusion.

One of those 'conditions' appears to be that queer youth conforms to the cultural definitions of innocent (and ideally non-sexual) childhood. But a further 'condition' can be identified by examining in more detail exactly what homophobic bullying is identified to be the cause of. What this line of enquiry reveals is that while it is indeed homophobia that is identified as the problem and not homosexuality, at the same time, there is no change as to *what* is problematized but merely the cause, and the formal and explicit rejection of homophobia in this way masks a series of heteronormative concerns. Examples of this trend can be identified within the empirical literature about homophobic bullying and in a variety of other cultural texts.

Rivers' work calculates the impact of homophobic bullying against assessments of 'psychopathology in adulthood' – a concept that, among other things, is evaluated by relationship status and duration of relationships.[24] This seemingly neutral psychological assessment is emblematic of a form of child developmentalism which has been subject to sustained critique by numerous theorists of childhood. As Walkerdine argues: 'The subject is not made social, but rather the social is the site for the production of discursive practices which produce the possibility of being a subject'.[25] Consequently while Rivers, as quoted above, argues that research should explore in more detail why some victims of bullying appear able to 'successfully negotiate adulthood', the critical questions left unanswered are what does that 'adulthood' look like? And who defines it?

These critical perspectives have a particular resonance with the concerns of queer theorists. Sedgwick, for example, in *The Epistemology of the Closet* demonstrated how the removal of homosexuality from the catalogue of psychological disorders has been followed by the discovery and inclusion of new ('DSM-recognized') pathologies. And these neutral scientific perceptions cohere with and enable dominant political discourses' new-found concern with homophobia. Rivers' use of relationships as an indicator of 'successful adulthood' is significant here. Within new 'psychological disorders' the inability to form 'stable' adult relationships is frequently a key component and this problematization coheres with the widespread political support for the Civil Partnership Act (CPA). For support was frequently premised, often explicitly, on the view that it would enable and support lesbian and gays to establish stable relationships. Indeed some conservative politicians explicitly linked their new found 'regret' about the notorious Section 28 and support for the CPA with concern about promiscuity among gay men. This approach is also adopted by some marriage-equality advocates *within* the LGBT community. Lisa Duggan argues that 'many have couched their advocacy in language that glorifies marital bliss, sometimes echoing the "family values" rhetoric of their opponents'. As an example she quotes the *Roadmap to Equality: A Freedom to Marry Educational Guide* which states that: 'Denying marriage rights to lesbian and gay couples *keeps them in a state of permanent adolescence*'.[26]

In a similar vein in relation to the Civil Partnership Act 2004 in the UK, Stychin argues that:

> there is a message within the Act ... that the encouragement of the rights and responsibilities of civil partnership through law will provide a disincentive for 'irresponsible' behaviour. In the context of New Labour politics, irresponsibility seems to include promiscuous sex, relationship breakdown at will, and the selfishness of living alone (or perhaps even living with friends and acquaintances).[27]

Stychin's analysis of debates about the Civil Partnership Act went beyond sexual practice to incorporate broader economic calculations; and the extent to which 'stable relationships' cohered with neo-liberal discourses about privatization of care. Echoes of this can also be identified here. Rivers' assessment of psychopathology in adulthood also includes employment status and this linkage reinforces Viv Ellis's observation that concern about homophobic bullying cohered neatly with New Labour's managerialist calculations and broader education reforms premised on clearly identifiable outcomes and audits of economic citizenship. In this vein he asks rhetorically:

> Is it a coincidence that recent policy and guidance from both a neo-liberal government and from the voluntary sector focus on how risky and disruptive identities might be *managed safely to ensure the production of auditable outcomes*?[28]

Another cultural text which provides insight into the extent to which the rejection of homophobia coheres with heteronormative understandings of 'perversity' are narratives of sport. The empirical literature on homophobic bullying frequently reveals that sports and changing rooms are the most feared places within the school.[29] And the Conservative Party's key policy document about children, which acknowledged homophobic bullying, was entitled 'More Ball Games'; a title that presents a reassuring image of normal stable childhood. But in this context what is noticeable is that other cultural texts present a tantalizing representation of a post-homophobic world within which the playing of sports features highly – in order to present a reassuring image of normal stable homosexuality. An example of this is two soap operas, *Eastenders* on BBC1 and *The Archers* on Radio 4. In both these programmes the public broadcasting company, in an almost Reithian educational role, portrays their resolutely 'out and proud' gay characters playing sports alongside the heterosexual male members of their respectively urban and rural communities (Christian playing Five-a-Side-Football in the former and Adam playing cricket in the latter). And in both contexts the gay characters are star players in their teams. That liberation is linked (and conditional on) a particular performance of masculinity is not surprising. Sedgwick reminded us long ago that 'the gay movement has never been quick to attend to the issues concerning effeminate boys'.[30]

Within this post-homophobic 'queer' developmentalist framework, homophobia takes on, with a twist, the psychoanalytical role formally played, albeit often in crude ways, by the concept of 'arrested development'. 'Arrested development', used to explain the origins of homosexuality, is for many LGBT rights campaigners highly problematic. For speaking of homosexuality in terms of development (even if in a morally positive sense and even if applied equally to heterosexuality) challenges the innateness of homosexuality which is both an article of faith and strategically essential for human rights claims within a liberal political paradigm (a point made by numerous queer critiques). Yet the argument here is that 'arrested development' has not been rejected but reformulated. Development into successful normal adulthood is not 'arrested' by parental or maternal attachment but, rather, by homophobia itself. In other words the developmental question now is not, 'what makes someone homosexual?' but, instead, 'what makes someone behave in a way that fails to conform to heteronormative behaviour?'. Homosexuality can not and ought not to be 'cured', but the attributes and behaviours of those whose lives have been 'blighted' by homophobia can be.

This (re)turn to developmentalism is particularly invasive. Reece, a critical family law scholar, has analysed this reconfiguration as a form of '(post) liberalism'. This concept is distinct from both conservative morality and laissez faire liberalism to the extent that it imposes a model of 'responsibility' that demands that the individual *internalize* responsibility rather than simply conform to juridical commands. Within this model 'psychological norms have replaced social norms, and therapeutic correctness has become the new standard of good behaviour'.[31] So instead of 'straight good/gay bad' we have 'responsible sexuality good' and 'irresponsible sexuality bad' (who you do it with no longer matters). Increasingly therapeutic correctness requires us to explain our deviancy by childhood trauma; liberated from homophobia by the state the injunction is to 'grow up' – once provided with equal rights there will no longer be any excuses for their 'permanent state of adolescence'. It is then a highly conditional riposte to Edelman's 'the child is antithetical to the queer'; for the answer is not only that even queers have their 'Tiny Tim', but that they must connect with them and explain themselves through them.

In this context it is worth noting that much of the research on homophobic bullying draws on *adult* lesbian and gay accounts of their childhoods[32] and, similarly, the numerous incidents of queer theorists drawing on their own personal narratives.[33] What is important to note here is that homophobic bullying is identified not only as the cause of a wide range of personal outcomes but that they are potentially conflicting. As noted above, tackling homophobia can be seen as away of enabling gays to develop in accordance with heteronormative relationship models and ideals of masculinity. A very different reading is provided by queer theorist Juan Muñoz who perceives the 'hypermasculinity' of many forms of contemporary gay male culture as *itself* evidence of homophobia.[34] Similarly, sadomasochism can also be read as both caused by homophobia and external oppression and conversely as evidence of 'liberation' from heteronormativity.[35]

The aim here is not to attempt to arbitrate or judge these competing truth-claims but to be attuned to their discursive power and the extent to which they draw on an untheorized and developmentalist investment in the child as future. For in the use of the child in these strategies, there is here a queer paradox. In particular, in the self-avowed queer accounts that distant themselves from mainstream liberal LGBT rights' agendas the child represents a free, almost Rousseau-like child, who, brutalized by the social forces of homophobia, is forced to mask and alter his or her behaviour. This is, therefore, equally a project premised on *liberating* childhood in order to build a future – albeit a queer*er* one – while, at same time, opposing any notion of essentialism. As Lesnik-Oberstein and Thomson argue, queer theory premised on challenging heteronormativity is remarkably wedded to psychoanalytical discourse. For in the desire to affirm gayness the proto-gay child, 'is strangely destined and yet not destined'.

The point here is not that these are inherently problematic as political aims (for example they may be of strategic value in challenging sex education policies), but to question the investment in the child. As Lesnik-Oberstein and Thomson argue, the child:

> maintains a centripetal force as an occasion of pathos and of, moreover – and therefore? – an *anti-theoretical* moment, resistant to analysis, itself the figure deployed *as* resistance. The child as a figure that

operates through repetition, and therefore as the repeating figure, is made to found the 'real' beyond language as the always retrievable already-there.[36]

This repetition is abundantly in evidence here. For despite the self conscious and constant distinction made between queer theorists and LGBT rights reformers, the queer child is invoked here as much as a victim and has to do as much cultural work as the mainstream brutalized proto-gay child.

Challenging homophobia: legitimizing (lawful) violence?

Alongside the enabling and reinscribing of a (queer) developmentalist thinking homophobic bullying also enables and is heard through a legal and increasingly penal discourse. A key premise here is that the coupling of 'homophobic' with 'bullying' is not straightforward, but a linkage that plays a role in determining the legitimacy of the means used to challenge them.

Bullying narratives – individualistic, depoliticized and, increasingly, drawing on pathological explanations of inappropriate behaviour – cohere and lend themselves with great ease to legal discourse. Critical legal commentators have for many years examined the ways in which legal causation is distinct from factual causation, to the extent that it starts with the harm, identifies the individual perpetrator and then stops. In doing so it does not need to enquire in to broader, political and cultural factors that influenced the behaviour of the perpetrator. In this way, like bullying discourses, it simplifies and individualizes. The coupling of bullying with law, moreover, has been emphasized in recent years as law is increasingly resorted to as a means of redress. So, frequently in the name of children's rights, law has been used creatively to meet this challenge by civil law claims of negligence, quasi-criminal law sanctions in the form of school exclusions, as well as the criminal law.[37] In support of this, Furniss has argued that it challenges the extent to which 'teachers may see bulling as an inevitable part of growing up' and that failing to utilize the criminal law in particular, 'sends out the message that the bodily integrity of children is not as important as that of adults.'[38]

From these perspectives it is possible to view the intervention of law as a form not only of individual redress but as justice for all lesbian and gay children. However, hearing homophobic bullying through the discourse of school discipline lends itself to particular outcomes. For example in

More Ball Games the Conservative Party suggested that in tackling bullying there should be 'increased use of exclusions and firmer use of parent contracts', a policy that attracted all-party support in the 2010 General Election manifestos. Tackling homophobic bullying by policies of 'zero tolerance' reveal how it is made *speakable* through its ability to cohere with a 'law and order' discourse leading Harris to express concern that it could lead to the 'complete abandonment of the perpetrators of bullying'.[39]

Moreover increased assertions for ever more draconian school discipline in schools finds resonance with concerns of criminologists. In particular what Rutherford describes as the re-emergence of the 'eliminative ideal', which 'strives to solve present and emerging problems by getting rid of troublesome and disagreeable people with methods that are lawful and widely supported' and 'sits all too comfortably with contemporary pressures for social exclusion, with notions of a culture of containment'.[40]

The potential for 'lawful violence' in the context of challenging homophobia consequently coheres with calls to utilize both school discipline policies and the criminal law as a political tool in the demand for rights and protection by the state. And there are significant parallels here with LGBT campaigns for the recognition of homophobia as a form of hate crime. While demanding widespread support – often of an unquestionable 'common sense' nature – this recourse to law and the criminal model, like campaigns for gay marriage and gays in the military, has not been without its critics. Moran, in examining the ways in which criminal law institutionalizes emotions in the context of demands for hate crime legislation, has sought to encourage reflection on the 'alliances that lesbian and gay men are making with law and order'.[41] Visibility, naming and recognizing the violence of law is critical here, for hate crime, and in this context school disciplinary action against homophobic bullies, as acts done in the name of the law and order are emptied of and perceived indeed as the *opposite* of emotions and disorder. As Moran argues:

as dimensions of retribution, they become civilised by being made in the image of reason and rationality and are thereby made to disappear. Through this process they take their place as a part of law's legitimacy.[42]

This legitimation equally masks the 'heteronormative violence' of head teachers rigorously enforcing gendered dress codes: 'law's violence becomes good violence'.[43] But in relation to the disciplined, excluded, punished homophobic pupil the legitimate violence of law serves to not only mask its own homophobia but positions it elsewhere, outside, onto an 'uncivilised other'. Here school discipline and exclusions, as with criminal justice generally, have a hugely disproportionate classed dimension.[44] As Munt observes, shame is lifted off sexual perversion and onto the perpetrator and that:

> Violence is transposed onto these marginal spaces in a dis-
> cursive shift that empties middle class life of any account-
> ability...Dominant discourse has long conflated non-normative
> subjectivities with criminality and threat; indeed, there is a kind
> of discursive contagion operating in which shame is infectiously
> displaced.[45]

That liberal agendas in the name of human rights have served to cohere with and play a role in increasing hate underscores Wendy Brown's question: 'What kinds of attachments to unfreedom can be discerned in contemporary political formations ostensibly concerned with emancipation?'[46]

An increasing emphasis on dress codes is one example of an 'attach-ment to unfreedom'. Another is the attempt to contain and control the use of the word 'gay' within schools, the widespread use of which is a key factor in the ability to present homophobic bullying as being 'endemic'. The aim here is not to question the possibility of experienc-ing speech as harmful but by recognizing the context-specific meaning of speech to take seriously the views of many children that they 'don't mean it like that' and concerns that censorship necessarily propagates the language it seeks to forbid.[47]

Identifying potential concerns about lesbian and gay engagement with law and order agendas is not to argue against these forms of engagements but rather to be reflective about them, to question the implicit political alliances that underpin them and in doing so to locate lesbian and gay political agendas within broader social and economic structures.

Conclusion

It is, perhaps, easy to locate an analysis of homophobic bullying as a discourse, rather than simply as an empirical matter-of-fact tangible harm, within what some commentators have observed as the negative turn of post-structural work – as one that lacks or obscures 'politics' and avoids the messy pragmatics of activist struggles. It is, consequently, important to emphasize that nothing here should be taken as suggesting that real harms do not require real action. Rather, that the complexity of the issue requires a deeper analysis in order to inform action. With this in mind the aim here has been to identify that the construction of harms to children – of which homophobic bullying is merely one example of many – is inevitably and unavoidably always precisely that – a construction. It has endeavoured to demonstrate that examining the foundations of that construction – revealing the web of legal, psychological, sociological and criminological tales through which homophobic bullying is told, heard, enabled and made real – is not simply a theoretical project but itself inevitably and unavoidably a political project.

Notes

1. See for example I. Rivers, 'The Bullying of Sexual Minorities at School: Its Nature and Long Term Correlates', *Educational and Child Psychology* 18: 1, 2001, 33–46; I. Warwick, R. Goodrich, P. Aggleton and E. Chase, 'Homophobic Bullying and Schools – Responding to the Challenge', *Youth and Policy*, 91, 2006, 59–73.
2. DES, *Bullying: Don't Suffer in Silence*, 2002, London: DfES; DCSF, *Homophobic Bullying. Safe to Learn: Embedding Anti-bullying Work in Schools* (Ref: DCSF-00668–2007), 2007, Written by Stonewall for the Department and Educational Action Challenging Homophobia (EACH).
3. The Conservative Party, *More Ball Games: The Childhood Review* (2008); Catholic Education Service statement re: Education & Skills Select Committee report on bullying (26 March 2007), Statement issued in response to the House of Commons Education and Skills Committee Third Report of Session 2006-07 on bullying: http://www.cesew.org.uk/standard-news.asp?id=5254; Church of England, *Frequently Asked Questions: Do CoE Schools Encourage Homophobia?* (2010). http://www.cofe.anglican.org/info/education/faqcofeschools/#homophobia
4. A. Diduck and F. Kaganas, 'Incomplete Citizens: Changing Images of Post-Separation Children', *Modern Law Review*, 67: 6, 2004, 959–81, 981.
5. V. Walkerdine, 'Developmental Psychology and the Study of Childhood', in M. J. Kehily (ed.), *An Introduction to Childhood Studies* (Oxford: Oxford University Press, 2nd edn, 2009), pp. 112–23, p. 113.
6. See further: D. Monk, 'Problematising Home Education: Challenging "Parental Rights" and "Socialisation"', *Legal Studies*, 4, 2004, 568–98.
7. J. Bowlby, *Attachment and Loss. Volume 2, Separation: Anxiety and Anger* (Harmondsworth: Penguin, 1978; first published 1973 Hogarth Press and The Institute of Psycho-Analysis), p. 301.

8. D. Monk, 'Parental Responsibility and Education: Taking a Long View', in R. Probert, S. Gilmore and J. Herring (eds), *Parental Responsibility* (Oxford: Hart, 2009), pp. 143–64.
9. D. Archard, 'Can Child Abuse be Defined?' in M. King (ed.), *Moral Agendas for Children's Welfare* (London: Routledge, 1999) pp. 74–89, p. 75, p. 88.
10. DCSF/Stonewall, *Homophobic Bullying. Safe to Learn.*
11. I. Rivers, 'Social Exclusion, Absenteeism and Sexual Minority Youth', *Support for Learning*, 15: 1, 2000, 13–18; I. Warwick *et al.*, 'Homophobic Bullying and Schools – Responding to the Challenge'.
12. I. Warwick *et al.*, 'Homophobic Bullying and Schools – Responding to the Challenge'.
13. P. Holland, *Picturing Childhood: The Myth of the Child in Popular Imagery* (London: I. B. Tauris, 2004), p. 143 (emphasis added).
14. http://www.stonewall.org.uk/at_school/
15. V. Ellis, 'Sexualities and Schooling in England after Section 28: Measuring and Managing "At-Risk" Identities', *Journal of Gay and Lesbian Issues in Education*, 4: 3, 2007, 13–30, 23.
16. C. Piper, 'Historical Constructions of Childhood Innocence: Removing Sexuality', in E. Heinze (ed.), *Of Innocence and Autonomy: Children, Sex and Human Rights* (Aldershot: Ashgate, 2000), p. 40.
17. For a definition of this term see L. Berlant and M. Warner in 'Sex in Public', *Critical Inquiry*, 24, 1998, 547, 548: 'the institutions, structures of understanding, and practical orientations that make heterosexuality seem not only coherent — that is, organized as a sexuality — but also privileged. Its coherence is always provisional, and its privilege can take several (sometimes contradictory) forms: unmarked, as the basic idiom of the personal and the social; or marked as a natural state; or projected as an ideal or moral accomplishment. It consists less of norms that could be summarized as a body of doctrine than of a sense of rightness produced in contradictory manifestations...One of the most conspicuous differences is that it has no parallel, unlike heterosexuality, which organizes homosexuality as its opposite. Because homosexuality can never have the invisible, tacit, society-founding rightness that heterosexuality has', it would not be possible to speak of "homonormativity" in the same sense'.
18. I. Rivers and H. Cowie, 'Bullying and Homophobia in UK Schools: A Perspective on Factors Affecting Resilience and Recovery', *Journal of Lesbian and Gay Issues in Education*, 3:4, 2006, 11–43, 38. For a similar perspective from the US see: M. V. Blackburn, 'The Experiencing, Negotiation, Breaking, and Remaking of Gender Rules and Regulations by Queer Youth', *Journal of Gay and Lesbian Issues in Education*, 4: 2, 2007, 33–54.
19. S. Munt, *Queer Attachments: The Cultural Politics of Shame* (Aldershot: Ashgate, 2007), p. 95 (emphasis added).
20. T. Gill, *No Fear: Growing Up in a Risk Averse Society* (London: Calourse Gulbenkian Foundation, 2007).
21. S. Bruhm and N. Hurley (eds), *Curiouser: On the Queerness of Children* (Minneapolis: University of Minnesota Press, 2004), p. xiii.
22. J. D'Emilio, 'Capitalism and Gay Identity' in A. Snitow, C. Stansell and S. Thomson (eds), *Powers of Desire: The Politics of Sexuality*, pp. 100–13, p. 101;

S. Braveman, *Queer Fictions of the Past* (Cambridge: Cambridge University Press, 1997), p. 26.

23. L. Edelman, *No Future: Queer Theory and the Death Drive* (Durham, NC: Duke University Press, 2004), p. xiv.
24. Rivers and Cowie, 'Bullying and Homophobia in UK Schools', p. 29.
25. Walkerdine, 'Developmental Psychology and the Study of Childhood', p. 119.
26. L. Duggan, 'Beyond Gay Marriage' *The Nation*, 18 July 2005, available at: http://www.thenation.com/article/beyond-gay-marriage.
27. C. Stychin, 'Family Friendly? Rights, Responsibilities and Relationship Recognition', in A. Diduck and K. O'Donovan (eds), *Feminist Perspectives on Family Law* (London: Routledge-Cavendish, 2006), pp. 27–31, p. 30.
28. Ellis, 'Sexualities and Schooling in England after Section 28', 23.
29. Rivers, 'The Bullying of Sexual Minorities at School'; I. Warwick *et al.*, 'Homophobic Bullying and Schools'.
30. E. Sedgwick, 'How to Bring Up Your Kids Gay: The War on Effeminate Boys', *Social Text*, 29, 1991, 18–27, 20. The coupling of sporting prowess with liberation is not new. Most striking is the extent to which it mirrors constructions of Jewish masculinity, see: D. Boyarin, *Unheroic Conduct: The Rise of Heterosexuality and the Invention of the Jewish Man* (Berkeley: University of California Press, 1997).
31. H. Reece, *Divorcing Responsibly* (Oxford: Hart, 2003), p. 217
32. Rivers and Cowie, 'Bullying and Homophobia in UK Schools'.
33. See for example M. Warner, 'Tongues Untied: Memories of a Pentacostal Boyhood', in S. Bruhm and N. Hurley (eds), *Curiouser: On the Queerness of Children* (Minneapolis: University of Minnesota Press, 2004), pp. 215–24 and J. E. Muñoz, *Cruising Utopia* (New York: University of New York Press, 2009).
34. Muñoz, *Cruising Utopia*.
35. N. Sullivan, *A Critical Introduction to Queer Theory* (Edinburgh: Edinburgh University Press, 2003), p. 53.
36. K. Lesnik-Oberstein and S. Thomson, 'What Is Queer Theory Doing with the Child?', *Parallax* 8: 1, 2002, 35–46, 36.
37. N. Harris, 'Pupil Bullying, Mental Health and the Law in England', in N. Harris and P. Meredith (eds), *Education and Health: International Perspectives on Law and Policy* (Aldershot: Ashgate, 2005), pp. 31–58.
38. C. Furniss, 'Bullying in Schools: It's Not a Crime – Is It?', *Education and the Law* 12: 1, 2000, 9–29, 17, 24.
39. Harris, 'Pupil Bullying, Mental Health and the Law in England', p. 57.
40. A. Rutherford, 'Criminal Policy and the Eliminative Ideal', *Social Policy and Administration* 31: 5, 1997, 116–35. Zygmunt Bauman expresses a similar concern through the concept of disposability in *Liquid Love* (Cambridge, MA: Polity Press, 2003).
41. L. J. Moran, 'The Emotional Dimensions of Lesbian and Gay Demands for Hate Crime Reform', *McGill Law Journal*, 2004, 925–49, 925.
42. Moran, 'The Emotional Dimensions of Lesbian and Gay Demands for Hate Crime Reform', 942.

43. Moran, 'The Emotional Dimensions of Lesbian and Gay Demands for Hate Crime Reform', 942.
44. D. Monk, 'Reconstructing the Head Teacher: Legal Narratives and the Politics of School Exclusions', *Journal of Law and Society*, 32: 3, 2005, 399–423.
45. Munt, *Queer Attachments*, p. 99.
46. W. Brown, *States of Injury* (Princeton, NJ: Princeton University Press, 1995), p. xii.
47. See J. Butler, *Excitable Speech: A Politics of the Performative* (New York: Routledge, 1998), pp. 129–33.

4
Reading the 'Happy Child': Normative Discourse in Wellbeing Education

Hannah Anglin-Jaffe

This chapter offers a reading of recent policy documents and research around children's wellbeing and happiness.[1] In the last decade educational initiatives have been introduced to address the perceived wellbeing needs of children and young people. These include Social and Emotional Aspects of Learning in the UK context[2] and Promoting Alternative Thinking Strategies in the US.[3] This chapter aims to explore the relationship between ideas about childhood and education and to examine how these ideas have shaped these educational interventions. Changing expectations of education are explored through an analysis of the implications of placing the responsibility for children's happiness with schools. The perception that children and young people's wellbeing needs to be addressed within the context of the school is considered through discussions of educational values and the role of the teacher. Conceptualizations of children's wellbeing are analysed and the appropriateness of government devised interventions to tackle perceived emotional deficits and dysfunctions are debated. In particular this chapter is concerned with how recent wellbeing interventions position the child, the teacher and the school in particular discourses of normalized emotional and social interactions, with the result of pathologizing and marginalizing those who do not conform (both children and teachers).

The state of children's wellbeing and happiness is a growing area of research[4] with well publicized reports, such as UNICEF's *Report Card 7*,[5] highlighting an apparently growing problem with young people's satisfaction with their lives. The attention devoted to this area suggests a preoccupation with children's happiness, which in turn reveals collective anxieties about the state of childhood. The data in *Report Card 7* were widely publicized with the particular concern for the UK being the data for 'subjective wellbeing' in which young people rated their sense of personal wellbeing and in which the UK found itself at the bottom of the scale with the Netherlands at the top. A growing field of writers exploring the state of happiness argued that the affluence of Western cultures was leading to a growing malaise and that evidence for this could be found in the UNICEF data, with children in countries with a lower GDP than the UK having higher levels of subjective wellbeing than their UK counterparts.[6] The influence of this apparent widespread malaise on children was perceived as being particularly worrisome. Books such as *Toxic Childhood* by Sue Palmer spelt out this connection in the explicit subtitle: *How the Modern World is Damaging our Children and What We Can Do About It.*[7] This body of writing suggests that the modern world is detrimental to people's wellbeing with childhood vulnerable to its pernicious attacks. In this argument mental health problems and anti-social behaviour (seen as indicators of a lack of wellbeing) are not perceived as natural problems for children but instead as adult concerns that are alien to childhood. The implication is that the modern world imposes adult concerns onto the protected realm of childhood, with the result of growing emotional and behavioural problems among young people. In such discussions childhood is mobilized as an unexplored, unified idea. Whereas the adult world is constructed as complex and in need of explanation, childhood is transparent and self-evident. It is through such discussions that the importance of exploring the social nature of childhood becomes apparent. Karín Lesnik-Oberstein, for example, argues that 'the "child" is a *construction*, constructed and described in different, often clashing, terms'[8] and that these constructions are 'the production of systems of purpose, which are fuelled by need'.[9] Erica Burman helpfully describes these constructions as 'social imaginaries of childhood'.[10] Following this it is pertinent to ask in relation to discourses of wellbeing: how is the child being constructed in wellbeing education and to what purpose is this construction being deployed? Lesnik-Oberstein reads the cultural positioning of the child as 'the most stable, the most fixed, the unquestioned and unquestionable'[11] and this positioning can be read in discourses of wellbeing education that attempt to address a perceived instability in the state of childhood that is manifesting in unhappiness or behaviour that is labelled as troublesome. Underlying such discourse is an assumption about the homogeneity of childhood, which assumes 'a fundamental and crucial similarity of experience and consciousness'.[12] As Lesnik-Oberstein argues, like adults, children are subject to differences of class, gender, ethnicity, age and disability, to name a few. However, these differences have only been allowed to creep in around the edges of wellbeing policies, which reinforce school norms, rather than enabling an acceptance of a variety of different styles of behaviour and relating.

Lesnik-Oberstein argues that the child is frequently positioned in relation to conflicting ideas including 'power, freedom, nature, innocence, sexuality, and hope'.[13] In the discourse of 'toxic childhood' we can see the mobilization of children as synonymous with innocence and childhood as a carefree time, separate from adult, complex and troubling experiences. Furthermore, in this approach, the duty of adults is seen as being to protect this innocence. The problems with such discourses of innocence are wide reaching, but one implication is to further marginalize children whose experiences and lifestyles do not correspond with such imaginings.[14] These discourses of innocence and protection lie alongside contradictory discourse about endowing greater freedom to children through talk of rights and agency, which can be traced to the 'new social studies of childhood'.[15] This approach claims to reconceptualize childhood as a distinct phase of human experience (rather than as a deficit in relation to adulthood). In line with this way of thinking, children are seen as having their own perspectives on the world with the status of separate subjects and with their own accompanying rights (signified by developments such as the UN Convention on the Rights of the Child in 1989).[16] Children are thus seen as active social agents, who play a full role in their lives and who will experience a range of experiences and emotions. Wellbeing education policies buy into this approach through discussions of empowerment and agency. The idea of childhood as a state of full social agency appears to be in contradiction to the idea of childhood as a time to be protected from adult concerns. These contradictions are played out in the field of education, which on the one hand purports to enable the agency of the child and on the other addresses the child through discourses of protection. Children's wellbeing in particular is a site in which contradictory discourses co-exist, for example in the educational interventions that claim to 'empower' the child through asserting greater control and surveillance over their lives.

In research, specific markers of wellbeing encompass objective measurements that incorporate external cataloguing of behaviours as well as subjective measurements that include personal reflections on life satisfaction.[17] However, in educational discussions the term 'wellbeing' includes a slippage between a range of ideas and activities covering health, social inclusion and exclusion, mental health, lifestyle, community, social cohesion, individual happiness and academic achievement. Wellbeing education has developed in response to a perception of growing numbers of anti-social, depressed, anxious and unhappy young people and children. Unhappy young people are considered to be a particularly concerning social problem, signalling a breakdown in society. Young people and children who exhibit anti-social behaviour or who experience more mental health conditions such as anxiety and depression are thus pathologized and targeted through attempts to rehabilitate them into normal social practices. Young people are labelled as problematic through readings of their emotions as deviant. Megan Boler argues that 'certain emotions are culturally classified as "natural", benign, and normal, while others are seen as outlaw forms of political resistance'.[18] In an educational context certain emotions are considered to be compatible with learning and with the school culture, whereas others are labelled as disruptive and unconducive to learning. This has resulted in attempts by researchers and policy makers to understand and rectify what is troubling young people and causing them to be troublesome. Policy makers have turned their attention to the education system to reverse this perceived trend towards negative behaviours and feelings through interventions designed to modify behaviour and manage the emotions.

Research has explored the relationship between school practices and children's emotions, their mental health and their perceptions of their own wellbeing. For example, a study conducted by Gutman *et al.* proposed that positive experiences in school minimized the risk to children of experiencing negative changes in wellbeing from stressful life events.[19] Politicians have been quick to make the link between school practices and social change. Through the introduction of social policies such as *Every Child Matters* that explicitly address children's wellbeing and educational strategies such as the Social and Emotional Aspects of Learning politicians have sought to intervene and address these problems through schools.[20] However, placing the responsibility for 'children's and young people's happiness' with schools enacts a change to the core values and purpose of education under which the current system developed, in addition to placing further demands on already over-stretched teachers. This has resulted in a highly charged critique of these changes from those who see this as a negative move away from traditional school values and towards 'therapeutic education'. The main proponents of this critique are Frank Furedi and Ecclestone and Hayes, who have argued that bringing the emotions into the curriculum devalues traditional subjects, problematizes the role of the teacher and embeds a culture of dependency.[21] Furedi describes the 'institutionalization of happiness teaching [as]...fundamentally an anti-educational process'[22] arguing that this process works against the potential of education to 'excite the imagination and open children's eyes to knowledge and ideas'.[23] These critics highlight significant changes to educational practice, however, their intentions could be read as reactionary rather than emancipatory as their motivation is not to counteract the marginalization of disenfranchised groups, but to reclaim traditional values and educational practices.

As can be read in the above quotation, Frank Furedi is particularly concerned with the rise of 'happiness teaching' and other writers exploring children's wellbeing are often concerned with happiness and how it can be achieved. Nel Noddings has argued that 'The atmosphere of classrooms should reflect the universal desire for happiness'[24] however what constitutes happiness in the context of twenty-first century global change and insecurity is unclear. Arguing that happiness is a universal desire ignores the cultural assumptions that underpin aspirations and assessment of life satisfaction. Even within cultures there is diversity about what constitutes a successful, contented life and which living practices support wellbeing. As with any socially constructed value the usual stratifications of class, gender, ethnicity, experience and personality may all be factors that influence how happiness is understood. The media, arts, literature and advertising may also play a significant role in constructing images and ideas about happiness. For example, Fred Inglis described the hope of parents that their children would develop into happy and virtuous people and that this process might be supported through the reading of children's literature[25] and Morgan *et al.* explore the role television has played in the development of children's aspirations.[26] Some definitions of happiness allude to a process of self-assessment and comparison with others, for example, Ruut Veenhoven describes happiness as the '*degree to which an individual judges the overall quality of his life favourably*. In other words: how well he likes the life he leads (original emphasis)'.[27] This reinforces the argument that happiness is culturally dependent.

As social institutions, schools may play a role in creating, maintaining or disrupting happiness. Csikszentmihalyi and Hunter found that school activities rated below the average scores of happiness for the young people in their study.[28] Konu *et al.* found that school context had a significant impact on young people's wellbeing.[29] Gibbons and Silva found that young people's enjoyment at school was only loosely related to academic attainment[30] and this suggests that educational strategies such as the Social and Emotional Aspects of Learning in the UK that link wellbeing to standards might be at best ineffective and at worst contradictory. There is a potential conflict between the desire for schools to foster attainment and for schools to safeguard wellbeing. This conflict is a symptom of the contradictory demands placed on schools by governments keen to use the education system to right the many perceived wrongs of society. As Dewey argued 'All that society has accomplished for itself is put, through the agency of the school, at disposal of its future members. All its better thoughts of itself it hopes to realize through the new possibilities thus opened to its future self'.[31] Schools in this sense are vulnerable to the idealism of society. They are endowed with the power to transform present difficulties into future harmony and this is clearly the case in policies that seek to improve the emotional condition of individuals and communities. Others however, have recognized the limitations of schools to transcend the difficulties of the present. Mary Warnock when writing about the conflicts present in inclusive education policies argues that the ideals of society may not always easily fit with the ideals of schools.[32] Dewey however, also emphasizes the relationship between change in society and change in educational practice.[33] Considering wellbeing policy from this perspective, and the tensions between attainment and wellbeing, highlights the fragmentation of 'ideals' and the uncertainty which characterizes current social practices.[34]

Placing wellbeing into the sphere of the school adds an additional burden on to the role of the school and also adds additional practical and emotional burdens. Julie Allan has argued in relation to inclusive education policy that schools are increasingly experienced as 'territories of failure', characterized by confusion, guilt, frustration and exhaustion.[35] This is a particularly relevant argument as much of the wellbeing policies are directed at including children who are labelled as having social, emotional or behavioural difficulties or other special educational needs. It is these children whose behaviour schools and society most want to modify and whose emotions they most want to control. If schools are already at breaking point trying to include such children, wellbeing policies can be seen as a further attempt to placate staff. Allan cites Galbraith's concept of 'innocent fraud' in which insurmountable challenges are rebranded in order to appear achievable.[36] Allan highlights the popularity of simple, 'commonsense' guides for teachers, which attempt to convey complex ideas about inclusion in simple, technical language, which can be easily managed with 'techniques and methods'.[37] Such an approach can also be identified with wellbeing or happiness policies and publications.[38] Practice that attempts to simplify concepts of wellbeing and reduce them to easy, achievable methods, while avoiding the major structural inequalities in which schools function and negating the personal difficulties that troubled young people might be experiencing, places an impossible burden on teachers and schools, and places all the blame for difficulties on to individual children. Allan cites Lyotard's important critique of this desire for simplification, which he describes as a process which:

> Threatens to totalize experience, to reduce language to Newspeak, to rob thinking of its childhood and pedagogy of its philosophical moment. It is the 'demand' for reality (for unity, simplicity, communicability) and remedy: remedy for the parcelling and virtualization of culture, for the fragmentation of the life world and its derealisation into idioms, *petit recits*, and language games (original emphasis).[39]

We can read this demand for 'remedy' particularly in the claims made about wellbeing education. Weare and Gray, for example, state that such schemes have the benefits of: 'Greater educational and work success, improved behaviour, increased inclusion, improved learning, greater social cohesion, increased social capital, and improvements in mental health'.[40] Claiming that 'greater social cohesion' can be constructed through the teaching activities that make up wellbeing education (such as circle time) places huge power and influence into the hands of teachers and diminishes the role of other social factors, such as socio-economic status, in determining cohesion.

As a social institution schools are constituted through interactions between the participants, including the children, the teachers, parents, governors, cleaners, staff and local people. All of these participants may bring to their interactions with the school their own problems and frustrations. By introducing teaching that addresses wellbeing and happiness schools are being asked to smooth over these complex interactions and fluctuating emotions and to override the inequalities of a wider society. The introduction of teaching activities that aim to intervene in the emotions raises the question of ownership of emotional responses. The link to social cohesion that is made by Weare and Gray implies that individuals have a responsibility to regulate their emotions for the good of society.[41] In this sense, emotions are no longer the private concern of the individual but the collective responsibility of the group. Children may be held accountable for emotions that are considered undesirable in the classroom, enabling blaming and shaming practices to further marginalize them.

In order to analyse how such normalizing practices might be enacted in wellbeing education I will now explore the interventions in more depth. In the UK the Social and Emotional Aspects of Learning (SEAL) documentation formed part of the Labour government's wellbeing strategy, which was first rolled out in 2005 in the document *Excellence and Enjoyment: Social and Emotional Aspects of Learning*.[42] Lessons focused on the emotions and behaviour and included activities such as circle time. The SEAL guidance defined its project around five key aspects: self-awareness, managing feelings, motivation, empathy and social skills,[43] with smiley faced images (an inheritance from PATHS[44]) linked to each aspect. The linkage of 'feelings' with 'management' is particularly telling of the attempts to control young people's behaviours that underpins the guidance. The 'skill' of managing feelings is described as a process of recognizing and labelling feelings, as a first step, followed by sharing this feeling with others and then, in an advanced application, being able to use 'self-distraction or self-calming strategies in order to reduce its intensity'.[45] Lendrum *et al.* stated that in 2009 SEAL activities were in place in more than 60 per cent of primary schools in England.[46] The 2005 guidance document formed part of the overarching Primary National Strategy and was closely linked with policies around inclusion. The SEAL guidance emerged from The Primary Behaviour and Attendance Strategy pilot, which was carried out in 2003–5 with 25 local authorities.[47] One dimension of this pilot was to trial curriculum materials and interventions to develop children's social and emotional skills.[48] The pilot was then used to develop the SEAL guidance, however, significantly, it is possible to read a shift in the labelling of the strategy from an initial direct focus on problem behaviour in the pilot stage, to a more veiled and general focus on all children in the SEAL guidance. The guidance does not explicitly set out to tackle problem behaviour but instead has a more benign focus on 'inclusion' and deliberately states its aims in positive terms such as 'setting suitable challenges', 'responding to pupils' diverse learning needs' and 'overcoming potential barriers to learning'.[49] A diagram in the guidance reinforces how these aims are linked by an overarching concern for 'inclusion'.[50] A further line states that the materials will need to be adapted for individual children suggesting a strategy that is flexible and accommodating. By utilizing the discourse of inclusion the guidance attempts to mask the earlier emphasis on problem behaviour that clearly arose from a deficit approach in which 'disruptive behaviour' is described as 'difficult' and is perceived as having a 'negative impact on teaching and learning'.[51] However, the focus is not on changing the system to accommodate those perceived as 'difficult' but instead about changing these individuals in order to cause minimum disruption to the system. As Erica Burman argues in relation to emotional literacy programmes in schools: 'Here we see the social inclusion agenda writ both large and small – for the focus is always on altering the individual or smaller social structure to enable inclusion in the wider whole, rather than problematising the boundaries that define that whole'.[52] Particular responses in schools that are perceived of as undesirable (what is constantly referred to simply as 'behaviour') are further pathologized through the extrapolation that such patterns of interaction inevitably impact on so called future 'life chances'.[53] This inheritance can be read in the title of the guidance, which links 'Excellence' with 'Enjoyment' and, therefore, attempts to unite a focus on achievement and standards with pleasure and is reinforced by the cover image of apparently happy children doing star jumps.

Megan Boler argues that 'Behavioural and expressive conduct is developed according to socially enforced rules of power'[54] suggesting that what is deemed to be acceptable behaviour (that which does not need to be labelled as 'behaviour', due to its apparent transparency) is constructed through normalizing discourses enacted in everyday school interactions such as praise, censure or sanctions. In the discourse surrounding behaviour and the emotions in the documentation, there is a slippage between the two terms, with an assumption that 'behaviour' is the straightforward expression of 'internal' processes. The emotions of the child are, therefore, constructed as readable by school staff and accessible to modification (or manipulation). This construction of the child's emotional world can be read as a further attempt to control and contain certain young people. Attempting to challenge this, Boler writes of 'resistance' instead of 'behaviour' to describe the instances of emotional interaction in which young people may attempt to push back against the system. She describes resistance as the expression of emotions such as 'anger, passion, fear, and rigidity'.[55] It is these types of emotional responses however, that the SEAL activities appear to be designed to quell as resistance leads to disruption and frustration in classroom management. The guidance document, for example, writes of children being 'motivated' and 'equipped' to 'manage' strong feelings such as 'frustration, anger and anxiety' and also to 'promote calm and optimistic states'.[56] Here we can read a suppression of children's emotions and resistance strategies and a cultivation of a passive state. Burman describes this as the 'manufacturing of acquiescence'.[57] The guidance reinforces this with an image of a classroom wall display with the title 'Have you used any of these calming techniques today?' and with phrases such as 'Tell yourself to stop!' and 'Walk away'.[58] This cultivation of passivity sits alongside skills that appear to encourage action such as: 'recognise and stand up for their rights and the rights of others' and that appear to value differences: 'understand and value the differences and commonalities between people, respecting the right of others to have beliefs and values different from their own'.[59] These statements again employ the language of equal opportunities and inclusion but still maintain a focus on consensus.

The guidance signals an awareness of culturally divergent responses to emotions but contains this within an appendix, rather than incorporating this awareness into the main body of the materials. The appendix focuses on research that describes how non-Western peoples may respond or display emotions differently to Westerners, using examples drawn from studies comparing Indian and Japanese participants with American or English participants. In the examples, the Indian or Japanese response is described as 'different' whereas the English or American response is not analysed or described in detail and is therefore established as the transparent norm. Here is an example from the appendix:

> Japanese and American participants watching stress-inducing (bodily mutilation) films showed similar negative expressions when alone, but the Japanese participants were much more likely to *mask* their negative emotions with smiles when a scientist was present in the room. In fact, extensive research shows that people from *different* cultures have *different* cultural norms regarding what emotional expressions are acceptable (emphasis added).[60]

Here it is the Japanese who do the unexpected by 'masking' and who are the implied 'people from different cultures' and the American culture that is the norm. The treatment of perceived differences in this appendix may serve to reinforce the pathologization of diversity in classrooms, rather than encouraging the 'valuing of difference' as the above skill states.

The SEAL guidance makes the link to pre-existing international interventions such as PATHS (Promoting Alternative Thinking Strategies).[61] PATHS has a more explicit focus on targeting problematic behaviour and is aimed at individuals who have been labelled as difficult by their schools. PATHS is based on the work of Greenberg and Kusché.[62] Greenberg describes his work as addressing questions such as:

'How can we help children resist negative influences when they live in high risk neighbourhoods?' 'How can we improve children's academic outcomes when their families have experienced an intergenerational history of school failure?' [and] 'How can we help children control their emotions when their peers are bringing out the worst in them through teasing and taunting?'[63]

These questions are couched in a deficit view of particular lifestyles linked to class and race, in which certain areas are 'risky', families are 'failing' and peers are a negative influence. In Greenberg's language the pathologization of particular styles of interaction is clear as children are *'exposed* to high-risk situations' (my emphasis) and the language of moral panic can be read in the phrase 'difficulties [...] may spiral into longer-term poor outcomes'.[64] When Greenberg writes 'unless something is done'[65] it is clear that the PATHS programme can be read as an attempt to rehabilitate these problematic lifestyles in a language that is colonial and paternalistic. This is reinforced in the examples he cites of 'changing community level ecologies, attitudes, and behaviour' and improving the 'culture, attitudes, and relations in families, peer groups, and schools'.[66] Here we can read what Burman describes as 'the societal imperative to assess and clean up errant interiorities'[67] and it is this colonial desire that has been imported, albeit in a veiled and adapted form, into the SEAL guidance.

The SEAL teaching materials have been criticized by Ecclestone and Hayes[68] and Craig for their introduction of therapeutic elements into mainstream teaching. Ecclestone and Hayes argue that the activities are intrusive and Craig describes the guidance as 'a major psychological experiment on England's children which...could unwittingly backfire and undermine some young people's well-being in the longer term'.[69] The guidance focuses on making explicit and visible social and emotional interactions and responses. The materials in the Relationship Theme use language that suggests a degree of surveillance. For example, teachers are encouraged to *'notice* and *celebrate* children (or adults) who have been *observed'* (my emphasis) demonstrating the required skills.[70] Children are to be praised for disclosure: 'telling the truth, saying sorry'[71] and are to be taught to 'share their opinions'.[72] These 'opinions' sound more like personal confessions in the specific detail of the curriculum, through phrases such as 'I can tell you something that has made me jealous', 'I can express feelings of guilt', 'I can tell you about a time that I felt embarrassed and what it felt like' and 'I can tell you how I feel when I lose someone or something I care about'.[73] The guidance document includes an image of a classroom display with the title 'How do you feel today?' and with cut out flowers with the emotions 'excited' 'nervous' 'angry' and 'happy' on. Clothes pegs with children's names on are attached onto the different flowers suggesting that they have been invited to disclose and display their mood.[74] Here we can read what Burman describes as 'therapeutics' 'in the crudest sense that they share an understanding that thwarted emotions give rise to distress, and that analysing emotions can be transformative'.[75] It is this introduction of therapy into education that Ecclestone and Hayes find problematic, arguing that these practices 'infantilise children, making them suggestible to fears, problems or "uncomfortable feelings" that they may or may not face and they normalise the bad experiences of a minority of children as universal difficulties that "we all have"'.[76] They argue that classroom activities that focus on the emotions cultivate vulnerability in children and distract from other educational aims.

The SEAL guidance and materials also have implications for the ways in which teaching staff are positioned within a deficit discourse that dictates practice and implicates staff in problem behaviours. The materials state that they are for guidance only arguing 'the particular choice of learning objectives, teaching styles and access strategies lies with the informed professionalism of the teacher'.[77] In this quotation the materials apparently undermine their own usefulness, claiming that it is, of course, ultimately the teacher's job to make such decisions. However, the specificity of the guidance, down to suggested activities, timeframes, materials and learning outcomes, means that the role of the teacher is limited to minor decisions within an overarching and prescriptive curriculum. Therefore, the emphasis on 'professionalism' is perhaps anticipatory of the perceived affront by teachers who may feel that such documentation undermines their abilities and agency. The linkage of the term 'informed' with 'professionalism' is particularly telling of a strategy that presumes to know much more about human interactions than the staff and children it is directed at. It is this implication that teachers may not currently be 'informed' about these social and emotional aspects of learning, which includes schools and staff as part of the 'problem behaviour' that it sets out to resolve. It is the making 'explicit'[78] of what was presumably previously implicit in a teacher's role, which further undermines the capabilities of schools and staff.

According to the documentation, it is not just children who can enhance their social and emotional skills, staff are also targeted. For example, in the guidance for secondary schools it is stated that 'social and emotional skills are essential for all those who learn and *work* in schools' (emphasis added).[79] The guidance also states 'good professional practice by school staff... [is] challenging to develop unless both pupils and staff have social and emotional skills, and the ability to manage their own behaviour'.[80] The implication is that some staff exhibit behaviour that is equally problematic and as 'underdeveloped' as the children. The document also claims that a focus on social and emotional skills can help 'tackle' staff stress and improve morale and staff retention.[81] Staff stress is here constructed as an illegitimate response to difficulties and changing jobs is problematized rather than seen as a strategy for resisting this stress. As with young people, here we can read staff difficulties being firmly blamed on the individual and their failure to respond appropriately, rather than as a legitimate response to the injustices of the system. This is a further manifestation of policy that claims to include through discourse that further excludes those who do not conform.

This chapter has attempted to read how recent wellbeing interventions position the child, the teacher and the school in discourses of normalized emotional and social interaction, with the intention to follow Burman's call to 'analyse the models of writing emotions in circulation'.[82] Throughout the interventions analysed in this chapter an elision can be read between the various terms used to describe Social and Emotional Aspects of Learning including: personal and social development, emotional literacy, emotional intelligence, and social and emotional competence and social, emotional and behavioural skills.[83] In this elision it is possible to read varying manifestations of the same idea, presented through the use of different terms: literacy (educational), intelligence, development (psychology), competence (managerial) or skills (technical). Burman draws particular attention to the linkage of 'literacy' to the emotions, arguing that the construction of emotions as that which can be read and written engages 'a critical politics of pedagogy'.[84] It is this political mobilization of education that this chapter has sought to explore through an analysis of the pathologization of those on the margins through interventions that aim to tackle perceived emotional deviancy. Changing expectations of schooling mobilize particular constructions of the child and of the value of education. As education makes the 'mastery' of the emotions part of its rationale, it simultaneously creates more opportunities to position children as lacking, as 'other' and as deviant.

Notes

1. The author would like to acknowledge the contribution of Joanna Haynes, who through the suggestion of sources, feedback and discussion helped to shape the arguments within this chapter.
2. DfES, *Excellence and Enjoyment: Social and Emotional Aspects of Learning Guidance* (London: DfES, 2005); DCSF, *Social and Emotional Aspects of Learning for Secondary Schools (SEAL): Further Reading Booklet* (London: DSCF, 2007).
3. M. T. Greenberg and C. A. Kusché, *Promoting Social and Emotional Development in Deaf Children: The PATHS Project* (Seattle: University of Washington Press, 1993); C. A. Kusché and M. T. Greenberg, *The PATHS (Promoting Alternative Thinking Strategies) Curriculum* (South Deerfield: Channing-Bete, 1994).
4. A. Ben-Arieh, *Measuring and Monitoring the Well-Being of Young Children Around the World. Paper Commissioned for the EFA Global Monitoring Report 2007, Strong Foundations: Early Childhood Care and Education* (Paris: UNESCO, 2006).
5. UNICEF, *Child Poverty in Perspective, Report Card 7: An Overview of Child Well-being in Rich Countries* (Florence: Innocenti Research Centre, 2007).
6. J. De Graaf, *Affluenza: The All-Consuming Epidemic* (San Fransisco: Berret-Koehler, 2002); O. James, *Affluenza: How to be Successful and Stay Sane* (London: Vermilion, 2007); R. Layard *Happiness: Lessons from a New Science* (London: Penguin, 2006).
7. S. Palmer, *Toxic Childhood: How the Modern World is Damaging our Children and What We Can Do About It* (London: Orion, 2007).
8. K. Lesnik-Oberstein, *Children's Literature: Criticism and the Fictional Child* (Oxford: Oxford University Press, 1994), p. 9.
9. Lesnik-Oberstein, *Children's Literature: Criticism and the Fictional Child.*
10. E. Burman, *Developments: Child, Image, Nation* (Hove: Routledge, 2008), p. 11.
11. K. Lesnik-Oberstein and S. Thomson, 'What Is Queer Theory Doing with the Child?', *Parallax*, 8: 1, 2002, 35–46.
12. K. Lesnik-Oberstein 'The Psychopathology of Everyday Children's Literature Criticism', *Cultural Critique*, 45, Spring, 2000, 222–42, 223.
13. Lesnik-Oberstein, *Children's Literature: Criticism and the Fictional Child*, p. 29.
14. The problematic relationship between childhood and innocence has been explored in the following: J. Rose, *The Case of Peter Pan or the Impossibility of Children's Fiction*, series: Language, Discourse, Society, (eds), S. Heath and C. MacCabe (London: Macmillan, 1984, 2nd edn with new introductory essay, Philadelphia: University of Pennsylvania Press, 1992); J. Kincaid, *Child-Loving: The Erotic Child and Victorian Culture* (London: Routledge, 1992); J. Kincaid, *Erotic Innocence: The Culture of Child Molesting* (Durham, NC: Duke University Press, 1998).

15. M. Freeman and S. Mathison, *Resesarching Children's Experiences* (New York: Guildford Press, 2009). One of the prominent writers in this field is Jens Qvortrup, see for example: J. Qvortrup (ed.), *Studies in Modern Childhood: Society, Agency, Culture* (London: Palgrave Macmillan, 2005).
16. United Nations, *Conventions on the Rights of the Child* (New York: United Nations, 1989).
17. Ben-Arieh, *Measuring and Monitoring the Well-Being of Young Children Around the World.*
18. M. Boler, *Feeling Power: Emotions and Education* (New York: Routledge, 1999), p. 2.
19. L. Morrison Gutman, J. Brown, R. Akerman, and P. Obolenskaya, *Research Brief: Change in Wellbeing from Childhood to Adolescence: Risk and Resilience* (DCSF: London, 2010).
20. DfES, *Excellence and Enjoyment*; DCSF, *Social and Emotional Aspects of Learning for Secondary Schools*; DfES, *Every Child Matters: Change for Children* (London: DfES, 2003).
21. F. Furedi, *Therapy Culture: Cultivating Vulnerability in an Uncertain Age* (London: Routledge, 2004); F. Furedi, *Wasted: Why Education Isn't Educating* (Continuum: London, 2009); K. Ecclestone and D. Hayes, *The Dangerous Rise of Therapeutic Education* (London: Routledge, 2009).
22. Furedi, *Wasted*, p. 192.
23. Furedi, *Wasted*, p. 193.
24. N. Noddings, *Happiness and Education* (Cambridge: Cambridge University Press, 2005), p. 246.
25. F. Inglis, *The Promise of Happiness: Value and Meaning in Children's Fiction* (Cambridge: Cambridge University Press, 1982).
26. M. Morgan, J. Shanahan and N. Signorielli, 'Growing up with Television', in *Media Effects: Advances in Theory and Research* (3rd edn), Jennings Bryant and Mary Beth Oliver (eds), (New York: Routledge, 2009).
27. R. Veenhoven, 'Is Happiness Relative?', *Social Indicators Research*, 24, 1991, 1–34, 2.
28. M. Csikszentmihalyi and J. Hunter, 'Happiness in Everyday Life: The Uses of Experience Sampling', *Journal of Happiness Studies*, 4: 2, 2003, 185–99.
29. A. I Konu, T. P. Lintonen, and M. K. Rimpelä, 'Factors Associated with School Children's General Subjective Well-Being', *Health Education Research*, 17: 2, 2002, 155–65.
30. S. Gibbons and O. Silva, *School Quality, Child Wellbeing and Parents' Satisfaction* (London: Centre for the Economics of Education, 2009).
31. J. Dewey, *The Child and the Curriculum and the School and Society* (Chicago: Chicago University Press, 1956), p. 7.
32. M. Warnock, *Impact No. 11. Special Educational Needs: A New Look* (London: Philosophy of Education Society of Great Britain, 2005).
33. Dewey, *The Child and the Curriculum and the School and Society.*
34. A. Giddens, *Modernity and Self-Identity: Self and Society in the Late Modern Age* (Cambridge, MA: Polity Press, 1991).
35. J. Allan, *Rethinking Inclusive Education: the Philosophers of Difference in Practice*, (Dordrecht: Springer, 2008), p. 9.
36. Galbraith cited in Allan, *Rethinking Inclusive Education*, p. 18.
37. Allan, *Rethinking Inclusive Education*, p. 19.

38. See for example: P. Sharp, *Nurturing Emotional Literacy: A Practical Guide for Teachers, Parents and Those in the Caring Professions* (London: David Fulton, 2001).
39. Allan, *Rethinking Inclusive Education*, p. 18.
40. K. Weare and G. Gray, *What Works in Developing Children's Emotional and Social Competence and Wellbeing?* Research Report no. 456, (London: DfES, 2003), p. 6.
41. Weare and Gray, *What Works in Developing Children's Emotional and Social Competence and Wellbeing?*
42. DfES, *Excellence and Enjoyment*.
43. DfES, *Excellence and Enjoyment*.
44. M. Greenberg, 'Promoting Resilience in Children and Youth, Preventive Interventions and their Interface with Neuroscience', *Annals New York Academy of Sciences*, 1094, 2006, 139–50.
45. DfES, *Excellence and Enjoyment*, p. 7.
46. A. Lendrum, N. Humphrey, A. Kalambouka, and M. Wigelsworth, 'Implementing Primary Social and Emotional Aspects of Learning (SEAL) Small Group Interventions: Recommendations for Practitioners', *Emotional and Behavioural Difficulties*, 14: 3, 2009, 229–38.
47. S. Hallam, J. Rhamie and J. Shaw, *Evaluation of the Primary Behaviour and Attendance Pilot* (London: Institute of Education, 2006).
48. Hallam *et al.*, *Evaluation of the Primary Behaviour and Attendance Pilot*.
49. DfES, *Excellence and Enjoyment*, p. 1.
50. DfES, *Excellence and Enjoyment*, p. 1.
51. Hallam *et al.*, *Evaluation of the Primary Behaviour and Attendance Pilot*, p. 3.
52. E. Burman, 'Beyond "Emotional Literacy" in Feminist and Educational Research', *British Educational Research Journal*, 35: 1, 2009, 137–55, 146.
53. Hallam *et al.*, *Evaluation of the Primary Behaviour and Attendance Pilot*, p. 3.
54. M. Boler *Feeling Power*, p. 4.
55. Boler, *Feeling Power*, p. 2.
56. DfES, *Excellence and Enjoyment*, p. 7.
57. Burman, 'Beyond "Emotional Literacy" in Feminist and Educational Research', 140.
58. DfES, *Excellence and Enjoyment*, p. 7.
59. DfES, *Excellence and Enjoyment*, p. 7.
60. DfES, *Excellence and Enjoyment*, p. 62.
61. DfES, *Excellence and Enjoyment*.
62. M. T. Greenberg and C. A. Kusché, *Promoting Social and Emotional Development in Deaf Children: The PATHS Project*; C. A. Kusché and M. T. Greenberg *The PATHS (Promoting Alternative Thinking Strategies) Curriculum*.
63. Greenberg, 'Promoting Resilience in Children and Youth', 139–40.
64. Greenberg, 'Promoting Resilience in Children and Youth', 140.
65. Greenberg, 'Promoting Resilience in Children and Youth', 140.
66. Greenberg, 'Promoting Resilience in Children and Youth', 140.
67. Burman, 'Beyond "Emotional Literacy" in Feminist and Educational Research', 145.
68. K. Ecclestone and D. Hayes, *The Dangerous Rise of Therapeutic Education* (London: Routledge, 2009); C. Craig, *The Potential Dangers of a Systematic, Explicit Approach to Teaching Social and Emotional Skills (SEAL)* (Glasgow,

Centre for Confidence and Well-being, 2007), available at http://www.centreforconfidence.co.uk/docs/EI-SEAL_September_2007.pdf (accessed February, 2009); C. Craig, *Well-Being in Schools: The Curious Case of the Tail Wagging the Dog?* (Glasgow: Centre for Confidence and Well-being, 2009), available at: http://www.centreforconfidence.co.uk/docs/The_curiouscase.pdf (accessed February, 2009).

69. Craig, *The Potential Dangers of a Systematic, Explicit Approach to Teaching Social and Emotional Skills (SEAL)*, p. 4.
70. DfES, *Excellence and Enjoyment*, p. 1.
71. DfES, *Excellence and Enjoyment*, p. 1.
72. DfES, *Excellence and Enjoyment*, p. 2.
73. DfES, *Excellence and Enjoyment*, p. 4.
74. DfES, *Excellence and Enjoyment*, p. 9.
75. Burman, 'Beyond "Emotional Literacy" in Feminist and Educational Research', 139.
76. Ecclestone and Hayes, *The Dangerous Rise of Therapeutic Education*, p. 44.
77. DfES, *Excellence and Enjoyment*, p. 1.
78. DfES, *Excellence and Enjoyment*, p. 5.
79. DCSF, *Social and Emotional Aspects of Learning for Secondary Schools (SEAL)*, p. 8.
80. DCSF, *Social and Emotional Aspects of Learning for Secondary Schools (SEAL)*, p. 8.
81. DCSF, *Social and Emotional Aspects of Learning for Secondary Schools (SEAL)*, p. 9.
82. Burman, 'Beyond "Emotional Literacy" in Feminist and Educational Research', 150.
83. DfES, *Excellence and Enjoyment*.
84. Burman, 'Beyond "Emotional Literacy" in Feminist and Educational Research', 151.

5
Perspectives and Community: Constructions of Autism and Childhood

Helen Ainslie

The Curious Incident of the Dog in the Night-Time by Mark Haddon was first published in 2003.[1] For the next year or so it was to remain among the best-sellers' lists and become the material for numerous reviews, articles and media attention. One thing that puzzled me about *Curious Incident*, and the praise and media attention that it gained, was that it was supposedly the first book of its kind. The book has been described numerous times as 'groundbreaking' and was widely praised in the popular media for being cutting edge.[2] Yet, *Curious Incident* was in the company of many books which had already, previously, been described as having offered the insight into autism for which the Haddon text had been so acclaimed. In her article 'Autistic Autobiography or Autistic Life Narrative', Irene Rose states that 'people with autism have been committing their life experiences to print for over 20 years and since 1986 there has been a significant growth in the publication of autistic autobiography.'[3] For Irene Rose then, the availability of autistic 'life experiences' is not something new and contemporary; her article references several autistic autobiographies, for example, *Nobody Nowhere* by Donna Williams (first published in 1992) and *Thinking in Pictures: And Other Reports from My Life with Autism* by Temple Grandin (first published in 1995), to name just two. What interests me more, however, is not so much the question of whether or not *Curious Incident* really was the first of its kind, rather I wish here to think through the underpinning of this question which assumes the possibility of any kind of text being the 'voice' of autism.

In this chapter, I wish to analyse how the 'autistic' is constructed and constituted as an identity and a difference and think through the problems entailed in the notion of this identity[4] as coherent and unified. Therefore I will not be considering autism as a medical or psychological 'diagnosis' or 'condition'. I analyse some sections from Mark Haddon's *The Curious Incident of the Dog in the Night-Time* and consider how both childhood, or adolescence, and autism are constructed as identities in this text. The ideas that I am seeking to diverge from are those implicit in the comments discussed above, which are that autism has often been read in Haddon's text as either an extension of what Jacqueline Rose reads in the industry of Children's Fiction; that is, that *Curious Incident* really *is* the autistic,[5] or that *Curious Incident* is a fictional text and therefore should not be taken as a 'representation' of autism.[6] The parallel issues and problems around Children's Literature and the construction of childhood have been thoroughly outlined and discussed by Karín Lesnik-Oberstein[7] and Jacqueline Rose.[8] Lesnik-Oberstein sums up the aim of Children's Literature: 'How to find the *good* book for the child is children's literature criticism's purpose, whichever way it is dressed up'.[9] Rose makes a similar point about the aims and desires of children's literature criticism; referring to J. M. Barrie's *Peter Pan* she states that, as far as children's literature criticism is concerned, 'it represents the child, speaks to and for children, addresses them as a group which is knowable and exists for the book, much as the book (so the claim runs) exists for them.'[10] In other words, the child outside the book is supposed to read itself as the child inside the book. Both Rose and Lesnik-Oberstein question the possibility of such arguments in terms of what constitutes the identity 'child' and the supposed relationships between the 'real child reader' and the 'fictional child' in the text. In line with these arguments, my position when reading the Haddon text will be that rather than assuming that language reproduces or represents reality, language *produces* reality. I will be using Jacqueline Rose's argument that 'childhood' is a constructed, not an essential 'biological' identity, just as I am reading 'autism' in this way. Judith Butler too makes a similar argument in *Gender Trouble* in relation to gender. As she says, 'For the most part, feminist theory has assumed that there is some existing identity, understood through the category of women, who not only initiates feminist interests and goals within discourse, but constitutes the subject for whom political representation is pursued.'[11] Following on from these arguments, I will read a section of *Curious Incident* and analyse how it puts in place two different kinds of language: one language that is produced by the narrator and another kind that is produced by an other and used by the narration.

The basis for many of the reviews and critiques of *Curious Incident* was its apparently unique perspective: it was thought to offer an insight

into the mind of a 15-year-old boy called Christopher who has Asperger
Syndrome, a condition on the autistic spectrum. The idea is that
Christopher, as the narrator of the book, gives us an example of how
people with Asperger Syndrome see and experience the world. *Curious
Incident* has, however, also been critiqued for its acceptance as a fac-
tual account of an autistic mind. Irene Rose for instance in her article
'What Can We Do With *The Curious Incident of the Dog in the Night-
Time?*' comments:

> During my research into autistic autobiography it came to my atten-
> tion that Haddon's novel had crossed over from fiction into 'auto-
> biography' in many citations, most notably on the lists of clinical
> autism courses that list personal narratives and fictional narratives
> for students to read as background.[12]

Irene Rose's concern is that the novel has slipped seemingly unno-
ticed into the category of autobiography and is therefore taken to be
a 'real' account of an autistic perspective; the book is said to provide
a pedagogical function by being listed as 'course' background reading
material. Irene Rose's observation here introduces one of the predominant anxieties in the current research on autism and writing: representation. What kind of writing can represent autism? Who writes it? Who
do they write it for? How is this writing disseminated? What status does
literature have in relation to autism? In their article 'Understanding
Autism: Insights from Mind and Brain', Elisabeth L. Hill and Uta Frith
write:

> Only a few decades ago very few people had heard of autism, but
> now it is widely known that autism entails an inability to engage in
> ordinary social situations. Thanks to the film 'Rainman', everyone
> knows that not only are there children with autism but that these
> children grow up into adults.[13]

Here, the existence of autism is 'widely known' and so is its definition. Although Hill and Frith are writing in a scientific journal they
credit 'the film "Rainman"' with what they see as educating 'people'
about autism. Here then, the increase in wider knowledge about autism
is not to do with medical or scientific dissemination of information but
is connected to a popular fictional representation. The (dis)connection
between autism and its (mis)representation in fiction is the contentious
point in autism studies: does fiction liberate the autistic? Or does it

perpetuate myths and misunderstandings? The desire of much work in autism and cultural studies is to identify texts in which the autistic might represent itself, free from external narratives and processes which distort it. Before my reading of *Curious Incident* itself, I want to think through further some of the core issues and problems concerning ideas of representation by reading some sections from Stuart Murray's *Representing Autism: Culture, Narrative, Fascination*. In the introduction to his book, Murray explains why he chose a particular photograph for the front cover: 'I felt that the cover needed to signal both a sense of autism in and of itself, an idea of what the condition is, and that it also should draw some attention to its own methods of portraying such an idea.'[14]

Murray describes the photograph on the front cover:

> The photograph on the cover of this book was taken by Jane Bown at the Lindens, a school in Surrey for children with learning disabilities, in March 1966. ... The photograph comes, then, from an early moment in the proper appreciation of the nature of autism as a distinct condition. Two girls are on a rudimentary seesaw or swing boat, probably used in the school to help children interact with one another. From their positions the girls seem to be at rest, though it is possible they are moving. They seem to be displaying no awareness of each other; the girl on the left has her forehead on her knees while the girl on the right appears to have her whole head covered, apparently resting it on the metal frame of the swing boat.[15]

Murray first situates the photograph within a framework: who it was taken by, where, and the date it was taken. The contextualization here constructs a history of autism; the photo comes from a time when the diagnosis of autism was in its first phase. It is, then, according to Murray's reading, a signifier of the progression and advancement that has culminated in the current 'appreciation' of autism as a 'distinct condition'. There are two narratives here: one which can be read from the photo itself and one which provides what might be called the context for the photo. These two narratives intertwine in Murray's reading as the 'Lindens' school provides explanation for the 'seesaw' that the girls are on. Murray's description of the photo places it within a surrounding narrative which gives it meaning. It is the context which comes first and provides the point of reference for the content of the photo; I want to point this out as a specific function of Murray's reading because I do not wish to take for granted that 'context' can unquestionably stabilize the meaning of a text, as this would privilege 'context' as a fully mastered text; as if the meaning of 'context' is not itself subject to interpretation.

Murray states that the girls '*seem* to be displaying no awareness' (my emphasis) and that one girl 'appears' to have her head covered with it 'apparently' resting on the frame of the boat. Murray's narration thus sets up the description of the girls through a perspective which claims a knowledge of another viewpoint from which the girls may 'appear' differently; for instance, from another perspective they may appear aware of each other. Murray's formulations of the description of the photo mean that the girls are already set up as questionable; the interpretation of them is not stable and is subject to doubt. How the girls look may not actually be how they are and, for Murray, this is the point, as he explains: 'given that this book deals with representing autism, I thought it was appropriate to have an example of such a representation on the front'.[16] So, for Murray, it is certain that the photograph *is* a representation of autism, but what is under question is how this representation of autism itself is *read* to mean autism.

For Murray, the investigation into the meanings of this photo begins with the effect that it has on the reader. The photo offers a 'series of immediate challenges and questions' which are 'all pushing at one another during the time that the picture takes to register its effects on the viewer':

> What are the girls doing? Are they in the middle of something, or is an activity over or possibly about to start? Are they interacting with each other and is such a question in any way important? Is there anything in the photograph that conveys to viewers how the girls might be feeling? What appears to be the attitude of the photographer towards her subjects? Is this an intrusive picture? Does it seek to spectacularize the girls because of an assumed idea of their difference? Or is it maybe a photograph that catches the two girls being themselves, one that pays testimony to the selfhood of each of these two individuals? ... My sense is that, for many, the photograph might convey a sense of tiredness or even sadness.[17]

This reading is made up of a list of questions which circulate around the idea of an explanation or narrative to go with the photo; the photo by itself is not enough. The questions posit a whole, complete narrative which would explain the moment of the photo. The photo is, in Murray's reading, a fragment of a complete story that occurred in time and space. Viewing the photo is his attempt to hypothesize what might be the whole story out of the few certainties that are there. The latter questions are about the ethical status of the photo, the problem being that it may feed a voyeuristic interest. Although Murray settles on a tentative reading which 'many' might make, the photo for him has meaning because its meaning cannot be settled on; its meaning *is* that it serves to prompt uneasy readings, questions and counter-questions.

Murray connects these questions to the broader frame of the investigation in the whole book:

> These are only some of the initial questions prompted by Bown's photograph, but even to mention them here is to begin to enter into the debate that is at the heart of this book, a debate that asks how we read and respond to the varying representations of those with autism.[18]

Doubt and question apply for Murray to the narratives that can be formed around the photo as well as the processes of the production of those narratives and indeed any 'representations of those with autism.' However, it is the narratives that are for him doubtful productions, not the fact that they represent autism. What is at stake is the real autistic that risks, first, being lost beneath the narratives and possible misrepresentations, but also, the danger that the autistic might be reduced to narrative and therefore be deconstructed out of existence. For Murray, it is crucial that the real autistic remains beyond narrative. The underlying meaning of the photo as stabilized paradoxically precisely *by* mobile, questionable, unstable narratives is grounded by the term 'girls' in Murray's argument. I read a parallel problem of 'girls' and the autistic as being read by Murray as real and self-evident identities in the photograph. I will go on in this chapter to argue that, because Murray wishes to offer a reading of the 'girls' that resists what he takes to be sentimentalized misrepresentations of them that he senses in current readings of autistic representation, it means that Murray must also claim a knowledge of the real autistic in order to be able to extrapolate it from the sentimentalized version.[19]

The different readings which Murray finds in the photograph prompt his suggestion that: 'it is possible to read Bown's photograph as a document that actually asks its viewers to interrogate their own systems of critical reading and judgment.'[20] There is a notion here that representations of autism function as a lens for wider cultural and social questions to do with reading. I want to think about how the photo is seen by Murray to operate as a prompt for a wider interrogation. Murray posits a series of counter questions:

> Why *should* the girls' body positions convey sadness, or upset, or tiredness? Can we automatically assume that, just because the girls are not looking at each other, they are not interacting? What values and terms inherent to our own processes of looking are being queried in the picture? If we know that autism carries with it a strong element of difference, why should we assume we can map any instinctual sense of the girls that we might produce when looking at the photograph on to them without trying to recognize that difference? ... Maybe it captures a moment of pleasure for both girls, where those particular positions on that object create sensory satisfactions.[21]

Here Murray associates autism with 'difference' and, further on in the article, refers to the 'difference that autism undoubtedly contains'.[22] For Murray, then, autism 'contains' difference and difference is a 'strong element' of autism. Thus, autism is not constituted *as* difference. In one sense, then, the photo is about not assigning meaning to, or claiming knowledge of, the 'difference', emotions and experience of the girls; the girls signify experience, emotion and 'difference' but we cannot say for sure exactly what these might be. For Murray, the viewer might be ignorant of the feelings and experiences of the girls, but this is a different kind of ignorance to that which Murray claimed of the moment of the photo in 1966 when little was known about the 'distinct condition' of autism; contemporary ignorance is claimed to be aware of autism as an indefinable 'difference' and acknowledges its existence in the form of a question.

Although according to Murray's claims whether or not the girls are interacting with each other cannot be decided on and neither can what their 'positions convey', many of the readings and counter readings nevertheless rely on a presence or absence of interaction. What might this say about reading and criticism here? Can this picture, then, allow reflection on our own systems of reading as Murray suggests? My critique of Murray so far would suggest not. Partly because the possibility of such reflection depends on a neutral position from which to reflect; it would require us to step outside of the debate which 'we' created. Rather than creating an opening for this reflection to happen, I understand Murray's list of questions to be about the need already to attribute a narrative in order to read the photo at all. To state, as I did earlier, that the photo gathers meaning from its questionability presumes that any 'question' at all might be asked of it. However, the questionability suggested by Murray might rather be thought of as a choice of readings or equivocations about the photo: the girls are aware but they do not look like they are aware; the girls are not aware just as they look like they are not aware; the girls are aware and our system of reading 'awareness' needs questioning and analysis; the girls are not aware but why should their posture have to mean this? In my reading here, I have exchanged the term 'question' for 'possible narrative'. In this sense, reading (in Murray's critique) becomes a recovery whereby the whole story might be made possible by offering different narratives up to the photo, and so reading is to supplement the text with equivocal narratives. This suggests that the photo/text is at the centre of the narratives which circulate and supplement it. The problem with this reading is that the photo, or text, remains stable at the centre: certain things just *are* in the photo (such as 'girls' or 'autism'), even if aspects about them can be questioned.

Further, Murray is certain that autism is largely defined through 'difference' despite the fact that he does not think it can be claimed justifiably where, or if, this difference might be located in the photo. The problem is that, for Murray, autism *is* 'difference' but there is nothing that allows us to read and fix that difference in the photo. So, on one hand, Murray wishes to question 'our own processes of looking' and think about why we make assumptions about the readability of 'difference'; yet, he then goes on to offer an alternative explanation for the 'position' of the girls. Murray thus comments on, and critiques the process of, attaching possible narratives to the photo, yet, at the same time, participates in the debate as to what it may or may not mean.

The questionability of the photo serves to emphasize for Murray the certainty of the 'presence' of the girls. No matter what narratives are spun around them, the girls are *there* and autism is *there*:

Above all...the girls in Bown's photograph are *present*, and it is the fact of their presence that needs to be reckoned with, understood and listened to. It is autistic presence, in all its many forms, that is the core of all attempts to discuss agency and legitimacy in those subjects for whom autism is in some way part of their representational existence. It is also autistic presence that resists the many discourses that would simplify or ignore the condition. The material nature of such presence, the excess it creates when confronted with any idea of what 'normal' human activity or behaviour might be, stubbornly refuses to be reduced to any narrative – medical, social or cultural – that might seek to contain it without reference to its own terms. In the chapters of this book, such a conception of presence underpins all my discussions of how autism is represented in the various cultural forms which it features.[23]

There are two kinds of autism in Murray's reading: 'autistic presence' which is 'present' in the same way that the 'subject' is present; and 'autism' which is part of a 'representational existence'. Murray then distinguishes between a real, 'core' or 'material' autistic subject and a 'representational' one. Thus, Murray knows both the real 'core', 'material' autistic and also the 'representational' autistic. However, although they are distinguishable, they are still connected because the 'representational existence' is 'their[s]' and so belongs to the real autistic. It is the knowledge of the real, according to Murray's argument, which enables him to separate it from 'medical, social or cultural' 'discourses' that diminish the 'excess' that enables the real autistic to unsettle the boundaries of ' "normal" human activity'. The investment in recovering the 'core' from representations is then bound up with enabling a discussion about personhood, validity and citizenship. The presence of the girls and of autism leaves no choice for the reader but to be 'reckoned' with; presence must be read and accounted for. The 'obstacles' for Murray that must be overcome are the narratives which threaten to represent autism through metaphor. It is the girls' undeniable presence which provides the centre for narratives to circulate around; reading autism as discourse stops at the point where the presence of the autistic is undeniable. In Murray's argument, then, it is the limit of interpretation, as the point at which interpretation stops and the confrontation with reality begins, which is at stake.

In 'The Psychopathology of Everyday Children's Literature Criticism', Karín Lesnik-Oberstein considers the related issue of 'the use of children as emblems of their own supposed innocence'[24] in relation to protests in 1997–1998 surrounding the release of 'child-murderers who have completed their jail sentences and who are not subject to supervision because they were sentenced before the 1991 Criminal Justice Act, which introduced compulsory supervision for sex offenders'.[25] In thinking through what the presence of children in some of the protests might mean, Lesnik-Oberstein critiques a BBC Panorama programme on one particular protest which, despite interviewing one of the children, fails to 'address a problem in the involvement of children in protests against pedophiles'.[26] Lesnik-Oberstein continues:

> The children are protesting their own potential murder and are therefore presented as informed of and knowledgeable about their own forthcoming torture and abuse. The adults demonstrate, not because they are in the line of fire. Instead, their children enact for them 'being in the line of fire' and are employed in their own defence.[27]

Although in Murray's reading it is the 'presence' of the girls and thus the possibility of the girls' own advocacy that is said to be unquestionable, I still read the same issue that Lesnik-Oberstein reads in relation to the children in the protest. That is, that the child/girls are positioned as the site of responsibility for their own preservation. The girls' vulnerability is constituted by their potential for being the object of fascination and becoming consumed as spectacle. However the 'fact' that the girls are there, according to Murray, cannot be suppressed by concerns over their spectacularization. The reading of the girls as present and speaking for themselves supersedes the questions and obstacles about the production and consumption of the photo; thus, it can be used on the front cover because it can speak for itself. Murray claims that we should 'let' the girls provide the schema for the interpretation of the photo; thus, the reader must remain passive and not indulge in an overflow of pathos. However, this reading is in the difficult position of claiming that the girls can be emblematic of their own advocacy and should be left alone for that reason; yet, Murray is still required to explain this to us. In engaging in an analysis of a problematic encounter between the researcher and the autistic I then inevitably encounter the defence which is formulated by Lesnik-Oberstein in relation to children's literature critics as a 'conscious claim of intent to do good to or for the [autistic]'.[28] The problem here for me is not only that the autistic is therefore read as that which necessarily requires emancipation, but also that the demand is put onto the autistic that it tell 'us' how it might be emancipated. If I describe the problem of the critic who calls for the autistic/child to be free to *tell us* how to read them, understand them or even help them, I am critiquing work which claims to be impervious to criticism due to its unquestionably laudable intent to do good. This inviolate investment is then the limit of the critics' self-reflection; I read this limit to be entangled with the limit of interpretation as the 'real', which I discussed earlier.

My reading of *Curious Incident* will now pursue the notion that autism, for this novel, is the disruption of an assumed pure relationship between language and reality in which language is mobilized to encompass reality and refer to it directly. My reading will also identify this claimed pure relationship as coming from the point of view of a community. The autistic is positioned as not having access to this community because it does not possess this privileged kind of language. Therefore my reading of autism in *Curious Incident* is that it is constructed as a dislocation from a pure and direct language and the conventional community or society that this language belongs to. I will try to show that constructions of autism in this text rely on the idea that there is a pure relation between language, reality and reading which relies on an assumption that, ordinarily, reality is to be found in language. Following my critique of Murray I further critique the idea that language can be taken as a medium or a vehicle which can then be used to represent an 'other', in this case the other as the autistic. According to this view, language is something transparent: a carrier of meaning that either accurately reproduces the reality that pre-exists it, or misrepresents and distorts it. I will also look at illustrations of what the text defines as 'faces' and think about how I read picture, language and meaning as negotiated within this text to produce notions of reading and interpretation and a particular construction of autism.

On page 2 of *Curious Incident* the narration states: 'when I first met Siobhan, she showed me this picture

and I knew that it meant "sad", which is what I felt when I found the dead dog.'[29] Here, the narration is a 'me' and 'I'. This viewpoint is a singular, retrospective perspective. The lines are defined by the narration as a 'picture' which is then defined as 'sad'. The inverted commas mark the word 'sad' as different to, and separated from, the rest of the text. The inverted commas could also be read as speech marks, or as a quotation, in which case they posit a previous text. Either way, it is as if 'sad' is being quoted or taken from an other source and not produced primarily by the narration but been previously established by an other. The implication is that the language used by the narration to express 'what I felt' is not produced directly from its own perspective: it knows 'what I felt' because of an other.

Where does meaning reside in this section? There is a distinction made between 'picture' and words that formulates meaning as something that is either direct or that has to be translated: the 'picture' is one step removed from 'how I felt', whereas 'sad' is claimed to be exact and can meet it directly in an unmediated way, if not by the narration itself directly. Words are the point of reference by which both interpretation of the 'picture' and the articulation of 'what I felt' become possible. The picture and its corresponding word put in place a system whereby the former is interpreted by the latter. If language cannot be attached to the 'picture' then the 'picture' has no meaning. The 'picture' and 'what I felt' both correspond to the word 'sad', thus 'what I felt' and the picture only have something to do with each other because they are both articulated by the same word. The picture's meaning, then, is located in the kind of language that is not produced by the narration. From the point of view of the narration, this quoted kind of language is privileged over the 'picture' as the 'picture' means 'sad' yet it is 'sad' that is 'what I felt' and not the 'picture'.

The 'picture' and the 'sad' are set up as forms of discourse that are supplied to the narration as opposed to being produced by it. The 'picture' is 'shown' by 'Siobhan' and 'sad' is adopted from elsewhere. By making this claim I have necessarily set up two different kinds of language: that which is *produced* by the narration and that which is produced by an other and *used* by the narration. Reading meaning is constituted in this passage as knowing what the picture means, 'I knew that it meant "sad".' Therefore, the 'picture' is interpreted by the narration through its correspondence to this kind of pre-existing language. Reading meaning, here, is matching the picture with a corresponding word which comes from the provided kind of language. There is an idea here that there is only one meaning that the picture has. Reading, here, is to do with the process of matching the picture with the word. Therefore, the possibility of reading occurs because the two things, picture and word, exist. If the word and the picture are both set up as being supplied to the narration from elsewhere then the articulation of 'how I felt' is constituted by the provision of meaning and interpretation from an other. The language that is used by the narration is, then, a result of what has been supplied to it for the provision of reading as well as for the expression of the feeling 'sad'.

To move on and look at another section of the text: 'Then she showed me this picture

and I knew it meant "happy", like when I'm reading about the Apollo space missions.'[30] The 'picture' is the same as the 'sad' one except that the ends of the line in the circle tail upwards and not downwards. The distinction between 'sad' and 'happy' could, therefore be read from a difference in direction.

I now want to look at another reading of emotion in *Curious Incident*. In 'Art is a Lie That Tells the Truth: Autism in Literature', Meg Errington quotes the following section:

> Father said, 'Christopher you do understand that I love you?'
> And I said 'Yes,' because loving someone is helping them when they get into trouble and looking after them and telling them the truth and father looks after me when I get into trouble like coming to the police station, and he looks after me by cooking meals for me, and he always tells me the truth which means he loves me.[31]

Errington comments that 'We sense that Christopher cannot *feel* love even if he can define it'.[32] This claim necessarily involves identifying the word 'love' in *Curious Incident* as the same yet different to the 'love' that 'we' can 'feel'. In other words, Errington's argument relies on there being a single, stable reality that *is* 'love' which exists outside of and before language. It is the 'we' in this argument that functions to put in place this single, knowable, (what might be called objective) notion of 'love'. The 'we' functions to confirm this and is then constitutive of all readers and readings because there is only one way (a direct relation to reality) to read real 'love'. The word 'love', for Errington, is not subject to interpretation as a part of language, unlike the narration's use and 'definition' of it. Thus, the community that Errington instates discerns the language of definition from a language that can announce reality and feeling. This suggests that the word 'love' in *Curious Incident* is somehow mobilized as a piece of discourse that can only exist *as* discourse, whereas the 'love' quoted by Errington herself goes beyond this to feeling and, therefore, reality. To make the claim that Christopher 'cannot feel love' there has to be an assumption that his definition *should*, or ordinarily would, mean that he can 'feel love'. Errington's reading of the text depends, then, on a discrepancy between the language used by Christopher as narrator and the reality (known from the point of view of the community) that he cannot reproduce. This reproduction is assumed as possible because of a privileged relationship to language and the 'real' that, ordinarily, finds language to be equal to its referent. This, then, allows 'us' to read the language of a narration as lacking the 'real' and therefore having a limited relationship to it and, ultimately, as being autistic.

To return to my reading of *Curious Incident*: 'Then she drew some other pictures

but I was unable to say what these meant'.[33] The first two single pictures (which I looked at above) have a known meaning from the point of view of the narration, but meaning cannot be read in these 'other pictures' because it cannot be 'said'. It is tempting to resolve this by claiming that the last group of pictures is more 'difficult' or 'complex' because there are more of them and more lines going in different directions. Except, what would it be that gave these pictures the quality of being complex? It is interesting that 'happy' and 'sad' are used in the first instance, as it suggests the idea of opposites as readable and understandable as the lines go either up or down and have meaning as happy and sad. My reading here relies on an idea of scheme and system. It is the narration's inability to 'say' what they mean that prevents their meaning being articulated, so meaning here is something which must be spoken. That the pictures hold meaning is assumed as self-evident, yet the narration is limited in its reading because it is 'unable to say' what they mean. There is an idea of accessibility here. The narration does not have access to the meaning of the faces because it does not know the said language that they correspond to. Yet, the narration reads them as holding significance because it knows that there is a possibility of them being interpreted. There is also an idea of knowledge, here, that has to do with articulation through language: the pictures have meaning but that meaning, until it is said, is not accessible. The expression of meaning is then bound up with access to a certain kind of language: the accessibility to meaning, from the point of view of the narration, is limited because its knowledge of this other kind of language is limited. Therefore, an idea can be read in *Curious Incident* that there is potential meaning in the faces: meaning is not there (yet) because the narration cannot realize it by 'say[ing]'.

The system of 'picture', language and meaning is one that is constructed, from the narration's point of view, as precarious. The distinction between 'picture' and words shifts in the next quote:

> I got Siobhan to draw lots of these faces and then write down next to them exactly what they meant. I...took it out when I didn't understand what someone was saying. But it was difficult to decide which of the diagrams was most like the face they were making because people's faces move very quickly.[34]

The 'pictures' have shifted in their definition to 'faces'. The 'faces' are 'drawn' and 'what they meant' is 'written'. Meaning is something which the faces have but is articulated in the writing next to them. The faces and their meaning are supplied by Siobhan but are demanded by the narration. Thus, the narration claims the knowledge of a system of drawn faces and their written meaning, but cannot produce this system itself. So it is Siobhan that has and supplies the necessary tools for the interpretation of meaning. The narration knows that the lines that form the pictures are 'faces' (this seems to be self-evident), yet this is not what they mean. The pictures are grouped together in their definition, 'these faces', thus there is an idea of sameness here, they are all 'faces', yet the faces all have different meanings. The meaning of the face is written 'next to' it, this produces a notion of positioning that defines which 'face' refers to which piece of writing. So there is no implicit link between the drawings and their written meaning from the point of view of the narration; the latter refers to the former because of its spatial positioning in relation to it.

Reading the lines as 'picture', 'face', and 'diagrams', then, is not a problem for the narration. Yet, at the same time, this is not the same as knowing what they mean. 'People's faces' are used as a point of reference for the diagram and in turn written language, but can also be something that changes and obscures, 'it was difficult to decide which of the diagrams was most like the face they were making because people's faces move very quickly'. The definition of 'face', therefore, shifts in the text. The 'faces' that are drawn by Siobhan can also be a 'diagram'. This 'diagram' then refers to a different kind of 'face' that 'people' have when they are 'saying'. There is an idea of representation here; the diagrams represent the 'people's faces' in that they are 'like' them. So the two kinds of 'face' are similar and can refer to each other because of this similarity, but they are not the same. I have identified two different kinds of language here: saying and writing. Saying is a kind of language that interprets the pictures and 'people's faces', and it is writing that the narration requires to interpret 'what someone was saying'; however, both hold a meaning that is not self-evident. Writing is, then, privileged over 'saying' because it is direct and unproblematic for the narration and does not have to be supplemented by a 'face'.

I read in *Curious Incident*, therefore, an idea of communication that is constructed through the negation of understanding from the point of view of the narration. It is the 'I' that does not understand what 'someone' is 'saying'. (Mis)Communication is constructed through the idea of two identities: 'someone' and 'I'. To look at 'someone' more closely, this could be read as some one (as in one of some), which puts in place an idea of one identity out of a multiplicity of other identities, a community, whereas the 'I' is the singular point of view of the narration. Communication is then configured through what is said by one of a multiplicity of identities to the single 'I'. This pin-points my argument about the construction of autism in *Curious Incident*: the idea of a self that can only be defined as autistic under the condition that it is situated among a community that is constituted by a stable language and communication.

Notes

1. M. Haddon, *The Curious Incident of the Dog in the Night-Time* (London: Vintage, 2004; orig. pub. 2003).
2. For examples see: M. Errington, 'Art Is a Lie that Tells the Truth: Autism in Literature', *Books for Keeps*, 142, 2003, 12–13 and R. Gilbert, 'Watching the Detectives: Mark Haddon's *The Curious Incident of the Dog in the Night-Time* and Kevin Brooks' *Martyn Pig*', *Children's Literature in Education*, 36: 3, 2005, 241–53.
3. I. Rose, 'Autistic Autobiography or Autistic Life Narrative?', *Journal of Literary Disability*, 2: 1, 2008, 44–54, 54.
4. I am here considering autism specifically but in fact my position could refer to *any* 'identity' including, for instance, childhood.
5. See for instance M. Errington: 'Art Is a Lie That Tells the Truth: Autism in Literature'.

6. See for instance I. Rose: 'What Can We Do With *The Curious Incident of the Dog in the Night-Time?*, Popular Fiction and Representations of Disability', *Popular Narrative Media*, 1:1, 2008, 43–59.
7. See for instance K. Lesnik-Oberstein, *Children's Literature: Criticism and the Fictional Child* (Oxford: Clarendon Press, 1994).
8. J. Rose, *The Case of Peter Pan: Or the Impossibility of Children's Fiction* (London: Palgrave Macmillan, 1984).
9. Lesnik-Oberstein, *Children's Literature: Criticism and the Fictional Child*, p. 3.
10. Rose, *The Case of Peter Pan*, p. 1.
11. J. Butler, *Gender Trouble: Feminism and the Subversion of Identity* (New York: Routledge, 1990), p. 3.
12. I. Rose, 'What Can We Do With *The Curious Incident of the Dog in the Night-Time?*', 43.
13. E. Hill and U. Frith, 'Understanding Autism: Insights from Mind and Brain', *Philosophical Transactions: Biological Sciences*, 358: 1430, 2003, 281–9, 281.
14. S. Murray, *Representing Autism: Culture, Narrative, Fascination* (Liverpool: Liverpool University Press, 2008), p. xiv.
15. Murray, *Representing Autism*, p. xiii.
16. Murray, *Representing Autism*, p. xiii.
17. Murray, *Representing Autism*, p. xiv.
18. Murray, *Representing Autism*, p. xiv.
19. In 'The Psychopathology of Everyday Children's Literature Criticism' (*Cultural Critique* 45, 2000, 222–42), Karín Lesnik-Oberstein reads a similar problem in misreadings of Jacqueline Rose's seminal book *The Case of Peter Pan: Or the Impossibility of Children's Fiction*. Lesnik-Oberstein states: 'Most children's literature critics who refer to Rose consistently either refer to her most obvious point, that children are divided by class, ethnicity, and gender, or they misunderstand her main argument to mean only that children are "idealized" in children's literature and that she is therefore saying simply that this fiction has got it wrong about the child', 229.
20. Murray, *Representing Autism*, p. xv.
21. Murray, *Representing Autism*, p. xv.
22. Murray, *Representing Autism*, p. xvi.
23. Murray, *Representing Autism*, p. xviii.
24. Lesnik-Oberstein, 'The Psychopathology of Everyday Children's Literature Criticism', 234.
25. Lesnik-Oberstein, 'The Psychopathology of Everyday Children's Literature Criticism', 234.
26. Lesnik-Oberstein, 'The Psychopathology of Everyday Children's Literature Criticism', 236.
27. Lesnik-Oberstein, 'The Psychopathology of Everyday Children's Literature Criticism', 237.
28. Lesnik-Oberstein, 'The Psychopathology of Everyday Children's Literature Criticism', 233–4.
29. Haddon, *Curious Incident*, p. 2.
30. Haddon, *Curious Incident*, p. 2.
31. Errington, 'Art is a Lie that Tells the Truth: Autism in Literature', 13.
32. Errington, 'Art is a Lie that Tells the Truth: Autism in Literature', 13.
33. Haddon, *Curious Incident*, p. 2.
34. Haddon, *Curious Incident*, p. 3.

6
Bothering about Words: Children's Literature and Ideas of Simplicity and Instruction

Sarah Spooner

In this chapter I will focus on ideas of 'simplicity' of language in the construction of concepts of the child and childhood, using the work of Arthur Ransome as a case study. Children's literature critic Perry Nodelman highlights the ongoing nature of questions around these issues when he recently argued that children's literature:

> is not merely a complex literature as, say, much literary fiction for adults is; it is, more paradoxically, a complex literature in the context of its essential simplicity.
>
> But how, then, can one best work to understand or describe this literature? How can it be both simple and complicated? What are the specific natures of its simplicity and its complexity?[1]

This chapter follows Stephen Thomson's 'Substitute Communities, Authentic Voices: the Organic Writing of the Child' essay in *Children in Culture: Approaches to Childhood*, elaborating on many of the connections he makes between the concept of the child and the ideas of the language deemed appropriate for that child and the notions of simplicity, authenticity and the natural world that are associated with that language: 'writing for children easily becomes the pretext for recovery of a lost simplicity in writing. The texts that will facilitate this will [it is claimed] be shorn of the excess and clutter associated with adult civilization; they will speak to the child with a voice that is simple and direct'.[2]

Children's literature critics have not devoted much time to discussing the specifics of Arthur Ransome's prose, preferring to focus on characterization and to speculate on potential reasons for the appeal of his work to children. However, when his use of language is turned to, it is discussed in terms of its 'simplicity', its 'accuracy', its 'truth' and 'authenticity'. His writing is hailed as detailed description of real activities stemming from careful observation (his journalistic background is often mentioned). Arthur Ransome's prose is 'workmanlike' according to Fred Inglis: 'The writing is plain, wholesome and firm; it is undecorated and its cadences fix only the scene and no special attitude towards it'.[3] His writing indulges in 'no tricks' in the view of Marcus Crouch;[4] 'There is no "fine writing", only plain exact words conveying concrete images. One knows precisely what is happening and exactly how it comes about'.[5] Roland Chambers refers to the 'carefully drawn detail' and 'authority'.[6] Peter Hunt's *An Introduction to Children's Literature* describes 'Ransome's functional Defoe-like prose, concentrating on primary features of things rather than on emotive or value-laden words'.[7] Thus a consensus appears that Ransome's language is clear, plain and precise and, because of this very plainness and simplicity, self-evidently needs no further discussion. Arthur Ransome is perceived to be engaged in the act of describing 'real life' in a detailed and accurate way and therefore more concerned with things and actions than with words. This can serve to release the critic from the necessity of looking more closely at this 'simple' and 'plain' language and enable them to concentrate on evaluating Ransome by how effective and 'realistic' his descriptions of things are.

I would like to place this next to a quotation from Jacqueline Rose's *The Case of Peter Pan or The Impossibility of Children's Literature*:

> Nothing must obtrude, and no word must be spoken, in excess of those which are absolutely necessary to convince the child that the world in which he or she is being asked to participate is, unquestionably, real.[8]

Thus it can be seen how very closely this common portrait of Ransome's prose style I have depicted resembles Rose's outline of a customary attitude towards language in children's fiction. Rose briefly outlines a history of the development of children's fiction that draws attention to the language in which that fiction is written and highlights a process which she terms 'the increasing "narrativisation" of children's fiction', whereby the overt narrating presence within children's fiction has been gradually deposed in favour of an apparently less self-conscious notion of representation.

> Children's fiction has tended to inherit a very specific aesthetic theory, in which showing is better than telling: the ideal work lets

the characters and events speak for themselves. This is a 'realist' aesthetic which shares with Rousseau's theory of language the desire for a natural form of expression which seems to be produced automatically and without mediation out of that to which it refers. What it denies precisely is language – the fact that language does not simply reflect the world but is active in the constitution of that world.[9]

Thus we can see in Inglis' comment that the cadences of Ransome's writing 'fix only the scene and no special attitude towards it' the desire or belief that language can simultaneously 'fix' a scene, hold it stable, and at the same time display no attitude towards the scene that it is 'fixing'. Rose holds neither of these to be possible, maintaining instead that language is not a stable or stabilizing entity and neither is it neutral. Language does not 'fix' a scene that is in some way outside of it but is rather the material out of which that scene is constructed. The notion that language has an essential and direct relation to the physical objects that it describes is also traceable in the descriptions of Ransome's style as 'exact', 'precise' or 'accurate'.

Rose places Rousseau at the beginning of her narrative of the development of children's fiction and children's literature criticism, and notes that many of the assumptions, attitudes and problems discussed by Rousseau are still very much in evidence in contemporary discourses of the child. She particularly draws attention to the idea that language is something imperfect or degenerate that intervenes and contaminates the human relationship with the physical natural world. She detects 'a desire to hold the written word as closely as possible to the immediacy of the visual image' and allies this to a fundamental 'deep suspicion of written language' itself. So the preferable and purest form of language is deemed to be one that appears to most simply and directly reflect the world outside of it. The best form of language is one that does not draw attention to itself as language. This type of language is also deemed to be closer to a natural state and, therefore, more appropriate for the child, itself constructed as closer to a natural state than the adult. 'Innocence of the child and of the word – the concepts seem to draw on, or attract, each other', as Rose says. She traces a narrative of this recurring attitude to language and the child to present-day children's literature critics who cite/site children's books as the place of sanity, simplicity and truth amidst an adult literary world which is seen as false, sterile and utterly divorced from reality as a result of its linguistic self-consciousness.

This process can again be seen at work in some of the critical comments regarding Ransome's prose. Ransome 'never wastes words' according to Hugh Shelley.[10] As already stated, Crouch says Ransome's prose contains 'no tricks' and that he eschews ' "fine writing" ' – which Crouch places in inverted commas – in favour of telling the reader what is happening 'without fuss'. Similarly, Victor Watson notes 'moments of fine writing, unselfconscious, subdued and balanced', 'careful and unpretentious phrasing' and that 'Ransome's language makes no fuss about its moments of imaginative perception'.[11] The terminology in use here implies that the proper job of words is to simply 'show' the events, the real world, as transparently as possible, and that everything else is 'fuss', 'decoration' (to use Inglis' term); either a 'waste' or worse, a 'trick', and thereby gratuitous and somehow false. These descriptions set up an opposition between 'wholesome-ness' and 'trickery', with all the additional notions about morality that that implies. The inverted commas around Crouch's reference to ' "fine writing" ' signify a writing self-consciously, even pretentiously aware of itself, always with one eye on what others will think of it. This writing is, therefore, held not to be real or natural and is viewed as concerned more with itself than with 'truth'. Again, we see the recapitulation of the idea at work in the first quotation from Rose; that language should not be excessive, should not be aware of itself but rather render itself invisible in order to convince the reader that what it is saying is true. The simpler a language is, then the more authentic and near to truth it is believed to be.

One important facet of the perceived 'accuracy' and 'authenticity' of Arthur Ransome's work is the amount of time devoted to close and detailed descriptions of the performance of physical activities, from lighting a fire and erecting a tent to hoisting a sail and gutting a fish. Here is one example from *Swallows and Amazons*:

> Susan took a few handfuls of dry leaves and moss. She put them in the middle of her fireplace and built a little wigwam over them with bits of dried reeds from last year. It was like a little copy of the charcoal-burners' hut. Then she lit the moss and the reeds blazed up, while she built another wigwam over the reeds, this time of small sticks, all meeting at the middle over the blaze. When they caught fire and began to crackle she piled bigger sticks against the small ones. In a few minutes she had a strong fire.[12]

This description is detailed, carefully specific, ordered and pro-cedural: 'she put', 'then she', 'when they'. This is presumably what is meant by 'undecorated' language: there are no words over two syllables in length; there are few adjectives, the existing ones being repeated and mostly to do with size; there is one simile, carefully isolated in its own sentence and drawing attention to itself: 'it was like a little copy of'. The impression given is that nouns and prepositions have the dominant role in the passage, words that appear to have a direct relationship to things. However, the use of the term 'wigwam' complicates this. Initially appearing to me to be a 'simple', self-evident descriptive term for the shapes made out of the reeds and the sticks, it is actually a metaphor. Not only that, but the subsequent simile is of this metaphor; the 'little wigwam' is 'like a little copy of the charcoal burners hut'. A 'wigwam' is not the 'triangle' I initially glibly read it to denote, it is something else. As defined by the OED, a 'wigwam' is a term for 'a North American Indian's hut or tent of skins, mats or bark on poles' and 'a similar structure for children etc' that has its roots in Ojibwa and Algonquin words. Leaving aside the intriguing question of what 'children etc' could possibly mean, this definition of 'wigwam' includes nothing about shape, but instead details specificity of cultural origin – one that is explicitly not English – and of construction materials (interestingly, as it is construction materials that the quoted passage from the Ransome text is also preoccupied with).[13] So this descriptive term that initially appeared to me to be so obvious becomes, on closer examination, a metaphor derived from a different culture which, particularly given the much-mythologized nature of the North American Indian/ Red Indian/Native American culture in question, inevitably mobilizes ideas about colonialism.[14] So this ostensibly 'simple', 'undecorated' passage actually proves to be anything but. However, in prioritizing a discussion of the 'metaphor' in the passage in this way – singling it out for further discussion and explication – I am in some ways reproducing the notion that some language is simpler and less in need of discussion than other language that I am attempting to critique here. Why have I chosen to discuss this word, selected and defined by me as a 'metaphor', rather than, say, 'dried' or 'she' or 'began' or any of the other words in the passage? And indeed, in selecting it as a 'metaphor' in this way, am I in some way implying that the other words that I have categorized as non-metaphors have somehow a clearer and more unmediated relationship to the things that they are meant to represent?

The leisurely, carefully-reported-action-by-carefully-reported-action style of the above quote from *Swallows and Amazons* also gives a clue as to why, despite his language being so apparently un-noteworthy, so 'plain', and 'exact' and 'simple' and 'uncluttered',[15] Ransome's novels are unusually long by the standards of children's fiction. The shortest of the twelve, *The Picts and the Martyrs*, is 64,000 words long, while the longest, *Swallowdale*, hits 150,000, a fact that seems to contradict Shelley's reference to Ransome's 'marked economy of words'.[16] Many of these words are taken up by long, detailed, practically-emphasized descriptions of the minutiae of 'real life'. The preparation and consumption of meals and the routine of going to bed is given as much space as the more ostensibly plot-heavy or exciting moments such as the burglary of the houseboat and the battle with Captain Flint. This element of the texts has been interpreted as a further aid to verisimilitude, helping to create the idea that the texts are depicting 'real' events in a 'real' world. Hugh Shelley reads the leisurely pace as allowing room for the details of a normal, daily life, which for him then enables greater access to the characters of the children.[17] In this formulation, being given the apparently trivial or mundane moments of their day helps the reader to get to 'know' the characters better. Roland Chambers, in his recent biography of Ransome, points out the same association: 'Ransome's adventures became famous for their carefully drawn detail, the authority which convinced so many young readers that his heroes could be addressed in letters as real people'.[18] For John Rowe Townsend also the attention to detail is an aid to identification: '[Ransome] explains so authoritatively how everything was done...that the reader is convinced it actually happened, and almost that he or she was there at the time'.[19]

In this connection I will also quote a comment on the cover of my Penguin edition of *Peter Duck* from a contemporary review by Hugh Walpole, which describes the book as 'so well written that you don't realise it is written at all. The adventures just seem to occur to oneself'. Here again can be seen the notion that the most successful language is that which makes us surrender the awareness that we are reading and convinces us that it is actually happening, that it is real.

For many of these critics the language of technical, practical detail also serves another purpose; that of instruction. Hugh Shelley notes that:

> During the course of reading the saga one can learn how to skin a rabbit, tickle a trout, catch, clean and smoke eels, use semaphore, assay copper, keep milk cool, lay patterans, burn charcoal, make a map and take flashlight photographs.[20]

Learn is the key word here. It is as if, by reading Arthur Ransome's 'exact', 'precise' and 'realistic' prose, the reader has been given the ability to perform the activities laid out by that prose. Frank Eyre claims that any 'boy or girl who has read the whole series must have a pretty thorough knowledge of small-boat sailing'.[21] In this construction, the Ransome texts serve as teachers, while Michelle Landsberg's recollections of what the books meant to her as a child construct them as initiators into a specific, and indeed special, type of knowledge:

> Ardently, I learned to sail and semaphore from the Swallows and Amazons. Thirty years later, when I finally had a chance to sit at the tiller of a dinghy, I knew the heft, the feel and the arcane language as though I were a secret inhabitant of a nautical world. As, indeed, I was.[22]

Here the Ransome books serve as educational tool again, as well as object of nostalgia. Ransome is not only praised for the 'accuracy' of his language, but also for the accuracy of the technical details with which his books are filled. He focuses on the mechanics of 'how' things happen as much as on what happens itself. The novel that tells of adventures brings itself nearer to reality by instructing on how those adventures are performed. It becomes a 'How to...' text; in Rose's terminology, it constructs itself as showing rather than telling. In Linklater's words, Ransome 'makes a tale of adventure into a handbook to adventure'.[23]

The particular technical language of sailing is granted a privileged position in Ransome's work, even as his characters accord a privileged position to those who can sail. The distinctive sailing jargon adds a further dimension to a discussion of Ransome's much-vaunted plain and simple prose:

> Susan had got the sail ready. On the yard there was a strop (which is really a loop) that hooked on a hook on one side of an iron ring called a traveller, because it moved up and down the mast. The halyard ran from the traveller up to the top of the mast, through a sheave (which is a hole with a little wheel in it), and then down again. John hooked the strop on the traveller and hauled away on the halyard. Up went the brown sail until the traveller was nearly at the top of the mast. Then John made the halyard fast on the cleats, which were simply pegs, underneath the thwart which served to hold the mast up.[24]

This jargon-heavy passage from *Swallows and Amazons* could almost come from a sailing instruction manual, so specific is the language. Yet a closer look at the passage raises a number of complexities that I offer as important issues in reading the passage, but not as questions to which I can provide answers. I am not a sailor, and what strikes me instantly is why some of these words such as strop and sheave, are explained here, while others – halyard, thwart – are not. Why are some of the explanations in parentheses while others, for example those of the traveller and the cleats, occur in the main body of the text? Also, as neither the word strop nor sheave appear anywhere else in the text, why is it felt needful to introduce and explain them at all? Why are the parenthetic explanations in the present tense: a 'sheave *is* a hole with a wheel in it', while the cleats '*were* simply pegs'? (one seems to read as more universal, a once-for-all-time statement of fact, while the other seems to be more specific, referring to a particular occasion). And if a strop is 'really' a loop, as the first parenthesis claims, why not simply call it a loop in the first place? Might this not then mean that 'strop' is a metaphor of some kind? This last particular example is one where the use of a more ostensibly 'complex' word ('strop' rather than 'loop') is highlighted by the insertion of the more 'plain' or 'simple' word next to it. It serves to question the primacy placed on technical jargon by effec- tively stating that the jargon-word is not what the object 'really' is. The use of two different words for the same object in the passage also calls into question the very idea that there is any inherent, 'natural' relation- ship between word and object, which is an idea apparently held dear by those depicting Ransome's 'plain' and 'accurate' language. In the same way, the 'cleats' 'were *simply* pegs', indicating 'cleat' as complex term that can or has to be translated into 'simpler' language in order to enable comprehension. But what is it about the terms 'pegs' or 'loop' that enable them to be seen as 'simpler' than 'strop' or 'cleats' at all? The only thing that might enable them to be read in this way in this passage is their relationship to each other, where one apparently serves to define or explain the other. So here, then, 'simple' seems to be to do with position and relation rather than anything inherent or essential. The whole foregoing discussion has highlighted the idea of 'simple' lan- guage as if it was a self-evident thing, able to be identified by everyone, requiring no further definitions or explanations of the criteria used in reaching this judgement, but closer examination shows that to be far from the case. How can any language be 'simpler' than any other?

It is notable that the existence of passages like the above does not lead Ransome's critics to call into question their statements about his 'plain', 'simple', 'accurate' language. This is perhaps because the techni- calities of the frequently unexplained sailing jargon also serve to add a further layer of obscure verisimilitude to the texts, functioning in much the same way as the medical terminology thrown around in TV medical dramas such as *Casualty* and *ER*. Often incomprehensible, it nevertheless contributes to the notion that the readers or viewers are entering into a pre-existing world. While phrases like 'Never forget to mouse the sisterhooks when you fasten the main halliard to the yard'[25] are no more inherently lucid than 'Twas brillig, and the slithy toves did gyre and gimble in the wabe',[26] they are still seen by the critics to be participating in the discourse of a real, practical world graspable by language. The words are still taken to be clearly related to things, but merely things and words outside the reach of that particular viewer or reader. As such, the particular lack of comprehension engendered by the jargon does not work to call into question the link made by these critics between word and object, and thereby does not query the stability, the concreteness, of language. However, once the idea that language bears a clear and obvious relationship to anything outside of itself is questioned or cast aside, then the notion that any language is simpler than any other language has to be queried or cast aside also as it seems to fundamentally rest on the notion that some words bear a clearer and more obvious relationship to things than others and are, therefore, easier to understand. This then in its turn calls into question many of the distinctions and judgements made about language, including those between 'plain' and 'decorative' language, and between 'jargon' and 'non-jargon'. 'Simplicity' is not inherent, it is imposed; it is a result of reading and interpretation, not something that stands free from it.

Further to Shelley's quote on 'doing', an emphasis on 'doing' things rather than reading about them is one available to be read throughout the *Swallows and Amazons* series, with its stress on practical activities in the outdoors, and many children's literature critics have directed attention to this emphasis. Hugh Shelley's monograph says that people who dislike Ransome's books are those 'who do not enjoy doing things for themselves', and recounts a list of the activities that a child can 'learn' from reading these books: 'During the course of the saga one can learn how to skin a rabbit, tickle a trout, catch, clean and smoke eels, use semaphore, assay copper, keep milk cool, lay patterans, burn charcoal, make a map and take flashlight photographs'.[27] Significantly, all of these listed activities are practical, outdoor-based physical activities, rather than mental or intellectual ones. The Latin declensions of Ransome's *Missee Lee*, for example, are not on the list. Marcus Crouch and Alec Ellis's 1977 *Chosen for Children*, a compilation of Carnegie Medal winners, again highlights the practical dimension of *Pigeon Post*, the first Carnegie Medal winner in 1936, describing Ransome's books as 'wonderful, practical handbooks' 'to self-reliant sensible children in getting the best out of a country holiday'.[28] The physical and rural nature of many of the activities in Shelley's list of things one can learn from the Ransome texts brings in further connections between learning and landscape, an idea of learning by doing frequently visible in educational texts from Rousseau onwards.

I have already said something about what I am terming the discourse of 'doing' in my discussion of the way Ransome's language is characterized by children's literature critics. It resides in the descriptions of Ransome's prose as 'wholesome', 'plain', 'simple' and 'accurate' which participate in an idea of language having a direct relationship to a world outside of itself, and that this relationship is best or clearest rendered in what could be viewed as un-ornate, un-self-conscious language. As Jacqueline Rose points out, this idea contains within it a fundamental 'deep suspicion of language itself'. Another key term is the description of Ransome's prose as 'functional', which begs questions as to the nature and purpose of that 'function', and which has an important relationship to ideas about education. Ransome's writing, primarily working with verbs and nouns, is depicted as dealing in 'objects', and whether that object is a stick or a halyard, it can still be seen as having an unmediated relationship with an 'immediate' world outside of words.

Many of the components of the interrelated group of ideas pertaining to the child and nature and their relationship to each other and the society around them can be seen in evidence in the *Swallows and Amazons* books. All twelve of the books are primarily rural in location, containing only fleeting visits to more urban areas, and the activities performed in these locations are the outdoor-based ones of camping, sailing, fishing, exploring, gold-prospecting, mountain-climbing, bird-watching, sledging, the list could go on. Leaving aside those scenes taking place in the cabins of boats, there are actually very few indoor scenes in the entire series.[29] Nancy's comment, 'You know what it's like. Dark at tea-time and sleeping indoors: nothing ever happens in the winter holidays'[30] makes clear that indoor activities are rated as 'nothing', non-events. Everything that counts as a 'happening' occurs out of doors. (It also makes the assumption that this is a universal belief, likely to be shared by everyone: 'you know what it's like'). The emphasis throughout is on physical activity in the outdoors. Great emphasis is placed on knowing how to perform these physical activities, with practical knowledge based upon experience more valued than a theoretical knowledge gained from books. This is particularly in evidence with the entry of the two explicitly city-bred children, Dick and Dorothea Callum, into the series in *Winter Holiday*. While the Swallows and Amazons appear to be largely preoccupied with what they will 'be' and 'do', Dick and Dorothea, on their first introduction to the Lake Country, instead describe themselves as 'looking at things': ' "there are a million other things we want to look at, too," said Dorothea. "We want to look at everything" '.[31] An early exchange between Dick and Roger can serve as an introduction to their differences:

> 'Do you really know all about the stars?'
> 'I only know a few of them,' said Dick.
> 'I know the saucepan and the Pole star,' said Roger.
> 'The saucepan?'
> 'The one you find the Pole by.'
> 'It's much more like a saucepan than some of the things they call it,' said Dick. 'I've got a book that has them all in, all the constellations, at least'.[32]

Dick's knowledge of and ability to identify stars is here gleaned from a book, while Roger's is through practical usage and function, namely direction finding. His name for the constellation is based on an idea of its physical appearance, derived from his practical experience of it, rather than a more abstract 'proper' name given to it in textbooks. Dick acknowledges that Roger's name for it is closer to an idea of mimetic representation, of what it looks like, than the names given to it in his book. Roger's name, itself derived from a functional object, obtained from practical experience, is thus constructed as less abstract and somehow closer to the object in question.

In *Winter Holiday* Dick and Dorothea's lack of knowledge and experience of the outdoor activities that the Swallows and Amazons take to be second nature is constantly re-iterated, casting doubt on their abilities and making them seem consequently lacking in sense.[33]

> He thought of Dorothea, a little town girl, not tough like themselves, out all day in that blinding storm. He thought of Dick, who was full of good ideas but was nearly always thinking of the wrong one. They could both skate like anything, but, in weather like today's, could anybody trust them to know what to do?[34]

They cannot sail, they do not know Morse code, they cannot tie proper knots, Dorothea cannot fulfil her desire to be 'useful' in helping to collect water because she forgets her gloves and they cannot even put the cork back into a message bottle properly: 'I'm sure I never shoved the cork in like that' (p. 307). Their lack of knowledge of and competence in these activities nearly prohibits their acceptance into the group:

> 'An astronomer might be quite useful.'
> 'But what's *she* going to do?'
> 'We'll soon know if they're any good' (p. 47, emphasis in original)

but the issue is 'settled' or saved by their knowledge of skating acquired in an 'indoor skating rink close by the University buildings at home' which prompts Nancy to confirm their acceptance: 'Of course, you ought to be in the Polar expedition. Not one of us can skate like that' (p. 63). So, both their entry into the already established Swallows and Amazons group and their potential exclusion from it are based around the ability to perform physical, practical activities. The Callums' skating ability in fact introduces a temporary hierarchy reversal into the group, placing them ahead of the established, competent group members. The Amazons know 'enough about skating to know that skating was to Dick as natural and easy a thing as sailing their little *Amazon* was to them' (p. 63). Not only does this episode place the newcomers in the position of having more knowledge than the longer-established group members, albeit temporarily, and thus having knowledge to exchange ('You teach me how to twiddle round and go backwards and I'll teach you signalling'), but the parallel with sailing – the core physical activity of the books – importantly makes it 'natural' knowledge. Sailing the *Amazon* for Nancy and Peggy and skating for Dick are said to be 'natural' and 'easy', thus seemingly instinctive and experiential rather than painstakingly learned.

Much of *Winter Holiday* is told from the perspective of Dorothea, who is continually conscious of the practical superiority of the more experienced Swallows and Amazons, afraid of what they will think of her and wishing to prove the worth of herself and her brother to them. She was 'a little shy of skating with these Arctic explorers who knew all about ships and could signal in half a dozen different ways. She thought they would probably be as much better than Dick and her at skating as they were at everything else' (p. 62). The repeated reiteration of her concerns over their lack of knowledge, uselessness and thus their potential lack of acceptance into the group makes clear the importance of such knowledge in constructing an idea of belonging. Victor Watson describes *Winter Holiday* as 'a quest for meaning in a bewildering world of coded messages' and as 'a process of initiation into languages and codes' with the text's diagrams and illustrations 'reinforc[ing] the point that meaning, and access to it, lie at the heart of the story'.[35] The winter landscape itself becomes another set of 'signs to be interpreted', another 'code to be cracked', while Dick and Dorothea also have to learn the code of the Swallows and Amazons. The latter's horror at Dorothea's use of newspaper to light a fire ('"You'd better come along with us at once," said Nancy, "and see how to make a fire and how to light it with one match and no paper at all"') and Dick's inability to see that they cannot go to the North Pole in a rowing-boat (because 'rowing boats don't count') construct the Callums' lack of knowledge and experience as much as social faux pas as simple physical ineptitude. The ability to sail, to tie proper sailor's knots, to read Morse code and to light fires in the approved manner, grants entry into a particular social world, and fears of exclusion from this world and of doing the wrong thing according to its precepts is an ever-present fear for Dorothea.[36]

An alternative standard is offered in later text *The Picts and the Martyrs* against which Dorothea can measure her lack of practical, rural knowledge and still find herself wanting. In this text, Dick and Dorothea, invited to stay at Nancy and Peggy's house by the Lake, are driven into hiding by the coming of the Blacketts' Great Aunt, having to fend for themselves in a disused cottage in the woods. Here, the model for behaviour is not idealized explorers, pirates or gold-hunters, but rather a notion of an ancient British rural way of life. Dick initially suggests they could be badgers: 'In lots of places people think they're extinct. But they aren't. Only they never let themselves be seen', but Dorothea then substitutes 'Picts':

'Picts?' said Nancy.
'Ancient Britons,' said Dorothea. 'Prehistorics. Original inhabitants. They had to hide from the invaders and went on living secretly in caves and in the end people thought they were fairies and used to leave milk outside the door for them. Something like that'.[37]

So this text then mobilizes an idea of an ancient rural people, native to the region, living secretly and in close connection to the land. The easy movement from badgers to Picts gives an impression of a people very close to the status of animals in their closeness to the land. Like many of the other narrative models used by the children in the series, this Picts model again includes an emphasis on being first, with the Picts as 'original inhabitants': 'She and Dick were the only people in the world. And Dick was asleep. She had the world to herself'.[38] But as original inhabitants, they are under threat from incoming 'invaders' from whom they have to hide, putting a different complexion on the colonial/imperial narratives from which so many of the other behavioural models in the books are drawn. However, as in many of the other texts, their status as first is complicated by reminders of the presence of others, in this case, signs of another user of the cottage in which they are staying. This other user turns out to be a young local boy, Jacky Warriner, the farmer's son who delivers their milk. Described as 'a better Pict than either of us', it is Jacky who spotlights Dorothea's sense of inadequacy over her inability to be a proper Pict.

> Somehow, the hut did not seem as much theirs as it had been. Jacky had been there first, and had done the thing better than they could hope to do it, living on trout and rabbits and having his own store of nuts like any squirrel.
>
> 'All the nicest houses have been lived in for hundreds of years,' said Dorothea suddenly.
>
> 'That boy was a sort of Pict, too,' said Dick. 'It sounded as if nobody knew he'd been here'.[39]

Despite being younger than Dick and Dorothea, Jacky repeatedly displays his superior knowledge of what she constructs as proper Pictish living, using the cottage secretly without anyone being aware, knowing how to keep milk cool, having a more practical cooking knowledge, and, most importantly, being able to gather food from the land (as opposed to buying it in tins or having to obtain it from the Blackett family's Cook). He teaches them to 'guddle' trout, catching them without the aid of artificial implements such as a fishing rod, instead relying on hands, 'artful'-ness and local knowledge. He also provides them with a rabbit, treating with scorn Dick's statement that they don't have a gun: ' "Gun? What for? You don't want a gun for rabbits" '. The trout provides them with what Dorothea calls 'our first real meal', with 'real' constituted as 'food that we got for ourselves', and she acknowledges that 'if Jacky was living here instead of us ... I'm perfectly sure he'd manage without any bought stuff at all. There were no shops for the Picts. And no things in tins'.[40] Despite Dick's assertion that the Picts would have used things in tins if they could have got them, Jacky's abilities remain the model. As a local, more working-class boy, as well as a younger one, his superior knowledge comes from direct, personal, practical experience as opposed to anything derived from books. Knowledgeable through experience, catching food without artificial aids, Jacky is constructed as closer to the land than Dick and Dorothea, purveyor of a truer, more authentic knowledge about a way of living constructed as far in the past, yet towards which Dick and Dorothea continually look as a measure for themselves and their interaction with the world around them.

The episode with Jacky's rabbit particularly highlights the Callums' town-bred inadequacies. Once presented with this gift from the land, the problems Dick and Dorothea encounter in its preparation and cooking become extensive. '[T]hat rabbit, in the mind of an inexperienced cook, was bulking bigger than an elephant.'[41] Dorothea's own trepidation regarding cooking the rabbit only adds to her doubts about her own authenticity as a proper Pict:

'It looks awfully dead,' said Dorothea.
'But it *is*,' said Dick.
'I wonder how I ought to begin.'
'There's probably a scientific way,' said Dick. 'Of getting the skin off, I mean'.
Dorothea took the rabbit from the peg. Its eyes were dull, and its fur felt cold to her unwilling touch.
'They're a lot nicer running about'.
'I know,' said Dick. 'So is everything. Even tinned pemmican was running about once, and sardines were swimming and bananas were growing on trees. But we eat them just the same.'
'Picts wouldn't think twice about it. Jacky didn't'.[42]

Dick points out the inauthenticity of their usual food, just as 'dead' as the rabbit whose corpse they are confronted with, but simply brought to them in a less obviously dead form which allows them to forget its previous status as 'running about', while Dorothea's distaste for the dead rabbit is a further violation of the code of Pictish behaviour she has set for herself. Jacky also provides them with an onion as the best thing to cook a rabbit with, but Dick and Dorothea don't know how to prepare the rabbit for the cooking stage as it is still intact with its skin on. Rejecting the idea of asking for advice from the Blackett's Cook, among others, on the grounds that 'we oughtn't to have to ask people everything' and 'I think I ought to learn' (especially as Nancy characterizes it as 'jolly useful' and, as already stated, Dorothea is frequently preoccupied with achieving the status of useful and with doing things in the ways her chosen models would approve), Dorothea decides to turn to a cookery book for advice. 'Books always help a lot', agrees Dick. However, despite informing them of 'about a dozen ways' to cook rabbits – 'Stew ... Fricassée ... Boiled ... Jugged' – the book is notably unhelpful in addressing the main areas of concern, namely how to skin it and remove its insides. The book participates in the inauthentic, non-Pictish world of food highlighted earlier, where 'the rabbits and things all seem to be born naked and ready for cooking'. 'Picts don't buy rabbits ready trussed like the picture. What do they do?'.[43] Deciding that a Pict would 'skin it with a flint knife', '[n]o. Bronze I should think', Dick ends up taking the rabbit into the wood to remove 'things' from its insides, from which he returns 'looking very green', and then they improvise a skinning process which degenerates into a 'messy' 'tug of war'. Even after this, the book proves to be of limited use, as 'lack of this and lack of that made it impossible to follow exactly any single one of the recipes in the book', so she incorporates bits from them all, which leaves her with such conflicting cooking times that she has to simply 'let it cook till it feels all right when we prod it'. So, the search in books for a 'scientific method' has to be replaced by an improvised, do-it-yourself approach, which is ultimately characterized as 'the real thing' by Nancy. The connection between the rabbit and books is also continued right through to the eating process, where Dorothea, whose preferred role throughout the series is the one of writer, 'felt about the eating of the first rabbit she had ever cooked much as if she were reading the proofs of her first book'.[44] Here, the rabbit is made analogous to a book, with the eating of this hand-cooked rabbit potentially holding as much satisfaction as encountering the proof of completion of someone's own written work. However, the specific written work consulted by Dorothea, the cookery book, proves to be inadequate in the face of the reality of the rabbit and its instructions have to be largely cast aside in favour of a more instinctual, hands-on approach.

In this chapter I have outlined just one of the discourses I believe to be at play in the Arthur Ransome texts. What I have termed the discourse of 'doing' places stress on the performance of physical actions and personal experience above what is constructed as a more distanced, theoretical knowledge. The children learn by close proximity to and immersion in the natural world around them, and judge others by their equal abilities in and experience of that world. This emphasis on physical actions is both to do with continued safety and survival in a selected world largely free from adult intervention and also to do with initiation and belonging, as a social as well as a survival rite. As I have argued from the start of this chapter, however, in line with the writings of critics such as Jacqueline Rose and Stephen Thomson, these discourses are not just readable in the works of Arthur Ransome, or indeed only in 'children's literature' and 'childhood' more generally – however fundamentally they may be enmeshed within them – but are at play in that wider ' "realist" aesthetic which shares with Rousseau's theory of language the desire for a natural form of expression which seems to be produced automatically and without mediation out of that to which it refers'.[45]

Notes

My title refers to the quote 'This was no time to bother about words', from: Arthur Ransome, *Peter Duck* (Harmondsworth: Puffin, 1982), p. 300.

1. P. Nodelman, 'Former Editor's Comments: Or, the Possibility of Growing Wiser', *Children's Literature Association Quarterly*, 35: 3, Fall, 2010, 230–42, 232.
2. S. Thomson, 'Substitute Communities, Authentic Voices: the Organic Writing of the Child', in K Lesnik-Oberstein (ed.), *Children in Culture: Approaches to Childhood* (Basingstoke and London; Palgrave Macmillan, 1998), pp. 248–73, p. 262.
3. F. Inglis, *The Promise of Happiness* (Cambridge: Cambridge University Press, 1981), p. 140.
4. M. Crouch, *Treasure Seekers and Borrowers* (London: The Library Association, 1962), p. 70.
5. M. Crouch, *The Nesbit Tradition* (London: Ernest Benn, 1972), p. 143.
6. R. Chambers, *The Last Englishman: The Double Life of Author Ransome* (London: Faber & Faber, 2009), p. 351.
7. P. Hunt, *An Introduction to Children's Literature* (Oxford: Oxford University Press, 1994), p. 123.
8. J. Rose, *The Case of Peter Pan or The Impossibility of Children's Literature* (Basingstoke: Palgrave Macmillan, 1992), p. 62.
9. Rose, *The Case of Peter Pan*, p. 59.
10. H. Shelley, *Arthur Ransome* (London: Bodley Head, 1960), p. 61.
11. V. Watson, *Reading Series Fiction: From Arthur Ransome to Gene Kemp* (London and New York: RoutledgeFalmer, 2000), p. 20.
12. A. Ransome, *Swallows and Amazons* (Harmondsworth: Puffin: 1980), p. 154.
13. By way of contrast, www.dictionary.com offers a definition of 'wigwam' as 'a Native American dwelling commonly having an arched or conical framework overlaid with bark, hides, or mats'. This definition similarly specifies construction materials but differs from the OED in including ideas about shape. However, these ideas remain relatively vague – 'commonly having an arched or conical framework' – and are still some distance away from the 'triangle' that I initially clearly read into the passage.
14. This is especially the case given the fact that the *Swallows and Amazons* texts are engaged in an ongoing examination of colonialism and its positions and narratives.
15. P. Hunt, *Approaching Arthur Ransome* (London: Jonathan Cape, 1992), p. 93.
16. Shelley, *Arthur Ransome*, p. 61.
17. Shelley, *Arthur Ransome*, pp. 26–7.

18. Chambers, *The Last Englishman*, p. 351.
19. J. R. Townsend, *Written for Children* (Harmondsworth: Penguin, 1965), p. 185.
20. Shelley, *Arthur Ransome*, p. 66.
21. F. Eyre, *British Children's Books in the Twentieth Century* (London: Longman, 1971), p. 92.
22. M. Landsberg, *The World of Children's Books* (London: Simon & Schuster, 1988), p. 123.
23. Eric Linklater, quoted in M. Crouch, *The Nesbit Tradition*, p. 19. However, a handbook is still a book, thereby instantly complicating any notions of learning by experience as superior to learning through language.
24. Ransome, *Swallows and Amazons*, p. 25.
25. A. Ransome, *The Picts and The Martyrs* (Harmondsworth: Puffin, 1981), p. 155.
26. L. Carroll, 'Jabberwocky', *Norton Anthology of English Literature*, II, 7th edn (New York: Norton, 2000), p. 1666.
27. Shelley, *Arthur Ransome*, p. 66.
28. M. Crouch and A. Ellis (eds), *Chosen for Children* (London: The Library Association, 1977), p. 4.
29. One apparent exception to this, with its school lessons given in a facsimile English parlour/schoolroom, would be *Missee Lee*. However, here the indoor lessons are experienced as a punishment and as a forced deviation from the norm.
30. A. Ransome, *Winter Holiday* (Harmondsworth: Puffin, 1983), p. 41.
31. Ransome, *Winter Holiday*, p. 16.
32. Ransome, *Winter Holiday*, p. 47.
33. They are also initially depicted as at a potential disadvantage to some readers in their lack of knowledge of information which those readers could already have obtained from earlier texts in the series. 'They did not even know the name of the island that lay there, with its leafless winter trees, and the tall pine tree above the little cliff at the northern end of it. It had been dark when they arrived, and everything was new to them' (Ransome, *Winter Holiday*, p. 17). To those already familiar with the books, this can be recognized as a reference to Wild Cat Island, a key location in some of the earlier texts, yet even without this familiarity, the 'even' of the first quoted sentence positions the lack of knowledge of the island's name as an extreme instance of the two characters' ignorance. They are placed almost as newborns in this world, seeing everything for the first time and thus unable to discriminate about what they are seeing.
34. Ransome, *Winter Holiday*, p. 311.
35. Watson, *Reading Series Fiction*, p. 24.
36. Ideas of inclusion and exclusion from this social grouping can also function in relation to the reader, who, by reading the detailed accounts in the texts, can 'learn' how to step a mast, light a fire properly, fill a kettle from a lake without getting scum on the water, and thus become honorary members of this world.
37. Ransome, *The Picts and The Martyrs*, p. 41. Her 'something like that' vagueness and uncertainty about her definition of Picts is worthy of note. She later seeks confirmation on the issue from her archaeology professor father,

who responds via a letter written by his wife that 'in a way you are right and in a way you are wrong'. He acknowledges that Dorothea's definition of the Picts used to be a theory among 'folklorists', but that it is 'an exploded theory'. However, 'most theories get exploded sooner or later' (p. 146). This is a view of history as less to do with static, ascertainable facts, but more as a succession of 'exploded theories'.

38. Ransome, *The Picts and the Martyrs*, p. 73.
39. Ransome, *The Picts and the Martyrs*, p. 123.
40. Ransome, *The Picts and the Martyrs*, p. 142.
41. Ransome, *The Picts and the Martyrs*, p. 180.
42. Ransome, *The Picts and the Martyrs*, pp. 147–8.
43. Ransome, *The Picts and the Martyrs*, p. 187. It is notable that in this passage the Picts have made the transition from the 'were' and the 'would' hitherto used to discuss them and are suddenly in the present tense: 'Picts don't', 'what do they do?'.
44. Ransome, *The Picts and the Martyrs*, p. 198.
45. Rose, *The Case of Peter Pan*, p. 59.

7
Irony and the Child

Sue Walsh

In *Irony's Edge* (1994) Linda Hutcheon examines a controversy around an exhibition at the Royal Ontario Museum in Toronto in 1989–90, entitled 'Into the Heart of Africa'.[1] In her discussion Hutcheon regards the 'irony' deployed by the exhibition as the source of the outcry that met it, the problem being, it is argued, that the irony was either not read or understood by many visitors to the exhibition, or it was regarded as utterly inappropriate. In two of the illustrations of the problem, children, as potential audience, are made reference to; once in the service of Hutcheon's own critique of the exhibition and once when she gives an account of some of the arguments made against it at the time by a protest group calling itself the Coalition for the Truth about Africa. The furore around the 'Into the Heart of Africa' exhibition has been much discussed since,[2] and is not itself my concern here, rather my primary interest in Hutcheon's discussion of the controversy is in the way the child is figured in relation to claims about irony.[3] Having said that, one of the issues that comes up forcefully in the analyses of the controversy, the question of the construction of race in putatively ironic terms, will be addressed more than once in this chapter, specifically in relation to the claimed effects of such constructions on children in the debates around whether *Adventures of Huckleberry Finn* should be required reading in schools in the US.

In her own critique of 'Into the Heart of Africa', Hutcheon takes issue with the Royal Ontario Museum's use of what she describes as 'an enormous, wall-sized enlargement of an image of a mounted British soldier thrusting his sword into the breast of an African warrior'.[4] Hutcheon suggests, by way of reference to an article written in 1991 by the exhibition's curator,[5] that this representation was intended to expose the brutality of the imperial project but that instead its effect was to provoke hostility against the exhibition for mobilizing such images. Hutcheon's own objections are articulated as follows:

> In today's culture, where visual images may indeed make more of an impression than printed text, and in an institution visited by schoolchildren of all ages and races who just might not stop to read the contextualizing accompanying texts, the placing and size of this image were, at the very least, signs of semiotic inattention or inexperience. While the relationship of text to image is a general problem for all museum exhibits, here it proved critical because many African Canadian visitors could not bring themselves to go beyond this violent representation of their race's history.[6]

Hutcheon's critique here is formulated along two prongs: the first deploys certain attenuated assumptions with respect to the visual image and how it is read or rather not read. Visual images, Hutcheon claims, *impose* themselves perhaps (the attenuation comes with the 'may indeed'), and have an *effect*, whereas 'text' (which means only writing here, while the 'image' is representation) must, but might not be read. On the one hand then, the 'printed text' holds the key as to how the image ought to be *read*, but is not, and as such it signals the image's inadequacy as (a/the) reality; on the other hand, that the image is constituted as a 'representation' validates the claim that it refers to a reality, however partially or faultily. Ultimately, Hutcheon faults the exhibition for its failure to grasp the affective power of the image, a power which here derives both from its unchallenged relationship to the real and from the claimed directness of its emotional communication with its audience.

The second prong of Hutcheon's critique concerns precisely the audience that is said to succumb to the effects of the visual image, and this is the point at which 'children' come into the discussion. 'Schoolchildren' are figured as particularly vulnerable here, and their vulnerability is presented as having to do with not reading, or perhaps it is the unpredictability of children 'who just might not stop to read' that constitutes their vulnerability. Implicitly, children must actively produce themselves as audience when it comes to written text whereas they are implicitly and unwittingly 'impressed' by the visual image. Reading then, is figured as a way of maintaining distance from, or 'contextualizing', the affective power of the visual image. In this notion of contextualization, the written text is figured as a stable meaning that must be added to the image, this meaning for the image is thus only available outside of itself, and its addition to the image must be performed by a conscious agential audience. The visual image's power to provoke an emotional response on the other hand, is direct, immediate and unavoidably and unconsciously acquiesced to, the nature of the affect[7] simply is what it is and is never put into question.

Hutcheon's formulation of 'schoolchildren' as potential audience also suggests that the very non-specificity of the category, in that it can encompass 'all ages and races', poses something of a problem. On the one hand different ages and races constitute different potential audiences, on the other hand these differences are subsumed under the supposed likely tendency to avoid reading. Indeed age and race are brought together here: children and African Canadians are both figured as non-readers, either through a likely predisposition, and here I am reading 'just might not stop' as producing the child as insufficiently (self-)reflective to be a reader (like Wordsworth's boy with his 'glad animal movements', whose perception is 'appetite' and 'feeling' as opposed to the adult with his 'remoter' relationship to the world 'by thought supplied'[8]); or through an inability (which is figured as originating in a racial identity) which amounts to a loss or lack of agency in the face of the affective violence of the image. The way in which the child here stands together with the African Canadian as vulnerable to the impositions of the image through an innate emotional response and a inability or unwillingness to read strikes me as a worrying corollary of Hutcheon's analysis.[9]

The second reference to children in Hutcheon's analysis of the 'Into the Heart of Africa' exhibition follows her description of a specific instance of what she terms 'ironic citational signaling', an instance which, she maintains, was 'mentioned in almost every public response to [the] exhibition':

> [A] missionary photograph of a (named and standing) white woman watching a number of (unnamed and crouching) black women doing washing [set against] its caption – 'Taken in Nigeria about 1910, this photograph shows missionary Mrs. Thomas Titcombe giving African women "a lesson in how to wash clothes". African labour was the mainstay of mission economies.'[10]

Following discussion of the status of this instance as irony, where the Coalition for the Truth about Africa is reported first as not regarding it as such and then as arguing that 'the subtleties of irony could not compete with the power of images of subjugation', while others are reported as finding the ironies to be 'didactic or heavy-handed',[11] it is interesting to note that Hutcheon goes on to ask the question as to whether 'the intended ironies implicitly rely too much on an audience that can be effectively and politically detached from the pain represented in the exhibition's visual images'[12] and later notes that 'the use of irony was read by some as belonging to a white culture's model of discourse.'[13] Despite the fact that Hutcheon treats this notion with some scepticism, her doubts are relegated to a footnote,[14] and this would indeed seem to be the logical outcome of Hutcheon's own formulations as I have analysed them above.

Where children once again appear in Hutcheon's account of the debates around the exhibition, it is in the reported reaction of the Coalition for the Truth about Africa to the aforementioned photograph and caption: 'African Canadian children came away from "Into the Heart of Africa" with a negative impression of black history, with the idea that Africans did not know how to wash their clothes or comb their hair before the whites arrived.'[15] Here African Canadian children, as both children and as representatives of their race, are figured as oblivious to irony, occupying the position of those who are most vulnerable in the face of irony and against whom irony constitutes the ultimate offence. The children, for the Coalition for the Truth about Africa, are held up to stand in the place of the Coalition's own affect, and through them the Coalition can lay claim to an unassailable and therefore privileged position of suffering against any who might claim, by arguing for the irony of the exhibition, that what is under question is not suffering but truth. Indeed, in the mobilization of the child, the Coalition equates suffering with truth and renders both uncontestable. At the same time, articulated in terms of defending children, the Coalition's objection to the exhibition maintains its claim to adulthood and agency, the very things it sees the exhibition as threatening.

Earlier in *Irony's Edge* Hutcheon expresses an uneasy scepticism about the implications of the idea that children simply lack the competence to detect and interpret irony, and argues that what may be at issue instead is whether the said children belong to the specific discursive community that 'provide[s] the context for both the deployment and attribution of irony'[16] in any particular instance. This would qualify the sense in which irony might be understood or claimed as belonging to a white culture's model of discourse but the examples I have analysed above tend to suggest rather that children often function in arguments around whether something is to be considered as ironic or not as baseline literalists who prove the unreadability of irony, and hence provoke questions as to whether it is indeed there, or, if irony is conceded as present, reveal its danger and suggest its dissembling nature. Hutcheon supports her critical attitude with respect to children's competence, or lack thereof, in understanding irony by reference to the work of developmental psychologist Ellen Winner, who finds that children have a rudimentary understanding of irony from a young age. Winner starts from the premise, evident from her characterization of metaphor and irony as non-literal language, that there is by contrast such a thing as literal language, a language that communicates its meaning directly and unambiguously, a language that refers directly to what is meant. This essentially privileges a certain reading or interpretation of any particular linguistic instance as the primary, usual, straightforward and implicitly 'correct' interpretation. Furthermore, the experiments Winner refers to in *The Point of Words* are conducted on the basis that 'adults do not ordinarily misunderstand metaphor and irony',[17] which inevitably produces an *a priori* distinction between child and adult on the basis that irony is understood by the latter though not necessarily by the former, before the understanding of irony is even investigated as a grounds for distinguishing between adult and child.

The accounts that Winner gives of how children arrive at an understanding of irony make it clear that the conception of irony that Winner is working with is something akin to what Wayne C. Booth would characterize as 'stable',[18] that is to say that it is irony defined as intentional,[19] limited and deploying a form of language in which what is said must be discounted in order to arrive at what is actually meant.[20] At the same time as being characterized as non-literal language, irony features according to Winner's argument both as that which involves a 'flouting of the maxims that ordinarily govern conversations'[21] and as 'an omnipresent principle of language, found in even the most ordinary conversations'.[22] At no point does there seem to be in her argument a sense that these two propositions may contradict each other or what such a contradiction might mean for investigations into how children come to learn about irony, in particular what it might mean for the underlying assumption that language use in children is primarily/originally literalist.

A further implication of Winner *et al.*'s approach becomes most clear when they advise that: 'Teachers of literature need to be sensitive to the specific kinds of problems children have with metaphor and irony in order to steer children toward appropriate interpretations of these major forms of nonliteral language.'[23] In other words teachers must predetermine what the appropriate interpretation of a piece of irony is; indeed the teachers must determine what counts and does not count as irony. This is precisely what research like Winner *et al.*'s must also inevitably do and the corollary of such research is the assessment that if children in particular age bands do not get the irony, predetermined as such by the researchers, they are immature or insufficiently developed as yet so to do. However, this approach cannot account for, or address the kinds of problems thrown up by the 'Into the Heart of Africa' exhibition which suggest that the inherent problems with irony are in establishing it as such (or as present), and then in the desire or requirement to fix its meaning and claim its stability.

Winner *et al.*'s closing advice to teachers would also seem to make a curious requirement of teachers if the understanding of irony is to be understood in developmental terms. After all, if the understanding of irony is a developmental issue, children should presumably achieve that understanding when they have reached the appropriate stage in development. Why then the requirement that the teacher supplement that development? Moreover, while Winner *et al.* can hardly be held responsible for the manner in which the antagonists of the 'Into the Heart of Africa' controversy conducted the debate, the common apprehension that the understanding of irony indicates the achievement of a certain developmental stage also has further unfortunate implications for the way irony is mobilized in arguments about the representation of race in supposedly ironic terms.

As I suggested above, one of the concerns I have with the way Winner *et al.*'s approach to irony is founded upon a supposed distinction between literal and non-literal language has to do with the way this approach tends to glance over the question of interpretation. The question of irony's presence would not seem to be at issue for Winner *et al.*: if irony is there it will be plain enough to those who are mature enough to grasp it. That this is the case is clear when Winner describes, in *The Point of Words*, a number of studies on the understanding of irony in the following terms: 'In several studies researchers have asked subjects to compare ironic and literal remarks to determine what people perceive to be the differences between using irony and a literal *equivalent*.'[24] This assumes that there *is* a literal equivalent to the ironic utterance and as such again effectively prejudges the interpretation of (the) irony. In the pages that follow the description of these studies this initial premise is somewhat undermined since there it is concluded that since people in the studies rated ironic compliments as equally insulting as ironic insults this shows that 'when a speaker says something negative to mean something positive, he never just means something positive but always means something critical as well'.[25] If this is the case it is hard to see how the claimed 'literal' remark could in any case be regarded as *equivalent* – but what becomes clear here, through the way the studies are described as set up, is an underpinning premise in the work of developmental psychologists as represented by Winner and the studies by Kaplan and associates on which she draws, that the meaning of an utterance can be determined independently of its form, since it is assumed, at least initially, that there can be an equivalence of meaning between two remarks formulated in quite different ways.

Since Winner's work is largely focused on children's responses to oral utterances, in thinking about the question of the competence of children in dealing with written irony, I now want to turn to two articles that deal specifically with children and their reading (or not) of irony; the first is Joseph O. Milner and Margie M. Milner's 2008 article on 'Emergent Readers' Recognition of Irony in *Good Dog, Carl*' in *Reading Psychology*, the second is Jon C. Stott's 1982 article for *Children's Literature in Education* entitled ' "It's Not What You Expect": Teaching Irony to Third Graders'.

As can be seen from the title of Milner and Milner's article, irony is conceived as straightforwardly and unambiguously present in the text used for the study, and as such reading is configured as 'recognition' of what is predetermined by the researchers as there. Milner and Milner offer the following account and interpretation of *Good Dog, Carl*, on which their study's findings are based:

> [The] book is built on irony from its first to last page. Those two pages, the first and the last, give us the simple print message, 'Look after the baby, Carl. I'll be back shortly' and then, 'Good Dog, Carl.' That simple request and commendation frame the picture book with parental language and orderly expectations. Inside the frame, adult print disappears, and we see the real life of Baby and good dog Carl. The irony of [the] book is that the mischief starts as soon as the orderly mother leaves the house, and most 2-year-old readers seem delighted by this outbreak. They do not miss a trick in tracking the pair's wild rumpus. They laugh and titter; they suck in their breath to see just what good dog Carl and Baby are up to.[26]

Interestingly, given my earlier discussion of conceptions of the visual image in the 'Into the Heart of Africa' exhibition, the claim to irony here lies in what is read as a contrast or opposition between the written text and the pictorial. Moreover, the pictorial is again not configured as text but, in this case, as 'real life'. While *Good Dog, Carl* can clearly be read as constructing written language as 'adult' and pictures, by contrast, as intrinsically comprehensible to the child pre-reader, the truth of this construction seems rather taken for granted by the researchers in this study. A further difficulty here is with a lack of clarity as far as the methodology of this study is concerned; Milner and Milner report that 'We found a group of nine 2- to 3-year-old children whose mothers or fathers read them *Good Dog, Carl* and then asked them the set of eight questions'[27] that were designed to 'tell us how much 2- to 3-year-old children understood when their parents read the book to them'.[28] One thing that is not clear here is what exactly was involved in the parents' 'reading' aloud of a picture book that does not employ more than twelve written words from beginning to end of the story. Though the implication is that the parents made no comment on the pictorial text, since it is claimed that 'No words are needed to tell emergent readers who are just forming their own rich worlds that the goings on here are out of bounds',[29] and that 'we have a silent set of 14 full pages that speak volumes about playful riot and friendly rebellion',[30] nevertheless this is far from certain, and even so a number of questions remain as to how then the 'reading' was conducted or performed, just two examples being: what account might be given of parental tone of voice in the reading of the available written text, and who turned the pages and when? Likewise there is no real discussion of how the test questions construct both the child pre-reader and an appropriate or correct reading. Prefaced by a 'Parent Statement' that frames the way the questions are to be introduced to the children, which reads 'Here are some questions about Carl. You can say yes to some and no to those that are not right', the following questions are listed:

1. Do you like Carl?
2. Does Carl look like a cat?
3. Does Carl misbehave and do naughty things when Mama is gone?
4. Can Carl drive a car?
5. Does Mama know that Carl does bad things?
6. Does Mama leave Carl at home with the Baby?
7. Do you think it's funny that Mama doesn't know Carl misbehaves or does naughty things?
8. Does the Baby have fun?[31]

Underlying this set of questions is a reading of the text which gives privileged place to reading as a process of identification. The children are called on to identify with 'Carl' and from the very outset it is assumed that they will do so; the rationale for the eighth question is given as 'a throwaway, a final opportunity to speak of their affection for Carl'.[32] In addition to this, even if we do not regard the formulation of question 3 as already embedding within it an interpretation predetermined as correct, questions 5 and 7 can be read as establishing that the appropriate interpretation of the picture book is that Carl does 'naughty things'. There are further issues here with the way the study constitutes some of the test questions as 'softball' or 'silly' and some as 'pivotal' or 'crucial'. Again it is interesting that the first question, identified as 'softball', is formulated around the presumed identification with Carl: 'hoping to limber up the children with an easy affirmative—most kids love Carl and love the mess he makes with Baby' (p. 398).[33] Likewise question 5 lays down the terms in which irony can be understood here with the claim that 'If Mama does know [that Carl has done bad things in her absence], there is no possibility of irony in the story'. This confines the reading of irony to a reading of the structure of the text and discounts a reading that would locate irony in a reading of the mother as making an intentionally ironic comment on behaviour she was well aware of. I am not here disputing Milner and Milner's reading of *Good Dog, Carl*, but rather questioning the assertion that believing that the Mother does know about Carl and Baby's behaviour in and of itself necessarily precludes an understanding or 'recognition' of irony.[34]

Whereas Milner and Milner conclude that their study 'sustains the finding that some fifth-grade children could recognize irony that even secondary students could not detect',[35] Jon C. Stott's earlier article for *Children's Literature in Education* equates the ability to read irony with readerly sophistication with all that that implies of the reader's education, refinement, development and ability to grasp complexity. The reading of irony here, and the sophistication of this reading, is all to do with 'perceiv[ing] discrepancies which are not clearly stated'[36] and as such it is about discerning the reality beneath the appearance. Nevertheless, and not incompatibly, for Stott, as for Milner and Milner and Winner *et al.*, irony is something that is predetermined as there waiting to be 'recognized' in the reader's achievement of the 'correct' reading. Irony here is explicitly glossed as 'stable', indeed a text employing what is categorized as 'stable irony' by Stott is chosen for his teaching exercise on the grounds that its 'relatively limited scope... is within the range of comprehension of children in the middle elementary grades'.[37] Stott also makes clear that his approach is based on Booth's arguments in *A Rhetoric of Irony*, and that consequently, for him, the reading of irony is anchored in establishing authorial intention: 'In order to perceive irony, ... the reader must be able to reconstruct the text to arrive at its intended, or true meaning', and that part of this process involves making a decision ' "about the author's knowledge or beliefs" '.[38] As Stott proceeds with his account of teaching irony to third graders (8–9-year-olds), it becomes clear that, as with Milner and Milner, reading is configured in terms of identification, and since irony is in part defined as a discrepancy between expectation and result,[39] questions aiming to elicit 'recognition' of the irony in the text (the picture book, *The Biggest Bear* by Lynd Ward) are articulated in the classroom in terms of a requirement on the child readers to identify with the character established by the teacher as the main character: ' "Was it what *you* or Johnny expected?" '[40] In addition to this, Stott, like Milner and Milner, also implicitly sets up the pictures as non-textual, as the reality, where the written text is not, for though he suggests that 'children should be given time to look carefully at the illustrations, noticing the absurdities in them',[41] the irony of the text is said to inhere in the gap between the pictorial text's representation of the reality and the written text's failure to meet it: 'Occasionally, the teacher can point out the ironic understatements of the text. For example, he might ask whether "pretty upset" accurately describes the neighbor's reaction.'[42] In both Stott and Milner and Milner I read a connection between the constitution of reading as identification and the constitution of pictures as non-textual; both of these configurations rely on reading as affective as opposed to analytical or interpretative,[43] and as is evident from J. Hillis Miller's description of the first side of what he calls 'the aporia of reading', the former is the mode of reading most commonly associated with the child: 'I am advocating, as the first side of the aporia of reading, an innocent, childlike abandonment to the act of reading, without suspicion, reservation, or interrogation.'[44]

At the end of ' "It's not what you expect" ' Stott gives the following account of the assumed benefits of the classroom exercises described and analysed in the body of his article:

> When I first taught Swift's 'A Modest Proposal' to university freshmen, I was surprised to find that several were shocked at what they thought to be that essay's sadistic message: they had read Swift literally and not ironically. Should my third grade students become university students, they are not likely to make that mistake.[45]

Here several things seem to me to be at issue. In the first place, despite Stott's assumption of a distinction between the ability of adults and children to read irony, 'several' first-year university students confound that expectation, unless university students are also to be considered as children. Second, there is little investigation here into why those 'several' students produced what to Stott was such an aberrant reading. This, I would argue, is because of the assumption in play that these students were simply not sophisticated readers and/or had not had their normal developmental processes adequately supplemented by the kind of elementary teaching that Stott develops and describes; but such an assumption puts a block on any potential questioning as to whether any other account of the scenario could be given.[46]

At this point I want to turn to the perennial controversy around the teaching of *Adventures of Huckleberry Finn* in American schools in order to draw the threads of my argument together. *Adventures of Huckleberry Finn* perhaps more than any other text is a site in which the implications of the interplay of constructions of irony and childhood together with the construction of race can be seen to operate at their most intractable. This is not, I would argue, so much to do with the attributes of the text itself (though these have their part to play), but rather with its positioning in the North American cultural scene, and specifically with the text's positioning within an American literary history promulgated and endorsed by the academic literary establishment, an aspect that has been most rigorously argued by Jonathan Arac in his seminal work *Huckleberry Finn as Idol and Target: The Functions of Criticism in Our Time.*[47] *Adventures of Huckleberry Finn* does not tend to draw the same kind of reactions in the UK, but then it is it is rarely taught at high school level in Britain,[48] and if it is, it will not be read as being about Britishness or what it means to be British (and so is no threat to British identity or complacency about race relations in Britain).[49] For my part, what I am interested in doing here, is in focusing more precisely on the constructions of childhood in relation to irony that are mobilized in the arguments and debates over the teaching of *Huck Finn* in schools. But before doing this I want to start by examining an observation made by the Australian children's literature critic Barbara Wall: 'My own experience as a child, a teacher, a reader and a researcher suggests that the language and the ironies of *Huckleberry Finn* are bewildering to children, and in many cases to adolescents too.'[50] Wall's assessment here is part of her judgment that *Huck Finn* should not be considered a book for children, and its irony specifically is one of the things that makes it not appropriate for children. Here again then, as with Stott, is the suggestion that irony is naturally beyond the child's ken – children do not get it. Wall implicitly constitutes children here as literalists unable to engage fully with a figurative language, and this conception of children is echoed in many of the critical assessments of *Adventures of Huckleberry Finn* where Twain is often praised for presenting such a convincingly literal-minded child narrator, the literal-mindedness being read as an index of the accuracy of Twain's portrayal of youth, a literal-mindedness that incidentally seems to be entirely compatible with Huck having rather elaborate superstitions.

A further problem with Wall's claim is that she omits to mention that given the kind of furore *Huck Finn* has periodically stirred up, it would seem that a great many adults also find the ironies of the novel bewildering. Indeed, if the child cannot read irony and neither can those who are critical of the novel (among whom there are a significant number of African American teachers and critics) a rather uncomfortable, but perhaps not entirely unpredictable parallel again starts to be drawn. However, the notion of irony being specifically and particularly difficult for children to engage with also plays a role in Leonard *et al.*'s *Satire or Evasion? Black Perspectives on Huckleberry Finn*, where it is argued that the novel 'poses its own obstinacies: readers can find the dialect inscrutable, the irony bewildering, and the repeated use of offensive language highly distasteful. For youthful readers, the puzzlements and shock are unavoidably magnified.'[51]

In the history of its criticism *Adventures of Huckleberry Finn* has often been defended against the charge of racism on the grounds of its irony. For example, in a relatively recent book addressing issues for the liberal arts classroom through readings of canonical American realist texts, Phillip Barrish admits, in his chapter on 'Mark Twain and the Secret Joys of Antiracist Pedagogy', that despite his own unease with this approach and in full acknowledgment of Arac's incisive criticism of the way

> [T]he idolatry of the book has served, and – remarkably – continues to serve, as an excuse for well-meaning white people to use the term *nigger* with the good conscience that comes from believing that their usage is sanctioned by their idol (whether Twain, or his book, or Huck) and is made safe by the technique of irony.[52]

that 'when it comes to the word "nigger" [he has] tended to resort to the Twain-uses-it-in-ironic-quotation-marks approach'.[53] And Arac also notes that despite the fact that academic discourse might be argued to no longer be operating with the notion that irony (or some ironies), is or can be 'stable', nevertheless 'the most insistent public claims made

for the value of *Huckleberry Finn* involve its moral stance as an achievement of irony.'[54]

But with respect to *that* word, in their introduction to *Satire or Evasion?*
Leonard and Tenney note that

> It is inevitable that black children in a classroom with whites should
> feel uncomfortable with the word and a book in which it appears so
> often, and that black parents should wish to protect their children
> from what the word represents. In the classroom, 'nigger' is embar-
> rassing and divisive at any grade level.[55]

The discussions around the teaching of *Huck Finn* in racially mixed
classes inevitably come back to the question of feeling. The emotions
provoked in the reading of this text become to a certain extent undis-
cussable and unsurpassable (or perhaps it is more accurate to say that
they constitute a wound that is returned to again and again, but to
no relief). The affect of the text produces its own 'truth', a truth that
cannot be challenged, since when it is, there is a danger that that challenge will find itself ranged with the crudest and most disrespectful
of responses to African American concerns. And yet, those approaches
that try to be sensitive to the feelings that erupt in response to *Huck
Finn* cannot avoid the problems it throws up simply by virtue of the
best of intentions.

> [W]hat I want to emphasize here is the necessity of open acknowledg-
> ment of the feelings of anyone who senses in this book any potential
> to offend. That potential might be present within the book itself; it
> might exist because of studying the book in an environment that
> one perceives as hostile; or it might be caused by misunderstanding
> the book. The precise cause of hurt feelings is not important at this
> point. What is important is recognition of such feelings. When my
> African-American students felt free to voice their most urgent con-
> cerns about *Huckleberry Finn*, and had their concerns validated by
> their white classmates, it was not long before their underlying affec-
> tion for the book became apparent.[56]

Here, Kay Puttock gives a thoughtful account of the range of elements
that might contribute to a reading of *Huck Finn* where pain may be experienced as result rather than pleasure. Moreover, Puttock insightfully
notes that 'At the least it should be conceded that there are elements in
the novel on which interpretive closure or critical agreement can never

be finally reached'.[57] And yet in the quotation above I am suspicious of the reported effects of such sensitivity. What if it had not resulted in the African American students making 'their underlying affection for the book apparent'? Underlying all this, it seems to me, is precisely a 'critical agreement' that the text is deserving of such affection and that it does have a specific value.[58]

A related issue can be read in Peaches Henry's discussion of the issues around the teaching of *Adventures of Huckleberry Finn* in *Satire or Evasion?* Here she argues that:

> The very profundity of the text renders the process of teaching it problematic and places special emphasis on teacher ability and attitude. Student cognitive and social maturity also takes on special significance in the face of such a complicated and subtle text.[59]

Once again the text is produced *a priori* as 'profound' and the ability to grasp this pre-established profundity is equated with maturity. Having discussed a number of critically contentious aspects of the novel and particularly its ending, Henry comes back to considering the appropriateness of addressing *Huck Finn* in the public school system:

> Given the powerlessness of highly discerning readers to resolve the novel in a way that unambiguously redeems Jim or Huck, how can students be expected to fare better with the novel's conclusion? Parents question the advisability of teaching to junior and senior high school students a text which requires such sophisticated interpretation in order for its moral statements to come clear.[60]

Here then it is worth noting the implicit requirement that the morality of the text must be (made to come) clear. The text can only be justified in the classroom if it can be said to have and promulgate an appropriate moral stance (on this point). Henry's formulation assumes, perhaps for the sake of argument, that the text does indeed make the appropriate moral statements but Henry also suggests that defences of *Huckleberry Finn* on such grounds involve 'vigorous critical acumen',[61] scholarly *attempts* to read the text in ways 'that would make it palatable'[62] going to 'ingenious lengths' and indulging in 'interpretative acrobatics'.[63] Here can be read a suspicion of such a wealth of critical analysis, which, even if it is not in itself too much for a text that in the end is regarded as unable to support this level of critical exegesis, it is firmly articulated as too much for the child reader.[64] For the child a certainty with respect to the text and its moral must be arrived at.

But the difficulty around grasping the moral of the novel could also be read as having to do with a certain repeated critical reliance on identification. Henry writes of the need unambiguously to redeem Jim or Huck for example, and earlier in the chapter she addresses a contentious passage in chapter 32 of the novel 'in which Huck lies to Aunt Sally about a steamboat explosion that hurt no one but "killed a nigger," and Aunt Sally callously responds, "Well, it's lucky, because sometimes people do get hurt".'[65] With respect to this passage Henry addresses herself to Leslie Fiedler's view that 'Huck does not get the joke – does not recognize the humor of the fact that he and Aunt Sally by "dehumanizing the Negro diminish their own humanity".' To this, Henry responds, 'It seems to Huck's foes (and to me) that if Huck does not get the joke, then there is no joke, and he becomes as culpable as Aunt Sally.'[66] The issue here is that Henry makes the reading of irony dependent on identification with Huck and this approach to the novel and to reading itself is evident throughout her chapter as she goes on to claim 'Huck (along with the reader) watches Jim emerge as a man whose sense of dignity and self-respect dwarf the minstrel mask,'[67] and also that 'The reader applauds Huck's acceptance of damnation for helping Jim and affixes all expectations for the rest of the novel to this climactic moment.'[68] In relation to the end of the novel which perhaps should disappoint if we identify with Huck at this point, as Henry suggests, Elaine and Harry Mensh observe that 'If we assess Huck as if he were a human being, his worth is lessened by his remaining racist; if we assess him as a character, this is not necessarily so.'[69]

In addition to this, Henry's approach does not really address what might be the consequences of attending to the novel's narration by Huck of himself and his adventures in the past. Interestingly, in view of my earlier discussions of the role the visual image has played in a variety of discussions around irony, in her discussion of Ralph Wiley's script for 'Spike Lee's *Huckleberry Finn*', Shelley Fisher Fishkin observes:

> I had long believed that part of Twain's genius in this book is letting the reader see things that Huck doesn't see, making Huck an endearing and engaging but ultimately unreliable narrator. In Wiley's script, the juxtaposition of the visual message the viewer gets, on the one hand, and the comically limited version of that *reality* that Huck (the narrator) communicates, on the other, captured that dramatic irony.[70]

Here then the visual medium of film (though what is under discussion here is an as yet unfilmed script) serves to stabilize the irony of the written text and once again the visual image is the 'reality' which is then limited in Huck's narration. But even if we accept Fishkin's interpretation of Wiley's script, this 'reality' is precisely not available in *Adventures of Huckleberry Finn*: the notion of the 'unreliable narrator' suggests, as Fishkin does, that somewhere in the text a reliable version, or the reality, is available, but where or how is this to be read in the written text? As Wayne Booth argues, 'dealing with any first-person narrative, we can explain away any fault, no matter how horrendous, if we assume in advance an *author* of unlimited wisdom, tact, and artistic skill.'[71] The claim to irony in *Huck Finn* would seem to me to rest rather on what disjunctures may be read between the narrating and the narrated Huck.

While I do not underestimate the difficulty of teaching, or being taught, *Adventures of Huckleberry Finn*, one aspect of the problem that strikes me is what I read as a particular issue to do with the *way* the text is taught. That is to say, even when it is acknowledged that the text is embroiled in controversy, there is, on the whole, an underlying acceptance that the text has both literary and moral value, since literary value is, in this context, assumed to be moral and vice versa. Thus, despite all apparent evidence to the contrary, it seems to me that *Adventures of Huckleberry Finn* is still largely taught as though there were no question as to how it could or should be interpreted, no controversy – nothing to see here. This is not an issue to be dealt with by replacing the text with another, though I agree with Leo Marx that 'to claim that [*Huckleberry Finn*] should be required reading because it is a great American book is unconvincing; we don't require students to read most great books,'[72] and, moreover, would argue that this in any case regards the question of what is a 'great book' as fixed and not itself subject to question or debate. But with respect to replacing the text with alternatives it might be noted that at Renton High School in Washington in 2003, one student who asked to be excused from reading *Huck Finn* was assigned Kate Chopin's *The Awakening* as a replacement.[73] What then might be the implications of this replacement, where at least one available reading is that 'the…liberation about which the book fantasizes is purchased on the backs of black women', since 'if Edna's children did not have a hired "quadroon" to care for them night and day, it is extremely unlikely that she would swim off into the sunset at the end' of the novel?[74] Rather the problem with *Huck Finn* seems in part to reside in two interlinked things: the expectation and demand that literature be morally improving, and the sense that no matter what, there is a correct interpretation – that the text is not *in the end* racist – which in the end must be arrived at. This is not about helping students to articulate their objections but consigns their objections to the level of affect, as that which can neither be analysed nor supported analytically, that which is left as feeling rather than intellectual argument.

Notes

1. L. Hutcheon, *Irony's Edge: The Theory and Politics of Irony* (London and New York: Routledge, 1994). The exhibition and its reception are discussed in the final chapter of the book, entitled 'The End(s) of Irony: The Politics of Appropriateness', pp. 176–209.
2. See T. C. Young Jr., 'Into the Heart of Africa: The Director's Perspective', *Curator: The Museum Journal*, 36: 3, September, 1993, 174–88; E. Mackey, 'Postmodernism and Cultural Politics in a Multicultural Nation: Contests over Truth in the *Into the Heart of Africa* Controversy', *Public Culture*, 7: 2, 1995, 403–31; S. R. Butler, *Contested Representations: Revisiting Into the Heart of Africa* (Amsterdam: Gordon and Breach, 1999); E. Schildkrout, 'Ambiguous Messages and Ironic Twists: *Into the Heart of Africa* and *The Other Museum*', in B. M. Carbonell (ed.), *Museum Studies: An Anthology of Contexts* (Malden, MA and Oxford: Blackwell, 2004), pp. 181–92.
3. My own position with respect to irony is informed by the following arguments by Kenneth Burke and Paul de Man respectively:
   > There is an implied sense of negativity in the ability to use words at all. For to use them properly, we must know that they are *not* the things they stand for. Next, since language is extended by metaphor which gradually becomes the kind of dead metaphor we call abstraction, one must know that metaphor is *not* literal. Further, we cannot use language maturely until we are spontaneously at home in irony. (K. Burke, *Language as Symbolic Action: Essays on Life, Literature, and Method* [Berkeley, Los Angeles and London: University of California Press, 1966], p. 12)

   > [T]ropes are not [to be] understood aesthetically, as ornament, nor are they [to be] understood semantically as a figurative meaning that derives from literal, proper denomination. Rather the reverse is the case. The trope is not a derived, marginal, or aberrant form of language but the linguistic paradigm par excellence. The figurative structure is not one linguistic mode among others but it characterizes language as such. (P. de Man, *Allegories of Reading: Figural Language in Rousseau, Nietzsche, Rilke, and Proust* [New Haven, CT and London: Yale University Press, 1979], p. 105)
4. Hutcheon, *Irony's Edge*, p. 188.
5. Hutcheon footnotes Jeanne Cannizzo's 1991 article, 'Exhibiting Cultures: "Into The Heart of Africa"', *Visual Anthropology Review*, 7: 1, 1991, 150–60.
6. Hutcheon, *Irony's Edge*, pp. 188–9.
7. For a related critique to my own here on the uses of 'affect' in theory, see: D. Caselli, 'Kindergarten Theory: Childhood, Affect, Critical Thought',

66ffort>6666t>6ort>6666

Feminist Theory (Special Issue on Childhood and Feminisms), 11: 3, 2010, 1–14.

8. W. Wordsworth, 'Lines Written a Few Miles above Tintern Abbey', in R. L. Brett and A. R. Jones (eds), *Wordsworth and Coleridge: Lyrical Ballads*, 2nd edn (London and New York: Routledge, 1996), pp. 113–19, p. 115.

9. It should be clear here that I am not attributing this to Hutcheon as any part of her intention, but as Hutcheon herself notes with respect to her discussion of the curator's purposes *vis-à-vis* her exhibition, intentions with respect to this issue may prove to be somewhat beside the point.

10. Hutcheon, *Irony's Edge*, p. 192.

11. Hutcheon, *Irony's Edge*, p. 193.

12. Hutcheon, *Irony's Edge*, p. 194.

13. Hutcheon, *Irony's Edge*, p. 195.

14. Hutcheon, *Irony's Edge*, p. 208, n. 33.

15. Hutcheon, *Irony's Edge*, p. 194, Hutcheon references the *Globe and Mail*, 20 June 1990.

16. Hutcheon, *Irony's Edge*, p. 18.

17. E. Winner, *The Point of Words: Children's Understanding of Metaphor and Irony* (Cambridge, MA and London: Harvard University Press, 1997), p. 54. This claim is made despite a later acknowledgement that adults as well as children are capable of 'mistaking' irony for deception (p. 149).

18. W. C. Booth, *A Rhetoric of Irony* (Chicago and London: University of Chicago Press, 1974).

19. Intentionality is a key point of focus for Winner throughout *The Point of Words*.

20. E. Winner, J. Levy, J. Kaplan and E. Rosenblatt, 'Children's Understanding of Nonliteral Language', *Journal of Aesthetic Education*, 22: 1, Spring, 1988, 51–63, 61.

21. Winner, *The Point of Words*, p. 27.

22. Winner, *The Point of Words*, p. 24.

23. Winner *et al.*, 'Children's Understanding of Nonliteral Language', 62.

24. Winner, *The Point of Words*, p. 155.

25. Winner, *The Point of Words*, p. 156.

26. J. O. Milner and M. M. Milner, 'Emergent Readers' Recognition of Irony in *Good Dog, Carl*', *Reading Psychology*, 29: 5, 2008, 395–404, 396–7.

27. Milner and Milner, 'Emergent Readers' Recognition of Irony in *Good Dog, Carl*', 400.

28. Milner and Milner, 'Emergent Readers' Recognition of Irony in *Good Dog, Carl*', 398.

29. Milner and Milner, 'Emergent Readers' Recognition of Irony in *Good Dog, Carl*', 397.

30. Milner and Milner, 'Emergent Readers' Recognition of Irony in *Good Dog, Carl*', 397.

31. Milner and Milner, 'Emergent Readers' Recognition of Irony in *Good Dog, Carl*', 399.

32. Milner and Milner, 'Emergent Readers' Recognition of Irony in *Good Dog, Carl*', 403.

33. Milner and Milner, 'Emergent Readers' Recognition of Irony in *Good Dog, Carl*', 398.

34. This article is also troubling in my view in terms of the conclusions it allows itself to draw on the basis of an extremely small sample of children, two groups of nine: 'a girl seemed to recognize the irony at an earlier age and two boys in the older cohort seemed to miss it. Girls in this small sample seemed more nimble in recognizing irony than the boys. This sustains the findings in older school-age children where boys did better with the irony in jokes and girls were better at stories' (Milner and Milner, p. 404).

35. Milner and Milner, 'Emergent Readers' Recognition of Irony in *Good Dog, Carl*', 404.

36. J. C. Stott, ' "It's Not What You Expect": Teaching Irony to Third Graders', *Children's Literature in Education*, 13: 4, 1982, 153–63, 153.

37. Stott, 'It's Not What You Expect', 154–5.

38. Stott, 'It's Not What You Expect', 154. The quote is from Booth, *A Rhetoric of Irony*, p. 11.

39. Stott, 'It's Not What You Expect', 153.

40. Stott, 'It's Not What You Expect', 157, emphasis added.

41. Stott, 'It's Not What You Expect', 157.

42. Stott, 'It's Not What You Expect', 157.

43. I am helped here in my thinking about identification by the work of Martin Barker in his chapter 'The Vicissitudes of Identification', where he argues as follows about the model of identity that the concept relies upon:

    [T]wo consequences...follow from 'identification'. When we 'identify', our self-consciousness is diminished, and our ability to appraise things rationally is reduced. ...

    Without those assumptions about loss of self-awareness and rationality, all we are left with is 'empathy'. But empathy has none of the power which 'identification' claimed for itself, ...'Identification' claimed that loss of self and or rationality made us vulnerable. That claim only makes sense within a larger model: a model in which rational judgment, self-awareness and critical thinking are seen as a 'veneer' over bubbling primal instincts, pre-rational elements held weakly in check by civilising influences. (M. Barker, *Comics: Ideology, Power and the Critics* [Manchester and New York: Manchester University Press, 1989], pp. 108–9).

44. J. H. Miller, *On Literature* (London and New York: Routledge, 2002), p. 119. The other side of the 'aporia of reading' is reading as interrogatory and demystificatory, and it is that kind of reading that can perceive irony according to Miller (pp. 122–3), though at the same time 'Sensitivity to irony seems to be unevenly distributed in the population', and while it 'is a requisite for good reading' it 'is by no means identical to intelligence. You get it or you don't get it' (p. 115).

45. Stott, 'It's Not What You Expect', 161.

46. By contrast, Lori Chamberlain writes that,

    In the classroom setting, lower-division writing students show a remarkable if not alarming inability to detect irony in their reading or to use it in their writing. Yet they are not unfamiliar with the trope; on the contrary, students – and women and the common people, for that matter – speak the language of irony all the time. They use it in talking with each other; they discern it in such popular sources as song lyrics or bumper stickers; and they may even, on occasion, enter their writing classes remarking how much they are looking forward to writing that day.

Chamberlain offers three possible reasons for the discrepancy she notes: the students fall foul of a lack of contextual information, their application of 'a limited or inappropriate set of reading conventions' to literary texts, and their lack of practice in critical reading and thinking (L. Chamberlain, 'Bombs and Other Exciting Devices, or the Problem of Teaching Irony', in P. Donahue and E. Quandahl (eds), *Reclaiming Pedagogy: The Rhetoric of the Classroom* [Carbondale and Edwardsville: Southern Illinois University Press, 1989], pp. 97–112, p. 102). Whilst Chamberlain writes that 'Irony – like all tropes – does not exist so much *in* the text as it does in the multiple voices in the text and in the reader's response to it' (p. 104), she nevertheless proceeds, as can be seen above, from the assumption that irony is there in the text waiting and requiring the right tools to be detected.

47. J. Arac, *Huckleberry Finn As Idol and Target: The Functions of Criticism in Our Time* (Madison and London: University of Wisconsin Press, 1997).
48. See D. Preen, 'Realistic Choices among the Prescribed Pre-Twentieth Century Writers', *English in Education*, 32: 3, September, 1998, 21–6.
49. Perhaps a parallel example in British literary history, although less urgent, is the controversy around the teaching and performing of *The Merchant of Venice*; likewise the role of *Othello* in performance in South Africa under apartheid.
50. B. Wall, *The Narrator's Voice* (London: Palgrave Macmillan, 1991), p. 116.
51. J. S. Leonard and T. A. Tenney, 'Introduction: The Controversy over *Huckleberry Finn*', in J. S. Leonard, T. A. Tenney and T. M. Davis (eds), *Satire or Evasion? Black Perspectives on Huckleberry Finn* (Durham, NC and London: Duke University Press, 1992), pp. 1–11, p. 9.
52. J. Arac, *Huckleberry Finn As Idol and Target*, p. 16, quoted in P. Barrish, *White Liberal Identity, Literary Pedagogy, and Classic American Realism* (Columbus: Ohio State University Press, 2005), pp. 35–56, p. 49. Wayne C. Booth, in an acknowledged revision of an earlier position (evident in *A Rhetoric of Fiction* where the 'successful reader' of *Huck Finn* is said to bring to the text convictions shared with Mark Twain [W. C. Booth, *A Rhetoric of Irony*, p. 141]) also argues in *The Company We Keep* that the appeal to irony is an inadequate defence of *Huck Finn* (W. C. Booth, *The Company We Keep: An Ethics of Fiction* [Berkeley, Los Angeles and London: University of California Press, 1988], pp. 470–2), and notes that many, if not most, critical readings that endorse the novel 'consider... "the reader"... to be plainly and simply the white reader' (p. 473).
53. Barrish, *White Liberal Identity, Literary Pedagogy, and Classic American Realism*, p. 49. The chapter on Twain is on pp. 35–56.
54. Arac, *Huckleberry Finn As Idol and* Target, pp. 32–3.
55. Leonard and Tenney, 'Introduction', in J. S. Leonard *et al.*, *Satire or Evasion?*, p. 5.
56. K. Puttock, 'Many Responses to the Many Voices of *Huckleberry Finn*', *The Lion and the Unicorn*, 16, 1992, 77–82, 79.
57. Puttock, 'Many Responses to the Many Voices of *Huckleberry Finn*, 81.

58. I do not have space here to address adequately the problem I also see in the idea that all that is necessary to address this issue is for white people to *validate* the concerns of black people.

59. P. Henry, 'The Struggle for Tolerance: Race and Censorship in *Huckleberry Finn*', in: J. S. Leonard *et al.*, *Satire or Evasion?*, pp. 25–48, p. 28.

60. Henry, 'The Struggle for Tolerance', p. 38.

61. Henry, 'The Struggle for Tolerance', p. 35.

62. Henry, 'The Struggle for Tolerance', p. 37.

63. Henry, 'The Struggle for Tolerance', p. 38.

64. In *The Company We Keep*, W. C. Booth also suggests that the critics he quotes in support of Twain 'have had to do too much of the work' (p. 474).

65. Henry, 'The Struggle for Tolerance', p. 31.

66. Henry, 'The Struggle for Tolerance', p. 31.

67. Henry, 'The Struggle for Tolerance', p. 35.

68. Henry, 'The Struggle for Tolerance', p. 36. In relation to this moment in the text (chapter 31), Arac addresses what he views as the 'idolatry' of readers like Henry through reference to Longinus' definition of 'the sublime' which 'produces, and depends on, a series of *identifications*, so that the words of a character, at a sublime moment, seem "the echo of a great soul" that is the author's, and in reading the sublime we are "uplifted," "as if we had ourselves produced" what we hear or read' (J. Arac, *Huckleberry Finn As Idol and Target*, p. 36).

69. E. Mensh and H. Mensh, *Black, White, and Huckleberry Finn: Re-imagining the American Dream* (Tuscaloosa and London: University of Alabama Press, 2000), p. 104.

70. S. Fisher Fishkin, 'In Praise of "Spike Lee's *Huckleberry Finn*" by Ralph Wiley' http://faculty.citadel.edu/leonard/od99wiley.htm (accessed 24 August 2010), emphasis added.

71. Booth, *The Company We Keep*, p. 470.

72. Leo Marx as quoted in Mensh and Mensh, *Black, White, and Huckleberry Finn*, p. 113.

73. G. Roberts, ' "Huck Finn" a masterpiece – or an insult', *Seattle Post-Intelligencer*, Weds Nov. 26, 2003 http://www.seattlepi.com/local/149979_huck26.html (accessed 24 August 2010).

74. E. Ammons, 'Women of Color in *The Awakening*', in K. Chopin, *The Awakening*, ed. M. Culley (New York and London: W. W. Norton, 1994), pp. 309–11, p. 310.

8
Fort/Da: A Reading of *Pictures of Innocence* by Anne Higonnet

Neil Cocks

Childhood and Construction

According to one recent account, art theory has, until recently, dismissed childhood.[1] Understood at once to be too trivial and too dangerous a focus for critical enquiry, a subject for 'second rate minds' that can too easily lead to the disclosure of unacceptable desire, childhood has languished on the margins of the discourse of art.[2] The account proceeds to claim that the last decade has seen this situation challenged, with a number of texts reading themselves as following innovations within the social sciences and approaching childhood as a 'construction', 'an abstract, shifting and heavily ideological *concept*'[3] rather than a reflection of a prior 'reality'. Such a move is understood as part of an ongoing critique of patriarchal normalization in art theory, the claim being made that 'just as class, gender, and race challenges to academic disciplines came first from art history's neighbouring fields of literary criticism and social history, so it has been with the subject of childhood'.[4]

This chapter will engage with the discourse of childhood as construction within recent art theory by focusing on one text that argues for it, *Pictures of Innocence: The History and Crisis of Ideal Childhood* by Anne Higonnet. I read Higonnet to be more concerned in making a consistent case for an approach based on construction than her contemporaries.[5] Unlike Patricia Holland, arguably the other most established recent reader of visual representations of children, who from the beginning of her *Picturing Childhood* is concerned with the promotion of 'childlike' values, and a childhood self representation that is not 'mediated by adulthood',[6] Higonnet attempts a reading of childhood as inevitably and always constructed. Thus although the text is in some sense a celebration of recent images of childhood, including those made by

147

children, no image or idea is read to be more or less 'real' than any other, more or less worthy. As Higonnet states, 'despite photography's realism, or the temptation to think that whatever is newer is more real, images of Knowing children are not intrinsically better or more honest... or more real than any other definition of childhood'.[7]

The 'Knowing children' Higonnet refers to are, for her text, the representatives of a late twentieth-century shift in visual culture, one that moves away from Romanticism, with its dualistic separation of childhood innocence and adult experience, its denial of the body and insistence upon the unselfconscious nature of children, to images that are bodily, self-aware and sexual. 'Knowing children' are understood to exist in the public realm, a category of subjects active in their own representation rather than passive objects of vision, rooted in a material existence, yet never available as raw identity, free from ideological and representational significance. Such a move enables a critique of both discourses that promote an idealized image of childhood, one detached from body, sexuality and self-consciousness, and a naturalized notion of a given representation as universal and necessary. Thus this double defence of materiality and construction can be read as having a certain ethical force, it is there to defend the child against ideology that denies the ideological.

Clementine and Apple

As a way to initiate a questioning of the model of construction utilized by *Pictures of Innocence*, I will offer a reading of two of the images the text classes as 'knowing'. The first, *Clementine* by Nicholas Nixon, is a close up side profile of the photographer's teenage daughter, the second, Nancy Honey's *The Apple of My Eye*, a view from behind another daughter, focused on the price tag of the brassiere she wears, with the mirror the teenager is looking into a distant blur.

For Higonnet, these two texts are significant because they demonstrate how 'photographers respond to Knowing children by looking at them very closely', 'at once tenderly intimate and objectively detached'.[8] Let us begin by stating that within this initial construction it is 'Knowing children' who initiate the process of representation, they exist as such prior to these images, as the artists 'respond' to them. This could suggest that the 'Knowing children' exist before their representations, which questions their status as construction, identity being independent of art. Conversely, it might be that the 'Knowing children' exist as representations prior to these specific representations, whether the children's self-representations, or that formed by another. This requires Higonnet to have knowledge of a construction prior to the specific construction offered by the artists, yet no evidence is given for this. What is clear is that, whether responding to prior reality or construction, the appeal to response allows a notion of fidelity. This art is successful in so far as it is true to something preceding it. Yet it is also read as ushering in a new identity, the images forming that which they apparently repeat. Although there is no attempt to read the problematic relationship between the constructive and the responsive and the unchanging identity they relate to, there is an idea of a divided vision, one that is both intimate and detached, as separate and impacted as the identity that leads to response, as closely bound to the observer as the construction that resists the real. The intimacy, as we shall see, is necessary for an appeal to the physicality of the 'Knowing child', and the adult desire for it, while the detachment allows the child the necessary distance that grants itself mastery.

In her reading of *Clementine*, Higonnet states that the figure in the photograph:

pays no attention to us, finger distractedly touching her gently smiling lip. No matter how closely we look, the child remains in her own world. The more attentive the camera becomes, the more elusive the child. Unlike Romantic children who are arranged and presented as a delightful spectacle to be enjoyed, Knowing children are neither available nor controllable. They themselves are looking at an inner world of the imaginary, or at the adult world.[9]

It would seem that despite the intimacy of the gaze, and the appeal to the image as constructing childhood, there is a childhood realm that exists apart from the image that can be looked on. There are, then, at least two worlds, the world of the seen, and that of the unseen. The more the child is shown by an attentive vision, the more of it that escapes such a showing. What the picture shows, apparently, is what it fails to show, a 'world' unavailable to sight that can be seen to be owned by the child.

For Higonnet, this image is about the rejection of a Romanticism defined in terms of the control of the child. The child is controlled through the idea that it can be shown in its entirety. To free the child is to insist on an art that partially defies representation. If the child in 'Knowing' art is that which is unavailable, it is an unavailability that is available as such. The adult can view the child and know nothing about what the child sees, while knowing it sees a world that is its own.

The adult can be sure that it is not controlling the child because there is an aspect of that child that it fails to see. It is this that guarantees its independence, its freedom; the failure of the photographer or viewer to see. As the child does not see the adult watching it, and its existence to itself is not something that can be seen, seeing a child is taken to be an unproblematic activity. The picture grants the right to look. Dichotomies of intimacy and detachment do not trouble such rights, they secure them. The father is intimate in his portraiture, but not too intimate. A young girl is seen by her father, but also by a camera, by a loving relation and an objective machine, which leads to an emotional as well as a 'documentary' truth.[10]

Not the least of my problems with this is that this supposedly anti-Romantic reading can be read as casting the child in the position of transcendence, one aspect of its being escaping the constructive through its radical unavailability. Those that view the picture will apparently look on the girl's physicality, to be sure, will be granted intimacy by a representation that cares little for the Romantic refusal of the child's body. Yet there is something more to her. Higonnet reads this unavailable portion as that which exceeds the Romantic, indeed, a move away from Romanticism is always constructed in terms of a move beyond which is also a move of addition:

> I do want to say at the outset that all of the photographers whose work I discuss have made photographs that celebrate their children's *pure beauty*, pictures every bit as Romantic as any made in the nineteenth century. My point, however, is that these photographers do what photographers did during the Romantic childhood, and much more.[11]

The problem with Romantic art that refuses the body is, apparently, that it also rejects transcendence, it is what it is and nothing more. In accepting the represented body, 'Knowing' art is always reaching beyond it, and in so doing transcends previous constructions. What is being moved beyond in this formulation is 'pure beauty', the idea here being, I think, that the purity is that of an aesthetic that cares little for the actual, material flesh of the child. I read Higonnet's text as moving between a number of contrary positions here; on the one hand the appeal to the thing-in-itself speaks of a kind of formalism, or a limited Romanticism, a notion of the pure, one that is opposed to the material, and any engagement with the transcendent Other. On the other, the thing-in-itself is the child's body, that confrontational materiality Romanticism does not wish to look at in detail, preferring to go beyond the body to the notion of the pure, always attempting to 'turn those bodies into something else'.[12] Which is to say that the image 'Clementine' is understood in terms of both material presence and partial absence. One way of understanding this confusion is that 'Knowing' and Romantic art are read in terms of their move beyond materiality, but in one the result is an absence that speaks of an absent presence, the other a flight from presence in its every aspect. I read such problematic constructions of physicality and transcendence repeated in the claim above that the child is 'looking at an inner world of the imaginary'. That which is unavailable and unrepresentable is still understood as physical. It is an 'inner world', one as much encased *within* the body as opposed to it, one that can be looked at.

I read comparable tensions in Higonnet's reading of the work of Nancy Honey who:

> captures the duality of the child's and adult's gaze with the title and forms of *The Apple of My Eye*. Like Nixon, Honey uses technique to express the look of the parent at a beloved child, the child so dearly seen, so closely identified with, that she is the 'apple' of her mother's own 'eye'. But *here the child turns away*, her look drawn to a mirror – another mirror, apart from her parent's photograph – by the sight of herself in something added to her body from child to adult: a brassiere. The parent's view, but not the child's, includes the brassiere's price tag. The parent's view is so close; the daughter's is more distant and less defined. The child looks out and away, while the parent fixates on the immediate material present.[13]

From the first, there is a move opposed to the transcendent, with the idea of art 'capturing' a particular gaze. Yet what is contained or controlled here is an expression of a particular parental look that, of necessity, must be understood as existing prior to its capture. This look is of 'the' parent, but at 'a' more generalized child. Thus the pre-existing gaze that works against the inclusivity of its capture lacks the specificity of the moment. The notion of the capture is also problematized by the claim that 'the child turns away'. The picture is one that is active, it has movement, existing within time. Moreover, the capture is only partial, as the child's gaze is directed at something apart from her parent's photograph. Just as in *Clementine*, the image contains something that transcends it. Oddly, this something that apparently exists 'apart' is still there in the photograph, only lacking focus. The reading finds it necessary to hallucinate an absence, that which is not included in the 'parent's view' that constitutes the frame, yet still available within it. The parental gaze is said to be focused on the 'immediate present'. Thus the nape of the daughter's neck, the price tag and the brassiere are granted a complete physicality. The available absence of the child's view is contrasted with an adult view in a way that grants that view immediacy. And that view, apparently, is one that any reader of this image has an unproblematic access to. The image allows us to read as a parent, which, it seems, is to read immediately, to be confronted by presence, to look upon the child that has all its focus taken up by something else, something that is both beyond and within the frame. Yet it also grants us access to another kind of presence; that of the child's image of itself. This image is made available through the mourning of its loss to sight. It is an absence that exists somewhere beyond the frame, the child 'looking out' onto the unrepresentable 'real' beyond the borders of the adult representation. The image outside of the frame is not truly lost, as it can be seen, lacking only focus.

It is claimed, then, that there are two visions collapsed within a single frame. Yet this duality enables a single privilege; when looking at the adult looking, the viewer is granted access to the immediate and the child's looking is understood in terms of an absence that takes on an extra-textual truth, one that is also accessible. The child is more than that which it perceives itself to be, more than what it is perceived to be by others. It is a plenitude, fully present, yet with the promise of more. This double advantage can also be read in the way in which, despite the adult gaze seeing only the physicality of the immediate present, what is present is not, apparently, a brassiere or a back, but an 'apple'. The adult looks with metaphor. This could be as much about the impossibility of seeing as the parent as the necessity of so doing; is the daughter contained within the eye, being part of the adult body, is it only the object of the daughter's gaze that exceeds the physical containment of the parent, is the child in actuality an apple, or is this an adult vision that cannot contain what the daughter truly is?

However one chooses to read metaphor, the notion of the child as apple problematizes Higonnet's attempt to differentiate Romantic and Knowing representations. Earlier in the text it has been claimed that although Romanticism makes an art 'centered on the child's body', 'the child's body does not exist because it is something else: a flower, a star, a fruit, whatever'.[14] In other words, at this stage metaphor is read as a refusal of the physicality of children, which is a refusal of sexuality and individuality. In *The Apple of My Eye* there is no such problem, apparently. Whereas in Romantic art the substitutive term eclipses all else, in Honey's image it is in turn eclipsed, *The Apple of My Eye* is a physical body, with nothing available beyond it as that is, apparently, what adult, immediate sight entails.[15] Yet in both formulas, metaphor ceases to work with the tension between two terms. Either the prior physicality is removed, leaving the escapism of 'purity' to itself, or the secondary substitution is removed, leaving material presence. In terms of the second formulation, that attributed to Honey's image, it is difficult to understand how the discrete adult vision can be maintained, as although, at one stage, it is only concerned with the immediate, dissolving the tension of metaphor, barred from the outward looking child realm, it is still read as the producer of metaphor, that which has knowledge of an outward gaze, an outside that is opposed to, yet synonymous with, the immediate.

Escape

In my reading, then, the 'duality' of vision that is collapsed into a single frame bestows a range of contradictory advantages. In so far as the adult vision confronts the materiality of the child, it refuses Romanticism's desire to move beyond the body. In so far as the child escapes the limiting gaze, it refuses Romanticism's desire for it to remain within the ideal. In so far as the adult looks on the materiality of the child, it engages the real. In so far as the child 'looks out', it confronts the real. We have a move in which the parent, adult, camera, or viewer, looks closely at a child, is confronted by its physicality, yet finds that something has escaped its gaze; the child's separateness.

If this is a narrative that could be read as repeated throughout *Pictures of Innocence*, it is equally available as a set of contradictory moves. For example, Higonnet begins her analysis with a reading of *Portrait of Mrs John Angerstein and her son John Julius William* by Thomas Lawrence. Initially the figures of mother and child in the painting are read as similar, testament to the infantilization of women within late eighteenth-century art. Higonnet proceeds to introduce differences, however; whereas Mrs John Angerstein 'faces the viewer with a distinctly come hither gaze...in comparison, John Julius William isn't paying much attention to anything'.[16] This 'Romantic child makes a good show of having no class, no gender, and no thoughts – of being socially, sexually, and psychically innocence.'[17] Thus a representation of an outward gaze is associated with sexuality, the specificity of social identity, and of consciousness, while a failure to gaze at a distinct object is the sign that these things are lacking. Or, rather, are shown to be lacking, 'show' being a mark of something less than wholly real here, even as the visibility of the gaze is read as necessary to the supposition of subjecthood.

This can be contrasted with Higonnet's reading of Nicholas Nixon's *Sam and Clementine*, a portrait of two children with the lower body of a boy sat high on a bed, a girl laying below him, gazing at a mirror, where 'her fixed stare at a small mirror contrasts with his anonymous physical presence', this being the sign of a 'Knowing child', the kind with 'bodies and passions of their own'.[18] Here not looking at the audience is indicative of consciousness, not, as in the case of John Julian William, a lack thereof. That is, perhaps, because the girl is looking at something. The gaze is 'fixed' on a mirror, it is stable, unswerving, certain. It is claimed that her 'looking dominates the picture'.[19] In a repetition of the move made in *The Apple of My Eye* and *Clementine*, the unavailability of the object of the child's gaze grants it independence from the viewer, a sense of subjecthood. Both Nixon's and Lawrence's images show contrasted figures, are conscious, the other unaware, one staring at something, the other staring a nothing, or deprived of the stare. Yet it seems that the girl and the mother should be understood as staring in a different way, as the mother has a 'come hither look' she is read as staring at the viewer. The girl is staring at something the viewer cannot see, absorbed in her own reflection. She looks to the left, Mrs John Angerstein to the front. This allows the girl to be read as escaping the gaze, even as she is being looked at. What she sees of herself is read as unavailable, she lacks the immediacy of presence granted to the anonymous boy. She escapes the gaze even as she is seen by it. So does the boy, however, as although he is viewed as immediate, his face remains unseen. The girl and boy can be read as representative of the duality between separateness and immediacy that Higonnet's construction of childhood requires, the girl being absent, the boy present. Yet the duality is within both figures, the girl's 'looking dominates the picture', the boy is incomplete. In contrast with this boy, John Julian William is not lacking in any sense. He is neither looking out or in. Instead his every aspect is read as contained within the text, completely available within it. Rather than leading to a sense of physicality, this seems to render him absent. As there is nothing beyond this text, there is no physicality to be desired, mourned or recovered. In contrast, Mrs John Angerstein's outward stare is read as making her available to a viewer in such a way that there is no subjectivity beyond the sexual, her stare focused on something apparently fully present to the viewer: themselves. The outward gaze constitutes the viewer.[20]

These images can be compared to Higonnet's reading of what she considers to be a defining Romantic image of childhood, *Penelope Boothby* by Joshua Reynolds, wherein the child portrayed 'glances ever so slightly aside; she is absorbed in childhood. We long for a childhood we cannot reach.'[21] This glance is like the gaze in both *Clementine* and *Sam and Clementine*, because it results in an 'absorption' that distances the child from the adult viewer. There is, however, a sense in which *Penelope Boothby* has more in common with John Julian William, as rather than a 'fixed' stare, we have a 'glance' to the side, a look that is absorbed within itself, without an object. In *Clementine*, the viewer is read as an adult, gazing on the physical body of the girl, in *Penelope Boothby* the child is 'nestled in an over sized fluffy cocoon'[22] made from clothes that are too big for her, concealing her body as they contrast it with the larger, more adult body such clothes are designed for. Thus the girl is 'absorbed' in a childhood which is utterly separate from adulthood, including, importantly, adult, bodily existence. She is read as 'unreachable' because, in every sense, lacking physicality. One difficulty with this comparative reading is that there is a sense in which *Clementine* is understood to be an image in which childhood is precisely that which escapes the body. The adult sees the physicality of the child, yet the closer it looks, the clearer the sense that the child has escaped the gaze, that the realm of childhood is that which cannot be seen. The girl in *Penelope Boothby* is absent, it would seem, but, unlike 'Knowing' images, this is not an absence that speaks of presence. She is absorbed, as contained within, but not 'absorbed' as entranced by a thing. We are to know that she is not looking at, the object of her looking is truly absent, not absent yet in some sense recoverable, as are, apparently, the objects of Mrs John Angerstein and the girls in *Clementine, Sam and Clementine* and *The Apple of My Eye*. Whereas these girls are understood in terms of psychological individuality and knowingness through their absorption, the fixity of vision which guaranteed them separation from the adult gaze, *Penelope Boothby* is not granted this privilege. There is, however, a sense in which she is still wholly available to sight, as she is unaware of being gazed upon; there is no issue, it would seem, in gazing upon her. Rather than resulting in a lack of physicality, this 'glance...ever so slightly to the side' places her in a world of activity, unlike the stillness of the gaze in *Clementine*. There the gaze was more certain, more knowable, yet the result is that it is only the figure in *Penelope Boothby* who is read as moving.

The tension between the notion that the lack of a fixed gaze will result in a diminished sense of presence, and that the partially represented body, especially that without a head, results in a present anonymity, forwarded respectively in Higonnet's reading of *Penelope Boothby* and *Sam and Clementine*, is further complicated by the interpretation of a 1902 Soap advertisement by Jessie Willcox Smith in which it is claimed the featured 'child is almost anonymous, because the head and shoulders we see reflected in the mirror are dim, and the child seems completely unaware of us'.[23] Here, as is the case for the boy in *Sam and Clementine*, a lack of a clear representation of a face leads to anonymity and physicality, although the 'dimness' rather than 'absence' makes this only 'almost' true. Rather than granting the immediacy of presence, however, this results in a situation in which:

> Neither the face or the soap matter; what matters is that an innocent, metaphorically clean, child uses soap in a cozy and very pretty middle-class home. The child is the prime object of our looking, but the desire we might feel is diffused into her surroundings.[24]

In *Sam and Clementine*, the lack of an observable face resulted in bodily presence, here it results in the unaware, unbodily child of *Penelope Boothby*. Moreover, in Nixon's image the unavailability of the head, and therefore the directed gaze, resulted in the fragment of body understood as a thing-in-itself, a materiality to be contrasted with the dominating absence of the girl's fixed stare. Here, a comparable lack results in diffusion, the move beyond the body to the surroundings. Rather than forcing the viewer to focus on their bodily presence this (almost) headless child allows the gaze to be directed elsewhere. The 'unawareness' of the child is what secures its Romantic status, the lack of recognition of the viewer being synonymous with a lack of any thought. This is a move repeated elsewhere, for example, in her analysis of *Los Chorros, Chenalho, Chiapas* by Jose Angel Rodriguez, Higonnet states that 'these children's oblivious innocence confirms a long western tradition of seeing anyone who isn't western as an innocent savage, a savage who remains perpetually a dependent child'.[25] A lack of awareness of the viewer is the sign of dependence, yet in *Clementine* and *The Apple of My Eye*, such a lack signals the independence of the child's vision, her radical separateness.

If *Clementine* and *The Apple of My Eye* seem to partake in the Romanticism they are variously read as opposing and supplementing, other images of Knowing childhood are on hand to offer what can be taken as a different construction. Such images are understood to show children staring 'out' at the viewer, rather than escaping the viewer's view through an inward gaze. One such is Sally Mann's *Jessie at 5*, which Higonnet claims 'insists on the vivid presence of its central child', featuring as it does a girl who 'snakes outward, flat torso naked, gaze unabashed, face made up with rouge and lipstick', an 'intensely physical' image.[26] Here, unlike in the reading of *Sam and Clementine*, the immediacy of physicality is not enabled by the absence of the head, or by anonymity as the child is named, her gaze visible and 'unabashed'. Despite its totality, this 'presence' is achieved through comparison, however, just as it was in *Sam and Clementine*, the central figure contrasted 'with girls on either side, both of them dressed in the traditional clothing of childhood innocence, both receding into the back ground, out of focus and oddly stiff, relics of an impossibly lost past'.[27] The 'out of focus', like the 'dim' image in the soap advertisement, but unlike the mirror in *The Apple of My Eye*, is that which is lost to an impossible extent, 'impossibility' absent, unrecoverable. It is these other children, in part, that grant the central girl her fullness of presence, one that does not require the notion required by other images of 'Knowing' children as, at one stage, absented from sight. The adult can fully encounter this child, but only because other children are absented in turn, made into metaphors for something else, something lost. The central girl is not a metaphor, it would seem, she is 'present' as herself. The lack of vitality that characterizes the other girls can be read through their apparent 'stiffness'. If the 'snaking' body of that which is present seems to have more in common with the glancing, Romantic *Penelope Boothby* than the fixed, Knowing *Clementine*, such a reading is challenged by the notion that this image achieves the level of 'art' by dint of its being 'sustained', 'consistent', and, above all, 'permanent'.[28] Thus, although *Jessie at 5* might be about the physicality and vibrancy of presence, it pertains to presence's immovability, its ironic lack of life. This threat is increased if it is compared to her reading of the female figure in *Portrait of Mrs John Angerstein and John Julian William*. There, the direct gaze spoke of a reductive availability, a lack of otherness. And here, it should be remembered, the necessity of the child to turn from us, to look elsewhere, to be other than wholly present.

According to Higonnet, a comparable image is Herb Ritts' *Vanity Fair* portrait of Courtney Love's daughter. Despite referencing certain Romantic tropes, the image is read as one whose

> innocence is also carnal, superficially because the child is naked, more fundamentally because the child confronts us with her being, and with her gaze. We see nothing but the figure, close and frontal,

with the head spatially dominating the body. She is not a cute object. She is a beautiful and knowing person.[29]

Although we 'see nothing but the figure', in the way that the boy in *Sam and Clementine* offered us nothing but his physicality, here the gaze is included within the category of figure and 'nothing but'. Rather than being placed on the outside of the body-in-itself, the gaze constitutes part of it, the head 'dominating' all else. This body is active, it moves, it confronts. It is not separate, in its own world, it engages with us, it crosses over, yet it is still separate from us. It 'is' 'beautiful', for example, this being a quality of body rather than perception, an objective fact.[30]

Such apparently visceral presences, such gazing materiality, can be contrasted with mid-twentieth century exercises in aesthetic formalism that Higonnet reads as falling within a Romantic paradigm. Take this description by Kathryn Harrison of one of Edward Weston's *Neil* images, photographs of torsos, bereft of the confrontational gaze: 'almost everything about him is ultimately withheld. There's no consummation between the viewer and viewed, which I think is powerful and compelling'.[31] This is an absence that, however 'powerful', is understood as premised on a denial of sexuality, and of individuality. In 'withholding' the child, one offers an image of it without depth, and this necessitates a denial of physicality as well as selfhood. It would seem that even an image which contains only a torso not only rejects any appeal to self consciousness, but also to physicality, a move opposed to the reading of *Sam and Clementine*.

Higonnet suggests that it is in the opposition to such superficiality and idealism that 'Knowing' art stakes its claim to originality; 'unlike Romantic images, Knowing images, for the first time in the history of art, endow children with psychological and physical individuality.'[32] It is, above all, a sense of physical existence and an inner life beyond that is lacking in a picture such as *Bubbles* by Millais, where 'the innocent child [...] is like a soap bubble: all beautiful surface, shimmering and empty. Do not touch.'[33] For me, there is a problem with the opposition being set up between *Bubbles* and *Clementine*, one arising from the relationship read between the Romantic surface, that which insists on not being touched, that which covers nothing, that which withholds, and the surface of the Knowing image which, in its various way, constitutes presence, and allows access to more. In *Clementine*, the image is apparently inspected in detail, yet something exists beyond such inspection, the world the child finds herself absorbed in, her own subjectivity, a vision that is its own. It could be said that this is because the surface we are being asked to look at is somehow genuinely that of the body, rather than a formalist essay in light and shade, a soap bubble, or some other displacement. To some extent this can be read in Higonnet's claims that 'there could be no better description of people in photographs than "the surface of living beings". The only reality a camera can record is light bouncing off surfaces. Knowledge supplies the rest.'[34] The surface is devoid of meaning here, it is physical, real, yet it lacks anything more, there can be no truth or meaning if one looks only to it. An initial problem with this is that Higonnet grants such a surface to all pictures, Romantic and Knowing. Moreover, within this construction, the image does not allow the viewer access to the physicality of flesh, only reflected light. Meaning, even the meaning of 'knowingness', is read as secondary. Yet, in *Clementine* the surface is understood to be bodily. Moreover, this bodily surface allows the image to grant the viewer some idea of that which lies beyond the representational borders, below the surface of the image, below the surface of the human subject. Yet this extra-textual something is read as opposed to the apparent physicality of the surface image, the surface flesh. This is not to be the kind of transcendent move offered by *Neil*. It is, instead, at least in my reading, a continuation of the material, as the girl is looking inwards, inside the body, inside the self, communing with her physicality, the solidity of inner identity, a fullness rather than an emptiness of being, that which apparently opposes the inner emptiness of Millais' bubbles. And, according to Higonnet's logic, the inner fullness, as opposed to such emptiness, is available as a command to touch.

Higonnet warns that Romantic art is dangerous because 'if childhood is understood as a blank slate, then adults can freely project their own fantasies onto children, whatever those fantasies might be.'[35] It is, then, essential for Knowing art to offer something more than nothing, to grant the child a palpable presence that resists being filled by adult desires because already in the condition of containment. One difficulty here is that absence keeps reasserting itself. Higonnet's reading of *Clementine*, for example, grants the surface of the image a physical presence while contrasting this to the separateness of the girl's subjectivity. Yet, at one stage of this argument, this separateness places this girl precisely in the dangerous position Higonnet reads in Romantic constructions. The girl is separate, as she is not simply part of adult fantasies, but, because she is separate, is the site for free projection. This becomes more problematic, however, as the part of *Clementine* that is present to us, again at one stage of the argument, is the physicality of the girl's body, a surface image that is read as having no higher meaning. Moreover, the absence so necessary to the separateness of the subject turns out to be an internal fullness, an absent physicality. In order to protect the child, she must be placed away from us, then given back, as both positions are unacceptable, as both having her and not having her are intolerable. Curiously, this game, for Higonnet, is about freeing the child from 'control'.[36]

Parental vision

Higonnet's reading engages with this threat, yet chooses to understand the tension between presence and absence introduced above in an alternative way. In her analysis, such a toing and froing between self and other is indicative of a way of seeing that troubles these very dualisms, understood as they are as central to the patriarchal gaze. Such a move is supported through reference to the work of Diana Fuss, for whom:

> identification can be rethought as a potent mode of 'self-recognition' but also self-alteration, at once self absorbed and engaged with the outside world: 'Identification' is the detour through the other that defines the self. This detour through the other follows no predetermined path, nor does it travel outside history and culture. Identification names the entry of history and culture into the subject, a subject that must bear the traces of each and every encounter with the outside world.[37]

In this reading, 'identification' breaks down the stability of the oppositions that have to be insisted upon if Higonnet's reading of adult visions of childhood is to be problematized. This paves the way for a vision of the child as other that is not opposed to the child seen as part of the self, which is why 'identification' is read by Higonnet as 'so essential to the problem of parenting'.[38] It is a move that Higonnet reads as particularly linked to a maternal vision, one that offers:

> An alternative to Freudian and Lacanian models of representation, a model that privileges identification and narcissism to break down oppositions between self and other, between symbolic and nonsymbolic. Introducing the concept of the 'matrixal gaze' [Bracha Lichtenberg Ettinger] proposes the mother's relationship to the unborn child who is both herself and another as her creative paradigm.[39]

Through engaging with such a paradigm, or even through focusing on older sons and daughters, 'these young artists' are 'reworking concepts of both identification and narcissism...turning femininity in on itself, producing symbolic distance within the very subjects previously consigned to the inchoate pre-symbolic.'[40]

This, then, is the theoretical grounding for the moves made above. The child can be present to the maternal viewer and yet remain separate because presence and separation are not as opposed as the symbolic would have us believe. In this understanding, the inward gaze encompasses the physical and external, it is constituted simultaneously through symbolic difference and non-symbolic immediacy. Yet, in terms of Higonnet's reading of *Clementine* and *The Apple of My Eye*, this results not in some kind of sustained collapsing of away and back, a form of spectrality, but in an insistence upon a complete otherness which is supplemented by an appeal to utter presence, the opposite terms required, at least at one stage, to be available as themselves. In other words, Higonnet needs, at some point, the child to be away and to be back, if away is to be back and back away.

In my reading, such problems arise whenever Higonnet attempts to appeal to a specific maternal, or even broader parental vision. For example, in discussing the late twentieth-century reassessment of the work of Julia Margaret Cameron, Higonnet claims that the critics:

> Mavor and Armstrong look at such pictures with the eyes of their time, which happens to be the eyes of loving and feminist mothers. Reinterpreting Cameron's technique, they explain her cracked negatives, hair shadows, and chemical blurs as signs of tactile presence which, far from spoiling the images, reinforce their haptic immediacy.[41]

To look as a mother, albeit one of a certain sort, is to desire, and gain access to, the physical. Although it could be argued that 'tactile presence' is read in terms of 'signs', thus breaking down the boundary between symbolic and non-symbolic, the idea here is one of a maternal vision that seeks out the touchable solidity of the real. The move is repeated with the idea that, in the images they produce, and are produced of them, 'new mother and father figures are intimately and vigorously involved in their children's physical existence.'[42] Again, the parental vision (fathers now included) is one that grants access to the physical real. The idea is that this physical intimacy grants parents a bonded relationship with their child, breaking down the barrier between self and other. Yet such a move can only be made through the introduction of another binary, hence the insistence upon a purely physical realm, one to be differentiated from that of formalism, distance and separation.[43]

An additional problem with Higonnet's reading of maternal or parental vision arises from its apparent exclusivity. This vision is a form of native sight, one that allows Higonnet to claim, in her reading of Sally Mann's *Last Light*, that 'as a parent it seems to me the child is achingly beautiful'.[44] The condition of being a parent is understood as enabling one to see in a particular way. Most often, as in the readings of *Clementine, The Apple of My Eye*, and the work of Mann and Cameron, this particular vision comes down to a concern with the materiality of the daughter or son being seen, the will, and the ability, to access its presence, while conceiving of its separateness. Yet the result of this is a vision that is curiously open to all. To read *Clementine* is not only to be confronted by the materiality of a young girl's existence, but to encounter that materiality as a father and, because of this, being able to see beyond the immediate parental vision.

In my reading, this difficulty undermines one of the ethical imperatives forwarded by the text, the proposition that 'the end of Romantic childhood entails the end to the utility of thinking about childhood in terms of rigidly opposed private and public values.'[45] I am not concerned with whether such a move would be beneficial, that being a judgement on the necessity of censorship and the validity of a certain construction of domestic privacy. Rather, my interest is with the way in which Higonnet reads a certain public vision as impossible, as to encounter *Clementine* is always, in these terms, to enact a private view, to see as Nicholas Nixon, father, even when one is seeing all that is denied him.[46]

According to Higonnet, the parental sight that allows a visceral encounter with material existence is not the only form of vision able to constitute the Knowing child, as non-parents engaging with the child's surface image can apparently achieve a comparable effect. The claim is made that 'new photographs recognise children's artifice',[47] and this separates the images they produce from Romantic traditions as the children in question are understood to be active in their own construction, rather than passive objects of the adult gaze. Because an artist such as 'Nan Goldin accepts children's displays of themselves', some idea of subjecthood, the child's own particular vision, can be displayed.[48] At this stage, Higonnet insists that such a move is necessary as children can never truly represent themselves as they do not have the artistic skill. However, in a work such as Goldin's *Io in Camouflage*, it is claimed that 'Photographer and subject together create the image...Pictures like this suggest that Knowing children's views of themselves may not be so different from the views attentive and unconventional photographers have of them.'[49] Children who cannot represent themselves in art can show themselves to others, and 'unconventional' artists can capture this show. Artists make children's own visions available because they share the same vision, the adult vision of a child's display having no important difference to that original display. Yet this necessitates that such an original display can somehow be accessed and known without being seen, or that we can access totally the child's own vision of its display through our adult vision of it.

As Higonnet's reading develops, it transpires that although children apparently lack the ability to represent themselves, they can be taught how to. Yet, for me, the readings of the images such educated children produce are problematic in a way comparable to those that focus on art formed through 'collaboration'. In claiming that 'there is nothing more brutal, carnal, tragic, or strange about any of the most controversial new photographs of children taken by adults than there is about the photographs children make of themselves',[50] Higonnet reads the defining quality of art as adjectival. Perspective is not an issue. Thus the art that children make of themselves is not to be differentiated from that of Knowing art, despite the majority of that art apparently being formed from a parental view.

For Higonnet, the parent, the collaborative artist and the child all produce work that displays the child as it constructs itself, each 'show how adults can value children for what they are instead of for what they are not'.[51] The vision of children, and children themselves, are separate from the vision of adults. Yet this is a qualitative separateness. Children are not to be taken to be unknowable, empty spaces open to adult projection. We know this because children can show us what they see and what they are. And what they see and what they are is exactly what we, as parents, and artists, and viewers of contemporary art, visualize them seeing, understand them as being. The vision of children is precisely that of adults. Again, the child must be thrown far from us, and then retrieved. Again and again this must happen, until, it would seem, in this process without end, difference and loss may be overcome, and separation achieved.

Notes

1. A. Higonnet, *Pictures of Innocence: The History and Crisis of Ideal Childhood* (London: Thames and Hudson, 1998); M. Brown (ed.), *Picturing Children:*

Constructions of Childhood between Rousseau and Freud (Aldershot: Ashgate, 2002); P. Holland, *Picturing Childhood: The Myth of the Child in Popular Imagery* (London: I.B. Tauris, 2004).

2. Higonnet, *Pictures of Innocence*, pp. 13–14.
3. Holland, *Picturing Childhood*, p. xiv.
4. Higonnet, *Pictures of Innocence*, p. 201.
5. The text was also chosen because, unlike *Picturing Childhood*, Patricia Holland's study of the image of the child in advertising and popular culture and *Picturing Children*, a collection of essays concerned with childhood in Fine Art, it has the broadest sweep, reading everything from Caravaggio to Geddes, Bon Jovi CD covers to the photography of Sally Mann. Also, *Pictures of Innocence* was first published in 1998, with subsequent texts regarding it as the seminal history of construction, see J. Milam, 'Sex Education and the Child: Gendering Erotic Response in Eighteenth-Century France', in M. Brown (ed.), *Picturing Children: Constructions of Childhood Between Rousseau and Freud* (Aldershot: Ashgate, 2002). pp. 45–53, p. 52 and Holland, *Picturing Childhood*, p. 22. If Philippe Ariès' *Centuries of Childhood* might be regarded as a better candidate, it is worth stressing that Higonnet is critical of that text, claiming that Ariès relies 'too much on images, which he uses liberally as social evidence' (Higonnet, *Pictures of Innocence*, p. 25).
6. Holland is keen to point out she is not arguing for a childhood self-representation that is qualitatively different from adulthood, just one that of necessity comes from a different point of view. Despite Holland's reading of child self-representation as an alternative rather than as authentic, *Picturing Childhood* is still concerned with the promotion of 'childhood's self representation that is not "mediated by adulthood" and the child's "right to wildness"'. In this, Holland can be read as offering a version of the 'Childist' approach to texts pioneered by Peter Hunt in *Criticism, Theory, and Children's Literature* (Oxford: Blackwell, 1991) and developed by Sebastien Chapleau in *New Voices in Children's Literature Criticism* (Lichfield: Pied Piper Publishing, 2004). For a reading of this, see K. Lesnik-Oberstein, 'Children's Literature: New Approaches', in K. Lesnik-Oberstein (ed.), *Children's Literature: New Approaches* (London: Palgrave, 2004), pp. 1–25 and N. Cocks, 'Response and Responsibility: "The Reader in the Book" by Aidan Chambers', in N. Cocks, *Student Centred: Education Freedom and the Idea of Audience* (Ashby-de-la-Zouch: Inkermen/Axis Series, 2009), pp. 45–75.
7. Higonnet, *Pictures of Innocence*, p. 209.
8. Higonnet, *Pictures of Innocence*, p. 210.
9. Higonnet, *Pictures of Innocence*, p. 210.
10. Higonnet, *Pictures of Innocence*, p. 173. Here, and below in my discussion of the parental gaze, I am following the reading of the child gazing 'out' of the image offered by Joe Kelleher in his 'Face to Face with Terror: Childhood in Film', in K. Lesnik-Oberstein (ed.), *Children in Culture: Approaches to Childhood* (Basingstoke: Macmillan, 1998), pp. 29–55.
11. Higonnet, *Pictures of Innocence*, p. 210.
12. Higonnet, *Pictures of Innocence*, p. 81.
13. Higonnet, *Pictures of Innocence*, p. 212.
14. Higonnet, *Pictures of Innocence*, p. 70.

15. What of 'Clementine' here? To what extent is the child read as opposed to its name, how might a child so opposed be written? To follow Higonnet's reasoning is to read 'Clementine' as both the name given to that apparent physical presence *there*, and that which is a refusal of it.
16. Higonnet, *Pictures of Innocence*, p. 24.
17. Higonnet, *Pictures of Innocence*, p. 24.
18. Higonnet, *Pictures of Innocence*, p. 207.
19. Higonnet, *Pictures of Innocence*, p. 207.
20. Again, see Kelleher, 'Face to Face with Terror', for an extended reading of this move.
21. Higonnet, *Pictures of Innocence*, p. 27.
22. Higonnet, *Pictures of Innocence*, p. 28.
23. Higonnet, *Pictures of Innocence*, p. 62.
24. Higonnet, *Pictures of Innocence*, p. 62.
25. Higonnet, *Pictures of Innocence*, p. 120.
26. Higonnet, *Pictures of Innocence*, p. 195.
27. Higonnet, *Pictures of Innocence*, p. 195.
28. Higonnet, *Pictures of Innocence*, p. 195.
29. Higonnet, *Pictures of Innocence*, p. 199.
30. Compare these two constructions with the following from a reading of what is considered a Romantic image, *A Little Bit of Heaven* by Bessie Pease Gutmann: 'We the viewers are situated intimately close to this charming baby, as if nothing else in the world existed for us' (Higonnet, *Pictures of Innocence*, p. 69). From this we can read what recoverable absence might be for Knowing portraits of full presence: everything in the world that is not present in the body that confronts us. Knowing images of full presence allow access to the lack that is the real, Romantic images of presence leave no room for anything but themselves.
31. Higonnet, *Pictures of Innocence*, p. 137.
32. Higonnet, *Pictures of Innocence*, p. 12.
33. Higonnet, *Pictures of Innocence*, p. 37.
34. Higonnet, *Pictures of Innocence*, p. 122.
35. Higonnet, *Pictures of Innocence*, p. 38.
36. Higonnet, *Pictures of Innocence*, p. 211.
37. Higonnet, *Pictures of Innocence*, p. 200. It is worth stressing that I am questioning the reading of Fuss by Higonnet, rather than offering any wider critique of texts by Fuss.
38. Higonnet, *Pictures of Innocence*, p. 200.
39. Higonnet, *Pictures of Innocence*, p. 201
40. Higonnet, *Pictures of Innocence*, p. 200.
41. Higonnet, *Pictures of Innocence*, p. 125.
42. Higonnet, *Pictures of Innocence*, p. 198.
43. For more on the maternal vision and its access to the physical, as well as childhood constructed in terms of physicality, see Higonnet, *Pictures of Innocence*, p. 205. I read Higonnet's construction of motherhood to be inconsistent, and lacking any sustained engagement with this inconsistency. Higonnet quotes Courtney Love with approval when she claims that there is a 'kind of mother's blood that makes you want to buy firearms when

you have a child' (p. 198), writes of a 'passion sprung from primary origins' (p. 205), when describing her own maternal feelings, yet also refers to what she reads as Sally Mann's belief that 'maternity is a role, complete with costume and props, and these girls aren't predestined to play it sweetly' (p. 204) while making no comment on contradiction between the various statements.

44. Higonnet, *Pictures of Innocence*, p. 202.
45. Higonnet, *Pictures of Innocence*, p. 223.
46. For a comparable discussion of claims made upon the child and how they relate to notions of parenthood and ownership, see S. Thomson, 'The Adjective, My Daughter: Staging T.S. Eliot's "Marina'", in K. Lesnik-Oberstein (ed.), 'Children in Literature', Special section of *The Yearbook of English Studies*, vol. 32 (Leeds: Maney Publishing, 2002), pp. 110–26.
47. Higonnet, *Pictures of Innocence*, p. 216.
48. Higonnet, *Pictures of Innocence*, p. 217.
49. Higonnet, *Pictures of Innocence*, p. 217. Compare this formulation to the notion that 'Photography's fidelity is to the values of that particular historical moment, not to some "real" truth about children' (p. 209). It would seem that the general historical moment Knowing art is true to is that which breaks with the conventions of the moment. The contradiction is not read through. Moreover, Higonnet seems to be relying on an appeal to what could be termed the sociological 'real'. There is a condition that image can have fidelity to, apparently, yet it is difficult to understand how this prior moment can be anything but the 'real', a condition now understood to be a procession of actualities. Far more could be written on this sociological 'real', particularly in terms of how it enables a notion of an existence apart from the representational, how, for example, it might be related to the idea that the Knowing art of Sheila Metzner 'represents an aesthetic transcendence of a painful physical reality' (pp. 214–15), or that 'photography has always included pictures of children whose realism is supposed to lead beyond bodies toward social conditions' (p. 117).
50. Higonnet, *Pictures of Innocence*, p. 217.
51. Higonnet, *Pictures of Innocence*, p. 224.

9
Television for Children: Problems of National Specificity and Globalization

Jonathan Bignell

In the developed nations of Europe, and in the USA, it has long been assumed that television should address children. Thus, notions of what 'children' are have been constructed, and children are routinely discussed as an audience category and as a market for programmes. A fundamental set of conceptions of childhood, originating in the late eighteenth century, links the unstated ideological assumptions of the great majority of programme producers, television programme buyers and executives, and parents, politicians and commentators.[1] In this respect, the chapter's focus on the construction of childhood in television has many links with the other chapters in this book. For adults' assumptions about childhood also inform literature that constructs children as textual subjects and addressees. Childhood has been seen as a life-stage in which emergent subjectivities are predisposed to immorality or amorality, and irrational behaviour, so that adult supervision of children's development is required. Conversely, the child is also understood as innocent, authentic and pure. Affected by these competing and contradictory discourses about childhood, adult television professionals who have produced and distributed animated programmes have addressed children in a range of ways.

The influence of public service television values has been strong in the UK, and powerfully influenced other West European television institutions making programmes that address and thus construct children. This is because of the early establishment of the BBC as a public service broadcaster in radio from 1922 and in television from 1936, and because of the broad acceptance of social-democratic ideologies in western European societies.[2] In early European television culture (until the

1960s), television for younger children was oriented towards a concept of playful education. Programmes aimed to connect with their play world, to stimulate their creativity and encourage them to discover the world in an experimental way.[3] The BBC and later the commercial public service broadcasters ITV and Channel 4 aimed to elevate the national audience's taste, intellectual appetite and knowledge, supplying diverse material for diverse audiences, including an audience sector categorized as children.[4] In Britain and in many other nations, the requirement for public service broadcasting for children stimulated both animated and live-action television. A range of public-service models existed in Western Europe and constructed similar notions of the child audience, and the more monolithic state-supervised television of Eastern Europe also promoted the development of children's programming.

In the USA, non-commercial television broadcasting has been overshadowed by the commercial networks, whose children's programmes have been reliant on funding from the makers of consumer products marketed to children, such as breakfast cereals or toys. Across the developed world, nevertheless, there are constructions of childhood and children that have been similar enough to facilitate the exchange of productions that are recognized as 'children's programmes'. Discourses about genre and audience have a homogenizing effect, and this is connected to commercial relationships of television exchange. Because of its international reach and public visibility in discourses about social policy, children's television is a paradigm case for debates about the role of the medium in subject-formation, ideology and the globalization of the media economy.[5] But transnational histories of the complexities of its production and exchange remain patchy, and often caught unproductively in debates about the influence of American television on other nations.[6] Throughout the history of British television there has been strong resistance to US programmes because of the fear of Americanization.[7] This applies especially to children, who are considered more vulnerable to the influence of the consumerism that is said to be embodied in many US toy-based series. Children are also regarded as susceptible to negative influence by the violent content in US children's programmes, especially cartoons. Indeed, in as much as their susceptibility to anti-social influence is what characterizes children in such policy debates, childhood itself could be understood as a construction that is legitimated by such ideas about vulnerability to media effects.

Since commercial television is associated with the USA as the dominant commercial broadcasting arrangement in the world, suspicion of commercial television has run alongside suspicion of US programming. This is especially the case for programme genres that construct youth audiences, such as pop music programmes and channels and imported US children's programming. Each of these genres had commercial success, and throughout the second half of the twentieth century the critique of Americanization, the defence of nationalism and the valuation of tradition have occurred around the totemic figures of the child and the teenager. In this context, the fact that the British and European animation[8] discussed in this chapter was not American could become a virtue in itself. Yet imported American fiction television for children, like *Lassie* (1954–73) or *Champion the Wonderhorse* (1955–6), set child characters and animals in narratives characterized by the threat and rescue format discussed below in a case study of Gerry Anderson's puppet series. The kinds of borrowing and mixing of forms discussed in this chapter's case studies undermine the possibilities for making distinctions between the programmes on the basis of their national cultural characteristics.

There have been consistent exchanges of programmes between European countries and between Europe and the USA. There are inequalities in production funding, and different roles of domestic and imported programming in national television cultures, and at both international and regional levels it has been argued that 'world patterns of communication flow, both in density and in direction, mirror the system of domination in the economic and political order.'[9] Globalization theses proposed by Herbert Schiller, for example, have argued that the globalization of communication in the second half of the twentieth century was determined by the commercial interests of US corporations, working in parallel with political and military interests.[10] This discourse connects cultural imperialism with the dynamics of colonialism, arguing that the colonial empires of Britain or France have been replaced by American-dominated commercial empires. Transnational studies of television cannot ignore the impact of the USA and the broadcast of animation for children in Britain has been dominated by US series. In the period discussed here, examples included *Scooby-Doo, Where Are You?* (1969), *Josie and the Pussycats* (1970), *The Harlem Globetrotters* (1970) and series based on pop celebrities such as *The Jackson Five* (1971) or *The Osmonds* (1972). Each of these series was screened in Britain in children's programming slots, either on weekday afternoons or Saturday mornings. In the early 1980s, exported US animation shown in the UK included *He-Man and the Masters of the Universe* (1983), whose success led to the subsequent *She-Ra: Princess of Power* (1985). These series were each repeated for several years and related toys and merchandising enhanced their cultural visibility. The link between programme import and commodity culture reinforced the stigmatization of US imports as an aspect of cultural imperialism and a supposed threat to the very concept of childhood.[11] Although the globalization of television trading appears to entail homogenization, in fact it also produces differentiation. Some programmes are regarded as inimical to childhood, while others are regarded as good for children.

Regional flows and institutional arrangements have been developed in Europe to foster and protect its television culture. These transnational relationships foster and protect a shared notion of childhood and children too, in as much as they facilitate the exchange of 'children's programmes' that are different from those that supposedly undermine childhood. The European Broadcasting Union (EBU) was formed in 1950 by 23 broadcasters across Europe and the Mediterranean and further national members and associate members subsequently joined (some of them outside Europe, from Canada, Japan, Mexico, Brazil, India and the USA). The EBU promotes members' co-operation and represents their legal, technical and programming interests, and runs the Eurovision network to pool programmes and co-ordinate joint programme purchases.[12] It was against this background that European programmes and programme-makers entered the British television landscape in the 1950s to the 1980s, in a period preceding the rise of international television channels for children (such as the Disney Channel) and cross-border broadcasting by satellite. This was still during the Cold War, in which boundaries between the television cultures of East and West might suggest that cross-border exchanges were rare. But in fact, hybridity, migration and exchange were evident and question conventional assumptions about the identities of programmes and broadcasting cultures.[13] The case studies later in this chapter demonstrate how programmes promoted and marketed as being for child audiences were both made in Britain according to the practices and formats of US programmes, and were imported into Britain from a range of continental European nations including East European countries.

Despite the introduction of quotas and subsidies, domestic production of children's programming in Europe has been vulnerable to competition from US imports because of its limited profitability on commercial channels and a focus by policy-makers on prestigious genres for adults, especially drama.[14] State-supervised channels broadcast a wider range of national, imported European and American programmes than commercial channels, with domestically produced series predominating over American series on both public and commercial channels. However, European drama has been constrained from import into Britain by considerations of language and cultural proximity[15] in ways that American programmes were not and freedom from these constraints made transnational children's animation possible and relatively common. The chapter charts this mainly in relation to stop-frame animation and puppet series, whose separation of image and sound tracks allows re-voicing[16] and assists their exportability. The exchange of programmes, formats and personnel is much easier in children's animation than in live-action series because of how it is made. Animation is made on film rather than video, so that technical work was not required to re-process programmes for the varied and incompatible transmission formats used across Europe and in the USA.[17] Animation requires the separation of image and sound tracks during the production process, allowing subsequent dubbing and re-voicing in different languages. The adaptability of re-voicing gets around the language obstacle that has restricted imports of continental programmes compared to US imports, which are already in English.

British viewers are very rarely offered opportunities to watch subtitled programmes, or programmes where live actors' dialogue is dubbed into English. The shared language of the UK and USA made import and export easier since processes of linguistic transformation were not needed, but translation is done in different ways in different television cultures and is also affected by the programmes' address to, and construction of, different sectors of that audience. In general, children's programmes construct a more youthful audience the more dubbing into local languages they use and the less subtitling they use. But once the audience is considered by the broadcaster to be of school age, subtitling takes over from dubbing. In some television territories such as the Netherlands or Greece, subtitling is common, whereas in Germany, Italy or Poland it is not. Conventional translation practices in programmes scheduled for children are closely related to national norms in audio-visual translation more broadly. But they are affected by specific assumptions about literacy and the relationship between spoken and written language that are part of ideologies that construct and subdivide the category of the child according to developmental and age-based criteria. In this way too, the notion of the child as audience and addressee for television programmes has both nationally specific and also transnational characteristics.

Transatlantic hybrids: Gerry Anderson and puppet science fiction in the 1960s

Animation has been dominated by US imports but there is a strong tradition of British and continental European animation.[18] In the 1960s in the UK, some producers aimed for export success by creating a transatlantic and internationalist fictional world, while others emphasized aspects of national specificity. This section discusses Gerry Anderson's 1960s puppet series, which have hybrid identities in their production for export to the USA and in the fictional worlds that they represent.[19] They were a compromise between Anderson's desire to make films for adults versus an available market for children's television puppet programmes and aimed to appeal to a cross-generational family audience. They were made on film, using novel effects, for a UK television production culture that still relied largely on live and videotaped production.[20] While commissioned by British ITV companies, the programmes were designed to be transatlantic products and had notable success in the USA, achieving national networked screening as well as syndication.[21] The transnational hero teams and security organizations featured in the series supported this internationalism, and simultaneously negotiated between the cultural meanings of Britishness and Americanness.[22] In many ways, therefore, Anderson's programmes are examples where difference is recognized and mobilized.

Anderson's puppet series were made with the backing of the television mogul Lew Grade, who ran the ITV company Associated Television (ATV) and whose Incorporated Television Company (ITC) was at the forefront of programme export to the USA.[23] Grade made programmes for the ATV region and also for supply to the national ITV network, thus covering the majority of their costs, but his ITC distribution arm also sold programmes to the US and other overseas markets to increase the programmes' profitability. Action and adventure drama aimed at family audiences, such as *The Adventures of Robin Hood* (1955) led the way in Grade's export sales, and were followed by programmes addressed to adults such as *The Avengers* (1961–9) and *The Prisoner* (1967–8). By the end of the 1960s, ITC had sold Anderson's children's series *Supercar* (1961), *Fireball XL5* (1962), *Stingray* (1964–5), *Thunderbirds* (1965–6), *Captain Scarlet and the Mysterons* (1967–8) and *Joe 90* (1968) to US broadcasters as well as to ITV in Britain and 60 per cent of Anderson's revenue derived from sales to the USA.[24]

Supercar could drive, fly, travel underwater, and go into space, piloted by the series' protagonist Mike Mercury, assisted by its inventors Professor

Popkiss and Doctor Beaker, 10 year-old Jimmy and Mitch the monkey. The series was set in the present day, but Anderson's increasing refinement of special effects led to further futuristic and technological series ideas. *Fireball XL5* (1962) was set in 2063, with Steve Zodiac piloting the eponymous flagship of the World Space Patrol. *Stingray* followed, set in 2064, in which WASP (the World Aquanaut Security Patrol) sent its flagship submarine Stingray to combat the alien technology of the underwater kingdom of Titanica. Titanica's cause was assisted by its terrestrial spy, agent X20. The series was sold by ITC for US syndication, and led to a further commission from Grade for a more ambitious format. *Thunderbirds* was a 50-minute episode series, enabling more complex storylines, more characters and more special effects. It was set in 2065 and featured the Tracy family leading the International Rescue organization from their secret Pacific island base. Each Tracy son piloted one of the vehicles, invented by 'Brains' Hackenbacker, that specialized in air, space, underwater or ground travel and had rescue capabilities. Anderson continued with *Captain Scarlet*, which began with a landing on Mars in 2068 by the Earth security organization Spectrum. Captains Scarlet and Black mistakenly destroyed a Mysteron city, triggering Mysteron revenge attacks against Earth. The Mysterons killed and duplicated Scarlet and Black in indestructible form, Black becoming a Mysteron agent and Scarlet leading Spectrum's operations from Cloudbase, its airborne military and communications centre. The protagonist of Anderson's next series, *Joe 90*, was the adopted nine year-old son of the scientist Professor McClaine. Joe and his father worked for WIN (the World Intelligence Network) and could transfer the brain patterns of selected individuals into Joe's special glasses from the BIG RAT (Brain Impulse Galvanoscope Record And Transfer). Thus Joe was able to undertake secret missions, such as stealing a Russian fighter plane, or driving a World Army tank to prevent a rogue state from activating a military base.

The production organization of these projects was a concrete instance of negotiation between British and American production norms. Each series was shot on film, paralleling the industrial practices developed in Hollywood. Filmed drama was the most common programme form among US imports to the UK, because it comprised the majority of primetime US network programming, but regulation and self-imposed quotas restricted US imports to about 15 per cent of programmes on any one channel. Pressure to sell British programmes to the USA[25] led to making programmes of about 25 or 50 minutes in length, to accommodate commercials on US television. US television had been broadcasting in colour since 1954, so the settings and design of Anderson's programmes were conceived with colour in mind. In Britain, BBC2 did not broadcast in colour until 1967 and BBC1 and ITV only from 1969. *Stingray* was the first British children's series made entirely in colour, because it was designed to appeal to the American market, but had to be screened on British television in black and white, as did each of the later series on first showing. Anderson's programmes resembled American ones in textual structure and production methods and used American or Canadian voice actors, as well as British performers. Many American performers and other media personnel came to Britain following US anti-Communist hysteria in the 1950s, and in the 1960s during the Vietnam War, creating a pool of overseas talent. Canadians could masquerade as Americans for voice work, and did not need work permits because they were Commonwealth citizens. Thus transatlantic voices could be used in Anderson's series to enhance their exportability. Puppet characters were designed to resemble American film actors, or international stars appearing in US films. *Supercar*'s antagonist Masterspy was based on the portly Sydney Greenstreet and his henchman Zarin sounded like Peter Lorre, thus recalling these actors' pairing in *The Maltese Falcon* (1941). In *Stingray*, Troy Tempest was based on the film star James Garner[26] and Captain Scarlet's characterization was expressed by his resemblance to Cary Grant both facially and in his voice.[27] In *Thunderbirds*, Jeff Tracy's sons Scott, Virgil, Alan, Gordon and John were named after the first US astronauts.[28] The transatlantic appeal of Anderson's childrens' series depended not only on their US-influenced production, but also on aesthetic features that signalled US popular cultural icons, and shared international references.

The audience categories discursively constructed for Anderson's programmes comprised separate groups identified as children or as adults, but the programmes were argued to bring these separate demographic groups together. The puppet series were conceived, scheduled and advertised as addressing children, but in the 1960s, British households would normally have only one television set and programmes were watched by mixed adult and child audiences, at least until the 9.00 pm 'watershed' when scheduling designed for adults began. Anderson's puppet adventures were planned to provide possibilities of fantasy and imagination that could entertain both child and adult audiences and bring them together in shared experiences. A promotional brochure for *Joe 90* claimed, for example, that this was 'fantasy adventure that will soon have every boy *and his Dad* playing JOE 90'.[29] The threats of war and environmental degradation in the 1960s, especially Cold War anxieties and speculation about technologization, were expressed in visually spectacular forms in Anderson's series, but also tamed by reassuring resolutions and by the domestic contexts in which they were watched. An associated culture of play and consumption promoted the programmes' imagery, characters and themes, for Anderson's series were supplemented by product ranges including comics, toy vehicles, dressing-up costumes, LP records, confectionary, badges and sheet music.[30] These products, like other toys and playthings, were predominantly purchased for children by adults and thus take part in the process of simultaneously establishing and also blurring the boundaries between adults and children.

Television for children is made by adults, for the group they define as other to themselves inasmuch as childhood and adulthood are distinct yet mutually defining. Children's television, therefore, commonly explores and expresses borderline states and boundaries between one zone and another. Television is both a homely medium watched in domestic space but its programming also connects children to the world beyond and Anderson's series reflected on the familiar and alien and on safety and danger. The format of each series included a base or home that signified safety and familiarity and there were pseudo-parental relationships between figures of authority and child characters or characters in a subordinate power-position. They addressed both child and adult audiences with storylines dealing with the mutually-defining roles of child and adult and with slippages between those roles. The protagonist of *Supercar* was accompanied by a child and an animal, *Fireball* featured the often-inept robot Robbie and the alien Zoonie in child-like roles and the premise of *Joe 90* was that a boy could masquerade as an adult with the aid of technology. John R. Cooke, for example, places Anderson's work, and *Joe 90* in particular, among a group of series in the 1960s and 1970s that 'mediated in their different ways the utopian hopes and dreams of a new Aquarian order of enlightenment and rationality led by the young'.[31] Childhood was a concept that was mobilized as both fragile and in need of protection, but also as a resource for future progress and social betterment.

By the mid-1960s, many adventure series, especially those produced for ITC, were deliberately international in setting and appeal, marketing both British pop culture and also the spatial mobility that British people began to aspire to, as affordable air travel and foreign holidays became accessible to them. In *Thunderbirds*, for example, the Britishness of Lady Penelope and her butler Parker were attractions to both British and US audiences in the context of the American Tracy family who surrounded them, and drew on the cultural meaning of 'cool Britannia'. Sylvia Anderson scripted Lady Penelope with 'not only the daring and panache of a secret agent but also the poise of a cool and beautiful aristocrat' and costume ideas for the puppet were based on Sylvia's interest in the Carnaby Street fashions of 1960s London.[32] The cultural meanings of the USA were contradictory, since consumer capitalism was associated with energy, progress and entrepreneurialism, but also acquisitiveness and the replacement of British imperial power by a new order of American cultural imperialism. The modernity represented by American youth culture and the ideology of opportunity could also entail disrespect for tradition, loss of national specificity and cultural colonization. The plurality of these meanings could be mapped onto the aesthetics of the American-influenced programmes that Anderson made.[33] Both programmes for children and for adults were regarded as both high and low in quality, and as both British and American in character, so they were discussed in conflicting and ambiguous ways. The London *Evening Standard* commented on 30 April 1960, for example, that ITV was a 'dull routine of cowboys, crime, murders, pop singers and half-wit quiz games',[34] condemning ITV programmes associated with the USA.

In Anderson's puppet series, British and American characters work together, usually for transnational organizations. *Supercar* and *Thunderbirds* feature non-state organizations that co-operate with apparently benevolent worldwide authorities. *Fireball XL5* introduced the pan-galactic World Space Patrol, and in *Stingray*, *Captain Scarlet*, and *Joe 90* the main characters work for a transnational government resembling the United Nations. This political context was rarely addressed directly and de-specified storylines so that conflict was represented as being between order and security versus disorder and disruption. The transnational organizations combated specific threats in futuristic settings, thus displacing the storylines from the nation in which the series were produced and facilitating export outside the UK. The domination of the futuristic security organizations by American and British personnel nevertheless signified their leadership of the imagined new world order, supporting the arguments of political elites since the Truman 'Doctrine' of 1947[35] for stable, free-market capitalism in the West and in the British Empire and Commonwealth. Anderson's protagonists help to secure the Free World and work towards a particular version of future global identity.

Looking East: British imports of European animated programmes in the 1970s–1980s

Programmes with hybrid origins across Europe were configured for British television, as a brief discussion of animated series from the 1970s and 1980s will show. Short animated children's programmes have been appealing to UK broadcasters, especially to the BBC where the absence of commercials led to a programme schedule that did not match the half-hour and one-hour slots that characterize US television. In the 1970s, for example, BBC children's programmes frequently had lengths such as 25 or 50 minutes and programmes did not customarily begin and end on the hour or half-hour. On BBC1, 'children's hour' in the 1970s ended at 5. 40 pm when the live broadcast of *Blue Peter* (1958-present) finished, leaving a short interval before the national news. Animation was useful for filling this gap and became very successful as a transitional buffer between children's programmes and the news's address to adults, gaining ratings of up to 10 million viewers. Moreover, as discussed at the beginning of this chapter, public service broadcasting rules created the need for programming categorized as being for children and thus constructing children as an audience group, but comparatively low budgets meant that resources were directed at prestige drama and domestically made animation and imports offered cheaper programmes that could be repeated in successive years.

Children's programming has been regularly exchanged, either in programme packages acquired at annual trade fairs, or under the auspices of the transnational organizations such as the EBU or Eurovision.[36] As I have argued, across the Western world there are shared assumptions that construct children as an audience group. A brief discussion of imported European animated programmes shown in Britain demonstrates some of these assumptions, such as that children enjoy puppetry and animation, that they identify with anthropomorphized animals and child-like characters and that they enjoy songs and music.

Textually, institutionally and economically, the notion of national origin conceals networks of textual borrowing and collaboration between individuals and firms. The best-known example of this hybrid production history and textual form is probably *The Magic Roundabout* (1965–71, 1974–7), in which an unseen adult narrates the adventures of animated child and animal characters who are seen in a magical garden. The series was produced by an émigré British animator, Ivor Wood, who learned his craft when working at the French studios run by Serge Danot. *The Magic Roundabout* was made by Wood and Danot for French broadcast as *Le Manège Enchanté*. It was modified significantly when screened in the different national context of Britain's early evening children's slot, because of the completely different storylines narrated by Brian Thompson that replaced their French predecessors. It is such complex national attributions that demand a more nuanced analysis of their hybrid components and multiple determinations than ascribing them simply to one national television context or to a generalized notion of globalization.

In a public service tradition similar to that of the UK, *Barnaby* was created in France and acquired for broadcast by BBC in Britain in 1973. The series was based on Olga Pouchine's books about the bear Colargol, written in the 1950s and subsequently popularized by Philips LP records in the 1960s.[37] The television adaptation, *Les aventures de Colargol*, was made by the French producer Albert Barillé's company Procidis and Polish animator Tadeuzs Wilkoz at the Semafor animation studios in Lodz, Poland. Music and songs were composed and recorded by French contributors. The programme was thus of hybrid nationality, crossing the Iron Curtain, before the 53 thirteen-minute episodes were translated by the British animation company Q3. *Les aventures de Colargol* was re-edited into 13 episodes and acquired by BBC for the 'Watch with Mother' slot formerly occupied by the French import *Hector's House* (*La Maison de Toutou*, 1965) and was re-titled *Barnaby*. Its stop-motion animation follows the adventures of a little bear who leaves the forest to begin a singing career and travel the world. His voice in the first episode is very discordant, but with the help of the King of the Birds he becomes melodic and is employed in Monsieur Pimoulou's circus. Escaping Pimoulou's cruelty, he goes to the North Pole and lands on the Moon. In Canada the series was renamed *Jeremy the Bear*, but in other European broadcasts of edited versions, in France, Poland, Norway and the Netherlands, for example, the protagonist retained the name of Colargol. The original French version had a story arc following Barnaby's travels and this led to different opening music and a different visual sequence at the beginning of each episode. The British and other edited versions disrupted narrative progression and adopted a consistent opening sequence and title music, turning the programme into a series of free-standing episodes. Like other transnational hybrids discussed later, *Barnaby* was an adaptation of an existing literary text, was produced with experienced Polish collaborators and different national versions significantly changed its form and structure. But the story of the bear's travels of discovery, adopting aspects of the idea of playful education, resonated sufficiently for the programme to be acquired for several national television channels.

Just as the creation of *The Magic Roundabout* was conditioned by the migration of Ivor Wood, *Ludwig* (BBC 1977) was produced by cross-border migration, in this case by the Czech documentary and current affairs director, editor and producer Mirek Lang and his son Peter. Lang migrated with his family to Britain in 1968 because his films were critical of the Soviet-supported Czech regime and Soviet forces had invaded the country that year. Mirek Lang failed to penetrate the British current affairs production culture, so he and Peter made short animations, which drew the attention of the BBC. The BBC commissioned *Ludwig*, a series of five-minute episodes made by the Langs with scripts by the British Jane Tann and Czech émigrée Susan Kodicek.[38] Episodes comprised the adventures of an egg-shaped creature whose exterior resembles the faceted surface of a diamond. Ludwig could be an alien[39] machine rather than a living entity, and he played music and drew pictures using mechanical limbs that emerge from his shell. Each episode began as Ludwig arrived in a forest by descending on a retractable helicopter rotor. He brought various objects out of his shell, most often musical instruments such as a violin or cello, which he then played. Throughout, Ludwig was secretly observed from the bushes, by a man with binoculars, wearing the tweed suit and deerstalker hat of an Edwardian naturalist, or perhaps Sherlock Holmes. The observer's voice provides the narration about Ludwig and the forest creatures' activities, while Ludwig is silent. Ludwig's name alludes to Ludwig van Beethoven, whose music was always used in the series, and is the German composer of the EU's anthem. The UK children's television industry could accommodate Lang as a Cold War émigré, whereas he was unable to work in adult current affairs programming. While the series alludes visually to British tropes (especially in the representation of the ambivalent naturalist-detective observer), its forest animals and setting and its music gesture towards broader European cultural frameworks that render the identification of national specificity problematic and draw from ideas of nature and discovery that again assimilate to playful education.

Semafor studios in Poland, where *Barnaby* was made, also produced *The Moomins*, an animated series based on the Finnish Tove Jansson's books. Though screened in Britain by ITV in 1983, the programme has a very complex international history of institutional collaborations leading to its production and subsequent transmission.[40] Semafor made the series between 1979 and 1982, financed jointly by Film Polski and the Austrian company Jupiter Films. The relatively liberal political regime in Poland after 1956 allowed collaborations between Polish and Western producers and imports of Western (including American) programmes to Poland. Originally there were 78 ten-minute Polish episodes (*Opowiadania Muminków*) based on Jansson's stories, re-edited for German broadcast into 28 half-hour episodes titled *Die Mumins*. These German episodes were edited again by the British company FilmFair into 100 five-minute stories and bought by the English Midland's broadcaster, Central Television, for screening on the ITV channel. The animation method combined painted backgrounds, flat felt cut-outs and three-dimensional puppet characters.[41] The unusual spatiality of the resulting films contributed to the uncanny tone of the series, which matches the current of menace in Jansson's books. The main characters were the Moomin family, resembling hippopotamuses, together with the Snork Maiden, the mouse-like Sniff and the vagabond Snufkin. Because the series was so significantly re-edited to produce its various export versions, the visual sequences were arranged in these versions in quite different ways. Thus quite different narration was added for each version and similarly the music accompanying the visual sequences took different forms and used different instrumentation.

Like *Barnaby*, *The Moomins* was based on an established literary property and its characters crossed national boundaries. But significant changes were made that show how the apparently stable identity of the Moomin fictional world was subject to reworking in ways that suggest how cultural difference operates alongside the transnational relationships of television exchange. The original Finnish publication was followed by a Polish film adaptation produced in collaboration with Austrians and the series came to Britain as a significantly different programme with new voice tracks and music, edited into much shorter episodes with abbreviated storylines. Some of the components of the Moomin brand, such as their name, visual appearance and character relationships persisted though such complex reworking, yet considerable changes were made to music, storyline, narration and the editing of visual sequences.

Hybridity and transnationality

The attribution of nationality is not a simple matter in children's television and this chapter has shown how from the 1960s to the 1980s children's television made by or acquired for British channels integrated national, European and transatlantic programme forms, personnel and business relationships. American television's production methods, personnel and attitudes to the audience have been both adopted and resisted in British television culture. In Gerry Anderson's science fiction series, US television was a model for British production practices and the programmes worked on a new sense of transnational community in futuristic settings. These strategies led to relatively successful attempts to sell British programming to US broadcasters in the 1960s. The boundaries between Britishness and Americanness shifted in dynamic ways, in relation to production, representation and reception. Imported US children's programmes in Britain have often been criticized on the grounds of quality, but Anderson's series were praised for their ability to reconfigure conventional action-adventure programme formats associated with the USA and sell those narrative forms back across the Atlantic. Children's programmes from continental Europe were comparatively cheap to acquire, professionally produced, and revoicing in English enabled them to be assimilated into British television schedules. The strength of the US domestic television industry has been the foundation of its success in exporting children's television as well as programmes for adult audiences, but the tendency to conflate American cultural exports with changes in popular culture in other nations is misleading. British and other European producers of children's television, and their programmes, played a considerable part in the processes of modernization and transnationalization that can also been seen in other cultural sectors such as the arts, fashion and architecture.

The circulation of children's television across borders has drawn on transnational conceptions of what childhood is and what child audiences want and need. That circulation has not been prevented by national regulatory regimes or political boundaries like the Iron Curtain, but of course these factors have operated as constraints. While discourses of national protectionism (usually protection of children from American television culture) have been significant, the child audience has been constructed as a transnational entity that could be addressed and provided for by transnational programming. But paradoxically, programmes originating abroad, or made for overseas markets, contributed to the perceived distinctiveness of children's television in Britain and there are many examples of programmes that are the hybrid products of different national television institutions, production staff and source materials. Similar points can be made about programmes made for adults, and the hybridization of cultures seen in cases of programme and format trading, and the transformation and exchange of programmes made possible by dubbing or subtitling, demonstrate that television accommodates and works with difference as well as homogeneity. These dynamic forces of difference and homogeneity are significant to transnational television in terms of both programmes and the organization of broadcasting institutions, technologies and professional cultures. In children's television, and especially in the animated programmes discussed here, re-voicing of sound tracks while maintaining a version of the original visual material, significantly obviated the 'language barrier' that affects programmes for adults acquired for British television from non-Anglophone producers. The absence of that linguistic barrier in British programmes for export to the USA has facilitated an important if still unequal transnational relationship. Working with largely unstated conceptions of children as a market and an audience category, national and transnational television cultures borrow from and exchange with each other, at the same time as they resist structures, modes of address and representations that are seen as uncomfortably other and unacceptable.

Notes

1. J. Bignell, 'Writing the Child in Media Theory', *Yearbook of English Studies*, 32 (Leeds: MHRA, 2002), pp. 127–39.
2. J. Bignell and A. Fickers (eds), *A European Television History* (New York: Blackwell, 2008), pp. 19–23.
3. See I. Bondejerg *et al.*, 'American Television: Point of Reference or European Nightmare?', in Bignell and Fickers (eds), *A European Television History*, pp. 170–3.
4. P. Scannell, 'Public Service Broadcasting: The History of a Concept', in A. Goodwin and G. Whannel (eds), *Understanding Television* (London: Routledge, 1990), pp. 11–29.
5. D. Lemish, *Children and Television: A Global Perspective* (Oxford: Blackwell, 2007).
6. See J. Wasko, M. Phillips and E. R Meehan (eds), *Dazzled by Disney?: A Global Disney Audiences Project* (London: Leicester University Press, 2001) for an investigation of US and non-US child viewers' conceptions of America and Americanization in relation to Disney.
7. For an outline of the history of British attitudes to imported American programmes, see Paul Rixon, *American Television on British Screens: A Story of Cultural Interaction* (Basingstoke: Palgrave Macmillan, 2006), pp. 32–58.
8. The term 'animation' is used broadly in this chapter to include filmed puppets animated by unseen operators, and drawn, sculpted or painted figures animated by stopping and starting the camera to produce an illusion of motion (stop-frame animation). The chapter does not consider cartoon animation in any detail.
9. J. Sinclair, E. Jacka and S. Cunningham, 'New Patterns in Global Television', in P. Marris and S. Thornham (eds), *The Media Reader* (Edinburgh: Edinburgh University Press, 1999), p. 173.

10. H. Schiller, *Mass Communications and American Empire* (New York: Augustus M. Kelly, 1969); H. Schiller, *Communication and Cultural Domination* (New York: M. E. Sharpe, 1976).
11. N. Postman, *The Disappearance of Childhood* (New York: Vintage, 1983).
12. J. Bourdon, 'Unhappy Engineers of the European Soul: The EBU and the Woes of Pan-European Television', *International Gazette of Communication* 69: 3, 2007, 263–80.
13. A more developed argument about the programmes discussed in this section can be found in J. Bignell, 'Migration, Translation and Hybridity: European Animation on British Television', *Journal of British Cinema and Television*, forthcoming 2011.
14. For a recent example of an organized defence of children's television in Britain against imports and reduced television provision for children, see the 'Memorandum from the Save Kids' TV Campaign to the Culture, Media & Sport Parliamentary Select Committee Regarding Public Service Media Content Inquiry', 18 January 2007, available at http://www.parliament.the-stationery-office.co.uk/pa/ld200910/ldselect/ldcomuni/37/37ii/pdf
15. Cultural proximity denotes the relative closeness or distance between different national or regional cultures, seen as a determinant of whether cultural products such as television programmes are readily assimilated and enjoyed by audiences in a different culture from the one that originated them.
16. The term re-voicing is used throughout to indicate the integration of new voice narration and character dialogue with a visual image track. Re-voicing is carried out after the visual sequences have been recorded, and replaces an original voice track that had been combined with them.
17. Domestic television sets in Europe and the USA (and elsewhere) produce pictures by means of a scanning beam of a certain number of horizontal lines, and the number of scanning lines varies widely. See A. Fickers, 'National Barriers for an *Imag(e)ined* European Community: The Technological Frames of Postwar Television Development in Europe', in J. Hojberg and H. Sondergard (eds), *European Film and Media Culture* (Copenhagen: Museum Tusculum Press and University of Copenhagen, 2006), pp. 15–36.
18. The British tradition is exemplified by Gordon Murray's *Camberwick Green* (1966) and its spin-offs *Trumpton* (1967) and *Chigley* (1969), the work of Cosgrove Hall on *Danger Mouse* (1981–92) and the Australian émigré Bob Godfrey on *Roobarb and Custard* (1974) and *Henry's Cat* (1983).
19. This chapter refers to Gerry Anderson as the creator of the programmes, to avoid complex explanation. The situation was much more complex; Gerry was mainly responsible for company management and planning special effects filming and his wife Sylvia for character origination and directing actors, while numerous collaborators worked on scripts and visual design, for example, and distinctive music for his series was composed by Barry Gray.
20. Videotape was used in television production after its invention in 1958, but in Britain it was not commonly used until the early1960s. Production on film was suited to programmes that used special effects or shooting in outside locations, but it was costly and children's programmes would be made

on videotape in enclosed studios wherever possible. Anderson's use of film is thus a significant choice.

21. Syndication refers to programmes being sold to a regional US television broadcaster for screening in that region. Sale to the national US networks (ABC, CBS and NBC) was much more lucrative.

22. The discussion of Anderson's programmes in this section is developed in more detail in J. Bignell, '"Anything Can Happen in the Next Half-Hour": Gerry Anderson's Transnational Science Fiction', in J. Leggott and T. Hochscherf (eds), *British Science Fiction in Film and Television* (Jefferson: McFarland, in press 2011).

23. For a brief account of Grade's commissioning of Anderson's programmes, see J. Bignell, 'And the Rest is History: Lew Grade, Creation Narratives and Television Historiography', in C. Johnson and R. Turnock (eds), *ITV Cultures: Independent Television Over Fifty Years* (Buckingham: Open University Press, 2005), pp. 57–70.

24. R. Sellers, *Cult TV: The Golden Age of ITC* (London: Plexus, 2006), p. 92.

25. This was a period in which export was crucial to British economic viability. Lew Grade was given Queen's Awards for Export in 1967 and 1969 for his success in television trading, in which the programmes discussed here were a part.

26. Sellers, *Cult TV*, pp. 89–90.

27. Captain Scarlet's voice was provided by the British actor Francis Matthews. Cary Grant was born in Britain, and his 'cool' and sophisticated persona in Hollywood films is connected to his émigré status.

28. S. Archer and S. Nicholls, *Gerry Anderson: The Authorised Biography* (London: Legend, 1996), p. 86.

29. Sellers, *Cult TV*, p. 113, emphasis in the original.

30. S. Anderson, *My FAB Years* (Neshannock, PA: Hermes, 2007), pp. 84–9.

31. J. R. Cooke, 'The Age of Aquarius: Utopia and Anti-Utopia in Late 1960s and Early 1970s British Science Fiction Television', in J. Cooke and P. Wright (eds), *British Science Fiction Television: A Hitchhiker's Guide* (London and New York: I. B. Tauris, 2006), p. 110.

32. Anderson, *My FAB Years*, p. 26, p. 30.

33. Similar negotiations with ideas of national identity were evident in ITC's live action series; see S. Neale, 'Transatlantic Ventures and *Robin Hood*', in Johnson and Turnock (eds), *ITV Cultures*, pp. 73–87.

34. Quoted in B. Sendall, *Independent Television in Britain*, vol. 1, *Origin and Foundation, 1946-62* (Basingstoke and New York: Macmillan, 1982), p. 371.

35. J. Kolko and G. Kolko, *The Limits of Power: The World and United States Foreign Policy, 1945–1954* (New York: Harper & Row, 1972).

36. On the institutional arrangements for programme sales, including international trade fairs, see J. Steemers, *Selling Television: British Television in the Global Marketplace* (London: BFI, 2004) and T. Havens, *Global Television Marketplace* (London: BFI, 2006).

37. S. Sheridan, *The A-Z of Classic Children's Television* (London: Reynolds & Hearn, 2004), pp. 52–3.

38. Sheridan, *The A-Z of Classic Children's Television*, pp. 149–51.

39. While protagonists in children's series are most often children, animals or adults in child-like roles, figuring the protagonist as an alien other is not

uncommon, for example in the pre-school series *Teletubbies*; see J. Bignell, 'Familiar Aliens: *Teletubbies* and Postmodern Childhood', *Screen* 46: 3, 2005, 373–88.

40. Sheridan, *The A-Z of Classic Children's Television*, pp. 162–9.
41. Because of the use of mixed two-dimensional and three-dimensional animation techniques using felt cut-outs, this series is sometimes referred to as 'the fuzzy-felt Moomins' to distinguish it from two earlier Japanese cartoon versions (1969, 1972) and a later Japanese cartoon version (1990) that was acquired for broadcast in the UK.

10
Out with Romany: Simulating the Natural in BBC Radio's Children's Hour 1932–1943

Simon Flynn

Natural History, or more broadly broadcasts related to 'nature' and the environment, was a constant thread throughout BBC radio's *Children's Hour* programme (1922–64). Internal Policy documents stressed the importance of inculcating in children the idea that they should be kind to animals and conserve the natural environment.[1] Hence, although *Children's Hour* adopted a mixed programming fare (stories, serials, music, poetry, competitions and 'Talks'), it was notable how many of the 'Talks' were on matters of 'natural history' and also how popular they seemed to have been (if the programme's twice yearly listeners' polls are anything to go by). Key figures who broadcast nationally on natural history matters would include: Romany (the Rev. George Bramwell Evens's *Out with Romany* broadcasts 1932–43), the Zoo Man (David Seth-Smith 1934–45), The Farmer (John Morgan c.1930s) and Nomad (Norman Ellison's *Wandering with Nomad* from 1945).[2]

In this chapter I will concentrate on perhaps the most popular of these broadcasters, George Bramwell Evens, who broadcast under the pseudonym 'Romany'. Although Bramwell Evens wrote many successful books under this name,[3] in this chapter I will concentrate specifically on his radio series, *Out with Romany* and, in particular, explore the way his broadcasts were acclaimed for their spontaneity and its participants' 'naturalness'. But such claims were thrown into relief when it was revealed that what seemed 'natural' in the programme was at every turn actually a product of studio-bound ingenuity. I will then examine the subsequent response to this revelation and the way that claims that the audience had been in some sense 'duped' or 'hoaxed' were especially shocking given the way the programme so clearly brought together the natural world, an idea of the child in nature and the child as natural.[4] Additionally, these discourses of the child and the natural were further mobilized by their relationship to the BBC's own internal policies about the need to be honest and truthful to its audience especially if part of that audience were children.

The Listener's Out with Romany reviews

In June 1943 *The Listener*'s Radio Drama critic, Herbert Farjeon (1887– 1945), brother of the children's poet and author Eleanor Farjeon, finished his column with praise for the *Children's Hour* radio programme *Out with Romany* in which the natural history writer and broadcaster 'Romany' went on one of his country rambles accompanied by two 'girls', Muriel and Doris, and his dog, Raq. Farjeon wrote:

> But Tuesday! I have omitted Tuesday only because 'Out with Romany', being supreme, must be separately praised. I can't, to be plain, praise it enough. Romany himself, conducting two little girls around the farmyard and the hedgerows, has much of the good, plain approach of Mr Middleton, with a fine birdlike eye for detail all his own. He alone would be good enough. But the two little girls! Who are these vocal geniuses? Have the voices of two children with their spontaneous wonderments, their unemphasised apprehensions, their quick, evanescent sympathies, their broken exclamations, unfinished sentences, half- laughs, interrupted interruptions, ever been, and will they ever be, more perfectly presented? To hear them getting on a horse, or asking 'Is that really true?' or just saying 'Oh' is childhood back again....The first Tuesday in every month is Romany's day. Remember that if you want a true taste of 'Holidays at Home'. Possibly, after my panegyric, you will be a little disappointed – that is the worst of praise – but you will be wrong. Here, I would hazard, is the B.B.C's best creation.[5]

Farjeon's commentary starts with praise for Romany, likening his 'plain' approach to that of Middleton (the BBC's gardening expert, C. H. Middleton). The word 'plain' here might be read as meaning 'clarity of expression' but has, of course, a number of other meanings: 'open in behaviour, free from evasion or subterfuge', and, most pertinent for this chapter, 'free from duplicity'. Moving beyond the comparison with Middleton, Farjeon suggests that Romany has a fine 'birdlike eye for detail all his own'. Literally, Romany's observations themselves are analogous with the 'natural'. Yet, what Farjeon really focuses on here are the voices of the 'two little girls'. His praise for the 'little girls' seems to suggest that as much as he knows they are 'vocal geniuses' and, hence, there is something being 'performed' here, their 'act' seems to correspond uncannily with his own idea of the child. In their voices he hears a confirmation of a construction of childhood which seems to derive from a Romantic notion of the child. The rhetorical question that he uses to structure his praise notably forecloses the possibility of disagreement. But such closure seems to be pre-requisite for the fantasy of a return to childhood that Farjeon suggests he experiences when listening to the 'two little girls'. But who is being addressed here? Who read *The Listener* in the early 1940s? Children? Unlikely. No, this is one adult writing to others telling them of his discovery of a programme which he believes captures the texture of childhood so well that it can effectively transport one back to one's childhood. The children are merely the vehicle through which adult listeners can re-visit their youthful selves.

Given the extravagance of Farjeon's praise for the series – 'Here, I would hazard, is the B.B.C.'s best creation' (Farjeon as *The Listener*'s radio critic – the BBC's own in-house magazine – is describing it as the 'BBC's' not simply *Children's Hour*'s 'best creation'), his final comments take on a slightly adversarial tone. He seems concerned that the excessive praise he has lavished on the programme may actually give adult listeners unrealistic expectations of it, hence his suggestion that, if they should they feel that programme doesn't deliver them back to their childhood as promised, the fault will lie with them and not the broadcast itself.

Such was Farjeon's enthusiasm for the series that a couple of months later, he returned to it in a piece entitled 'Spontaneity':

> Two months ago I wrote in high praise (but praise no higher than deserved) of Romany and the two child voices heard on First Tuesdays in the Children's Hour. On the first Tuesday of the present month I listened to them again, and was completely entranced. True, Romany might, perhaps, stress a little less the beauty of this or that miracle of Nature; but then we should miss the children chiming in with that over-quick accord which is half genuine appreciation and half reflex good manners blended with respect for age and a desire to be older. It is not only that the performance of these children is perfection, but that their dialogue is written with an instinctive and most sympathetic simplicity: as when Romany explains some natural phenomenon, and Muriel murmurs, 'I never thought of that', or when,

entering another field, Doris turns and exclaims, 'I didn't know you could see the farm from here'. There speaks a child, or no child ever spoke at all. Immediately, you are back again on one of your own early summer holidays, when the ball of your foot responded more sensitively to the spring of the turf, your brow more sensitively met the breeze.[6]

This second review continues in a similar vein to the first, except that Farjeon gently chides Romany's tendency to stress 'the beauty of this or that miracle of Nature'. But such criticism has to be tempered because, as we know, it is only through Romany that Farjeon hears the voices of the children. Again, as in the first review, the 'voices' are described as objects of adult desire and phantasy. Here though, there are subtle changes evident in the words Farjeon chooses to use. When listening to the programme he hears 'two child voices' *not* two children (or 'two little girls' as in the first review). The term 'children' is used later in the passage. Furthermore, the naturalization of the child intimated in the first review gives way to a clearer positioning of the voices as 'perform-ance' and to the suggestion that their success must be partly attributable not only to 'performance' but also to the dialogue that has been written for them. Although notably, whoever writes the dialogue – presumably an adult – is still seen to possess 'an instinctive and most sympathetic simplicity'.[7] Such is the skill with which the dialogue is written that it seems to perfectly coincide with Farjeon's idea of the child. So much so, that he declares, 'There speaks a child, or no child ever spoke at all.' He is commending the programme's construction of childhood because he suggests that it confirms his own idea of childhood. Furthermore, the proof of its brilliance is once again its ability to transport him or his reader 'back again on one of your own early summer holidays'.

The final paragraph in that week's column on radio broadcasts returned to the subject of *Out with Romany*:

But to my confession. The spontaneity in those Romany rambles of the children's interjections and interruptions, their overlappings of speech, their half-completion of sentences, is so faultless in timing that, when I wrote of them two months ago, only lack of space saved me from remarking that here must be a producer of real genius and of the most exacting standards, and that the rehearsals must be rig-orous and unremitting indeed to achieve such faultless results. And now I have learned that the two little girls attend no rehearsals at all. The performance you hear is the first-run through! The players are accustomed to each other, and that suffices. It must have been some similar factor that gave such spontaneity and life to the commedia dell'arte... A line of development is suggested which might be worth following up. The impromptu actor might acquire fresh vitality. A chancey adventure maybe, as producers may well point out; but there is no progress without experiment – and you can always scrap a record.[8]

Now Farjeon praises the programme still further because he has discovered that far from being meticulously rehearsed, 'the two little girls attend no rehearsals at all. The performance you hear is the first run-through!'. There are a number of points to make here. First, of course, the starting assumption is worth considering – if children who play children on radio have to rehearse to get it right what does this say about the 'nature' of childhood? Second, Farjeon's discovery of the 'spontaneity' of their performances – they are merely the 'first-run through', insinuates an essentialist notion of childhood which is then, in turn, negated by the re-theatricalization implied in the comparison with the *Commedia dell'arte*.

A week later, a tiny paragraph in *Radio Times* noted what a versatile broadcaster Doris Gambell was. An accomplished singer, she could tackle anything from high opera or variety to *The Children's Hour* with 'apparently equal ease'. In relation to her work for children, the column ended by noting that it was as 'Doris who always accompanies Muriel when "Out with Romany" in country lanes and fields'.[9] So, Doris wasn't a child at all, but an adult pretending to be one. This revelation, combined with Farjeon's ecstatic praise, prompted one listener to write into *Radio Times* the following week. The letter was printed under the title 'Hoax?' It read:

A PARAGRAPH in the RADIO TIMES of August 20, reveals that the two 'children' featured in 'Out with Romany' are not children at all, but adults, one of them a well-known singer. The dramatic critic of *The Listener* has recently been filling his column with raptures about the fresh, spontaneous voices of these 'children', so natural and unrehearsed, etc., etc.- Evidently, he and listeners in general, have been victims of a hoax which seems to go beyond what is permissible in broadcasting –[10]

This response, finishing with its condemnation that listeners had been 'victims of a hoax which seems to go beyond what is permissible in

broadcasting', as I will discuss later, says a great deal about this particular listener's expectations of the BBC, the BBC's children's programming and possibly the natural history genre too. Farjeon replied to this
criticism in the next edition of *The Listener*, writing:

> Shortly after my first eulogy of the acting of Doris and Muriel, the
> two little girls in this Children's Hour series, I received an anony-
> mous postcard stating that these parts were not played by little girls
> 'at all' but by grown-ups, and condemning the proceeding, in conse-
> quence, as a swindle.[11]

He then went on to quote the Brighton listener's charge, following it
with a denial that the programme counted as a hoax. He pointed out
that *Out with Romany* wasn't a hoax because

> the B.B.C. has never announced that the parts of Doris and Muriel are
> played by little girls. Is it then a hoax that the part of a little girl should
> not be played by a little girl? Is it a hoax that the part of Henry V
> should not be played by Henry V? Is Romany a fraud if he wasn't chris-
> tened Romany? And should not 'raptures about the fresh, spontaneous
> voices of these "children"', far from being diminished, be intensified
> by the discovery that it's all done by art and not by nature?[12]

Here the 'Romany broadcasts' are being re-framed discursively as the
product of art not nature, and a hoax is only a hoax if it has been
intentionally designed to mislead.[13] Farjeon as a dramatic critic for one
of the BBC's own publications, not surprisingly, went on to defend the
Corporation against any charge of 'misleading the public in this matter', writing:

> The B.B.C. is in no way guilty of misleading its public in this mat-
> ter; and it should be commended for its wisdom in preserving the
> anonymity of the performers in question hitherto. To those now
> 'in the know', they will never be quite the same again. Where
> illusion is the object, anonymity is invaluable. Let us have more
> of it.[14]

Here Farjeon cleverly turns the charge of hoaxing on its head by suggesting that the anonymity of the actors contributes to the programme's
sustaining of the illusion of the real. In doing this, Farjeon is now constructing it as the product of illusionism.

But these claims did not stop. Indeed, the controversy about the broadcasts eventually prompted Robert W. Reid, in a short article on the programme for *Radio Times*, to reveal one or two other secrets. Under two pictures of the suitably mature looking Muriel Levy and Doris Gambell, Reid wrote:

> There was lately a stirring in the nurseries and around the family tea-tables – and in the columns of the *RADIO TIMES* and *The Listener*, too. The question was: when is a hoax not a hoax?
>
> The thing really started twelve years ago when Romany and Muriel and Doris – and Raq – began their country walks and put over such a convincing show that you could almost smell the cattle-byre, the hedgerows, and the meadows as you sat listening at home – an effect largely due, of course, to the brilliant informality of Romany, Doris, and Muriel. They sounded – and still sound – like a very nice country uncle and a couple of his favourite schoolgirl nieces enjoying the great outdoors before going home to have muffins for tea.
>
> Then a listener made the horrifying discovery that Muriel and Doris are grown-ups and that *ipso facto* the schoolgirl part of the show must be a hoax. As a matter of fact, 'Out with Romany' has never made any pretence about the business. It was never suggested that two schoolgirls were taking part.[15]

But having defended the programme from this accusation of fakery, Reid had other disclosures to make:

> So having disposed of the hoax, the least we can do now is to tell you something of the behind-the-scenes story of the programme.
>
> In the first place, all those country rambles take place in a studio at the BBC's Northern headquarters. Romany comes up from his house in Cheshire or from his country wanderings with Raq, his grey and black cocker spaniel, at his heels. Usually Raq follows the broadcast with a mournful eye and an occasional snuffle. In the main, however, he is prepared to sit back on his haunches and leave matters to a nicely modulated gramophone record.
>
> As for Romany, Muriel, and Doris, 'brilliant informality' perhaps implies design, whereas much of that informality is a sheer accident. Romany's distracting habit of ignoring the 'mike' and wandering about achieves a marvellous effect of strolling away and coming back with another titbit of field gossip. Muriel and Doris are never conscious of trying to imitate children's voices. Much of that eager

curiosity with which they examine a flower or a plant is due to Romany's habit of unexpectedly producing that particular flower or plant from the depths of his jacket pocket and letting the girls actually see what they are talking about![16]

So there was no *Out with Romany*, more a case of 'in' with Romany. Furthermore, Romany didn't live in a caravan but in a house in Cheshire and his dog, Raq, was sometimes a recording or sometimes the sound engineer, Jack Hollinshead, imitating him.[17] These further revelations received a mixed response from correspondents in *Radio Times*. One listener wrote that far from feeling 'hoaxed', the fact that the Romany broadcasts do not actually take place out of doors, increased their admiration for the programme's 'realistic results'. Another, however, felt that the programme's demystification robbed her of its pleasure. A Mrs M. Carter of Chesterfield wrote, 'Why was the article on Romany's broadcast ever published? Why were we not allowed to go on enjoying those country rambles? For me, it is "goodbye" to one of my favourite programmes.'[18]

Finally the correspondence on this subject ended with a letter to *Radio Times* from Nan Macdonald, the programme's producer and the Organizer of *Children's Hour* in the North Region. She wrote:

> These programmes are broadcast all the year round at the same time of day, i.e. 5-30 pm., and in winter takes place *after dark*. Most listeners, therefore, if they thought about it, must have realised they were studio productions. But just as when we listen to Romeo and Juliet being broadcast, we allow ourselves to be carried away by the tragedy of the young lovers, and don't constantly remind ourselves that Juliet is not shut up in a tomb, but is merely Peggy Ashcroft standing in the studio reading from a script, so with the Romany programmes, the important thing is not where they are done, nor how they are done, but the atmosphere created by Romany and his friends. As these programmes will continue to be put on in exactly the same way as they have been for the last twenty years, we hope they will still carry an atmosphere of the countryside with them, and continue to bring enjoyment to many millions of listeners.[19]

Here Macdonald denies that any deception has gone on, but instead suggests that listeners must have been 'unthinking' or naive if they actually thought that the broadcasts happened out of doors. Furthermore, as with Farjeon's earlier defence, the programme is subtly re-framed as fictional rather than factual. Listeners must now suspend their disbelief. Sadly, MacDonald's hope for the programme would not be fulfilled because within a week of the publication of this letter, Romany died suddenly.[20]

But beyond this generic re-framing of the programme in the light of the knowledge that it was all studio based, it is worth pausing here to think about what, for example, might have caused the listener from Brighton to claim it 'seemed to go beyond what is permissible in broadcasting'. What does such a comment say about expectations of Public Service Broadcasting and broadcasting for Children?

The BBC – public service broadcasting

As Paddy Scannell and David Cardiff note, the BBC 'was animated from the beginning by a high sense of moral purpose which it realised in giving an educational and cultural lead to its listening public'.[21] John Reith, the first Director General of the BBC, wrote in his book *Broadcast Over Britain* (1924), 'Our responsibility is to carry into the greatest possible number of homes everything that is best in every human department of knowledge, endeavour and achievement, and to avoid the things which are, or may be, hurtful.'[22]

An important part of this agenda was broadcasting *to* children. It is notable that a children's programme (what we would later know as *Children's Hour*) was established very early on. The importance of such programming was that Reith believed that broadcasting was concerned with the construction of citizens. Additionally, the BBC had, of course, a financial interest in these citizens. Publicity material for *Children's Hour* often described child listeners as the 'licence holders of the future'.

As to how children's broadcasting should operate, Reith saw it as:

> to provide an hour of clean, wholesome humour, some light music and a judicious sprinkling of information attractively conveyed. Children – like grown-ups – hate to feel that they are being 'educated' ...[23]

This attitude meant that as much as the *Children's Hour* was seen as mainly for recreation and not for 'instruction or moral improvement',[24] at the same time the programme's Standing Instructions noted:

> if the organisers of the Children's Hour keep in mind the creation of the atmosphere of a good home and the presentation of real beauty in song, story, music and poetry on a plane attractive to the young,

they will inevitably, without self conscious efforts, raise the standard of culture in their young listeners, and the result will be educative in the best sense.[25]

But if these were the general principles of broadcasting for children, how should they be carried out in practice?

Over the years, there were a number of policy documents and published discussions that focused on how to address the child audience. These covered matters such as not talking down to the audience or finishing stories with a moral through to Post-War documents such as 'Entertaining the Young Listener' in the *BBC Quarterly* (1946–8) which stressed the sensitivity but also intelligence of child listeners. Notably, the latter article included the injunction, '... "you cannot – not you *must* not – cheat a child" should be foremost in the minds of all those who have regular contact with the younger generation, in the sphere of entertainment as in that of education.'[26] Here, prohibition ('cannot') replaces obligation ('*must* not'). As much as this statement should be 'foremost in the minds of those who have regular contact with the younger generation', one cannot help but read this emphasis on 'you' as also a regulatory address to parents and other adults that might be reading the *BBC Quarterly*. Such a statement also underlines a certain institutional ethics concerned with how broadcasters should address/ approach broadcasting to children.[27]

With this in mind I would like to return to *Out with Romany*, a programme in which some sort of cheating or deception seemed to be going on. Was it acceptable to pretend to be broadcasting from outside when you were in fact in the studio? The answer is provided by an internal memo from Derek McCulloch, the *Children's Hour* Organiser, to the North Region's *Children's Hour* in July 1937 (six years before the controversy over *Out with Romany*). In the memo, McCulloch complained about a feature programme on the subject of Hadrian's Wall, entitled 'The Roman Wall' presented by Joan Littlewood. This was a broadcast that passed itself off as an outside broadcast but which was in fact entirely studio-bound. In the memo, McCulloch wrote:

In the first place I think it is utterly wrong to convey the impression to listeners – and particularly to children – that they are listening to an O.B. [outside broadcast] when it is in fact quite clear that the performance is a studio one, i.e., in this case Hadrian's Wall purporting to be an O.B.[28]

Now it may be that the historical matter of this particular programme contributed to McCulloch's ire, but I think the more prominent issue here is the belief that it is wrong to deceive listeners that you are broadcasting outside when in fact you never left the studio – but this is especially bad, if you are broadcasting to children.

From this, I want to suggest *Children's Hour* was informed by a discourse of honesty to its child listeners and so deception must be condemned. But isn't all broadcasting about 'illusionism', a word which can be defined as 'a false belief' or – more problematically for a sound medium – 'of deceptive appearance'? Indeed, in radio, it is worth remembering that even what we 'read' discursively as 'factual' broadcasts rely on both the listener's interpretation of words and sounds as well as a series of techniques – sound montage/close miking which do not reflect so much as *constitute* the 'real'. From this we might ask, what is the difference between illusionism and deception?

There is, however, a third factor which follows from this prohibition on deceiving the child – a certain construction of the child as associated with innocence and moral purity. This is a notion of the child that is emphasized by the connections that are made between the 'child' and the 'natural'. Such a discourse, I would argue, constituted *Children's Hour* policy towards its child listeners. This discourse of the 'natural child' was also actively staged in the programme, *Out with Romany*. Indeed, the shock that surrounded the revelation that the 'Romany' broadcasts did not take place outside (not to mention the issue of Romany's 'child companions') was no doubt felt so strongly because the programme seemed to exemplify a celebration of the child in nature. *Out with Romany* was a programme that revelled in the 'natural' and effectively denied artifice or simulation. It was a programme that seemed to draw on Romantic discourses of the child. In thinking about this construction, it is instructive to consider the 'Romany' broadcasts in relation to one of the founding texts of Romanticism, Jean-Jacques Rousseau's *Emile* (1762).

Romany and Rousseau

'Romany' was the pseudonym of the Methodist minister George Bramwell Evens (1884–1943), a man of gypsy heritage. After contributing natural history columns to various northern newspapers, a chance meeting led to him being asked to audition for the Manchester *Children's Hour*. Not wanting to be announced as Uncle Bramwell, nor the Reverend Bramwell Evens, he decided to broadcast under the name

'Romany'. Broadcasting initially only to the Northern Region, he contributed a couple of short nature stories which were interspersed with the usual *Children's Hour* fare of songs and back chat from the Aunties and Uncles.

Gradually, however, Bramwell Evens's spot was enlarged and by the end of 1933 he was contributing a forty-five minute script that took the form of a ramble in the country usually accompanied by Muriel and Doris. Bramwell Evens's widow, Eunice, in her posthumous biography of her husband, provides a useful description of the programme when she writes:

> To describe what they saw on these walks to those who did not hear them is not easy, for though on paper the dialogue looked absurdly simple, it was their personalities which brought the scenes to life. The children are most likely to remember the exciting adventures as they waded the river to rescue the otters, climbed the belfry tower to watch the rooks or followed the tracks of the trapped badger, but others will recall with pleasure the natural way in which Romany would comment on the most commonplace things as they sauntered along. He would show them the beauty of the golden crops swaying in the breeze, the charm of a passing Admiral butterfly, the dew sparkling on the delicate tracery of a spider's web, the bronze and gold leaves of the shapely beech tree, the gossamer wings of a green dragon-fly, and the vividness of the red berries on the mountain ash. All this was interspersed with useful information given in such a delightful and such an amusing way that the child listener was not conscious that he was learning anything.[29]

This gives a flavour of the series, but it also demonstrates the way Romany exemplified a pedagogical discourse which can be traced back at least to Rousseau's programme for the education of children outlined in *Emile*.

Famously, in *Emile*, Rousseau constructs the child as an uncontaminated, spontaneous figure. He recommends that the child learn from direct experience in the natural environment (away from the contamination of culture). In Book II of *Emile*, Rousseau writes, 'Nature, not man, is his schoolmaster, and he learns all the quicker because he is not aware that he has any lesson to learn.'[30] *Out with Romany* in which two 'children' (I will qualify this category again later) accompany Romany on a nature ramble is similarly predicated on the appeal to some sort of spontaneous education by nature. Muriel and Doris often emphasize how they have attained 'knowledge' simply from 'walking'.

As for the child listener, if we take Muriel and Doris as figures with which the child is invited to identify (I stress 'invited'; we don't know how an 'actual child', whatever and whoever that would be, would respond to the programme), we could say a similar process of invisible 'education' happens. Here Romany's role and the radio as an instrument of education is typically disavowed. As Eunice Evens noted about the broadcasts, they were 'interspersed with useful information given in such a delightful and such an amusing way that the child listener was not conscious that he was learning anything'.[31]

Out with Romany can be aligned with Rousseau's pedagogy in a number of other respects too. Linguistically, for example, Romany's ideas are also reminiscent of Rousseau: in *Emile*, Rousseau makes much of the idea that children should experience objects not language, and this mistrust of language can be seen in Romany's preference for plain speaking. Eunice Evens notes that her husband valued 'honesty and reticence of speech that marks the true countryman – no fulsomeness, no superlatives, no exaggerations, no striving for effect'.[32] Similarly, the obituary for Romany printed in the *Yorkshire Post* in 1943 noted, 'Romany's great achievement was that he took his listeners away from the loudspeaker into the real lanes and fields and woods which never relied on word-painting for their existence.'[33] In this description, Romany is being aligned with 'plain speaking', implying a distrust perhaps also of the figurative – of 'word painting', and this again places him firmly in the philosophical tradition going back to Rousseau.

As Jacqueline Rose has pointed out, Rousseau's philosophy is one in which an attempt is made to 'retrieve a form of language or expression which would be uncontaminated by the intrusion of the verbal sign'.[34] Recognizing that there is no natural relation between the linguistic sign and the thing to which it refers, Rousseau, Rose writes, 'wish[ed] to by-pass this aspect of language *through* the child ... in the desire for some perfect or uncontaminated form of expression'.[35] Language, Rousseau believed, had gradually become abstract and has lost touch with the object or sentiment which it was originally intended to express. As Rose notes, '[i]n *Emile*, therefore, the child is being asked not only to retrieve a lost state of nature, but also to take language back to its pure and uncontaminated source in the objects of the immediate world.'[36]

Out with Romany evinces a similar attitude towards language in two ways. First, Romany's natural history seeks to avoid any sense of a technical, Latinate language. One example will suffice: in a 1940 episode

Doris spots some snap dragons to which Romany replies 'I'm glad you didn't call them antirrhinums. I hate big names for flowers, don't you?'. The 'big names' here suggest a more abstract language away from the natural. Second, a similar case can be made for the use of words taken from the Romani language that were used in the series, including words and phrases such as: Cushto Jukkal (good dog), Cushto Gry (good horse), Shuski/Shoshoi meaning rabbit, Canengro for hare, and Hotchi for Hedgehog. Significantly, most of these words are mainly nouns of animals or instructions to animals. They have an exotic, incantatory quality which fully exploits the aural medium and they can be seen as connoting a natural 'undegenerate' language. I am not suggesting there is some essential correlation between the Romani language culture and the 'natural'.[37] But, in *Out with Romany*, I would suggest, the use of these words does make such a link. So too does the knowledge that the British gypsy language is a primarily oral language. Furthermore, they are shown to be imbued with a transparency and 'presence' which English lacks. In one episode in 1937 Doris bemoans the fact that she has forgotten some of the Gypsy words, but she then says 'but I know what they mean when Romany uses them'. This suggests that 'meaning' is somehow considered to be immanent within them. These British gypsy words could also be seen as establishing a sort of code between broadcaster and listener. It is notable that at intervals throughout the years when *Out with Romany* was broadcast, Romany or Muriel and Doris would remind listeners of the meanings of the words.

A last point to make here concerns the use of gypsy culture in the series. *Out with Romany* is unusual in its positive treatment of the figure of the gypsy. Indeed, in both literature for children and literature about childhood from George Eliot to Enid Blyton and the US Magazine fiction such as *The Motor Girls Through New England*, gypsies tend to be constructed as a dangerous 'racial' other only too keen to lead children astray. Here though the racial 'other' is employed for his knowledge of the countryside – a knowledge which from a Romantic perspective might be seen as redemptive for the urban children. Indeed, Romany's broadcasts throughout the 1930s could be seen as the vanguard of the interest in the countryside. A 'movement' which, as David Matless has shown, would take on increased significance with the coming of WWII and the evacuation of children to the countryside.[38]

Another way in which the language of a series set out to suggest the 'natural' and the 'authentic' was in its use of regional accents, and Bramwell Evens's conscious selection of amateurs – non-actors who had appropriate accents.[39] (This pre-dated the North broadcaster Wilfred

Pickles's brief news reading job.) These included a woman from his church concerts and a BBC Manchester commissioner. As Eunice Evens observed, her husband was looking for:

> ordinary working-class people who had never stood in front of the microphone...his object was to preserve the illusionary character of the walks by not introducing those whose voices were well known to listeners, and to use simple, unsophisticated people as much like his own village friends as possible.[40]

Therefore, in everything we have seen so far, I am suggesting that the shock caused by the disclosure of artifice in *Out with Romany* can be seen as a reaction to the way the programme relentlessly deployed discourses of the 'natural' and the 'authentic'.

Constructing the real on radio

I now want to consider the artificiality of the programme and some of the strategies used to construct realism and whether they could be said to have misled its listeners. Steven Connor, writing on ventriloquism, notes that, 'the radio ventriloquist does what radio itself does: conjuring with sound a visible scenario in which we consent to be duped'.[41] Perhaps the controversy about the 'Romany' broadcasts is whether listeners *did* consent to be duped along with the status of such duplicity in broadcasting for children. Nan Macdonald, Herbert Farjeon and Eunice Evens all claimed that there was never any suggestion that the programme actually took place out of doors. An analysis of the scripts, however, suggests something different. In fact, there were two methods that were used to suggest that it was an 'outside broadcast'. First, the pre-1939 programmes generally started with an introduction from Muriel and Doris in the Manchester studio.

This pre-amble frequently consisted of prosaic but quotidian conversation between the pair as to whether to wear waterproofs. The very ordinariness of these comments, contributed to the reality-effect that the programme was seeking to construct.

Such an introduction also functioned to set up a relation between inside and outside. At this stage the programme's illusionistic strategy was to establish the outside of the walk in relation to the inside of the studio. Typically the movement to the outside would be signified by a script direction that read, 'an appreciable interval of silence.' Silence on radio is of course a form of signification which can be read in a number of ways. Here at the start of *Out with Romany* it seems to signify 'dead air', a point where nothing is happening. As Andrew Crisell suggests, in such a function, 'silence can resemble noise in acting as a framing mechanism, for it signifies the integrity of a programme or item by making a space around it.'[42] Of course, if silence persists for too long it is quite likely that it will be read as signifying the non-functioning of the radio station. But the silence at the beginning of the Romany programme served to signify the boundaries between inside and outside.

The next thing the listener would hear would be a gradual fading in of sound effects, perhaps the twitter of bird song at intervals. If this transition seemed quite subtle, at other points in the programme's history the shift from inside to outside was made far more explicit. One programme in 1937 started with an announcer saying:

> Muriel and Anna were in such a hurry to get over to see Romany – they wouldn't wait. So I will switch you over to the vardo or somewhere near. I expect we shall hear them talking about a lot of interesting things, I only wish I were out in the fields instead of being in the stuffy studio.[43]

Such a comment is still more or less used today in transition from studio to 'OB'. But in *Out with Romany* this sort of comment and other references to 'when we get back to the studio' make it difficult to sustain the claim that the series did not actively set out to construct an illusion.

From December 1938 there was a change in the style of the programme's introduction (this was also the year that the series went national). The studio preamble was dropped in favour of an announcer saying that we are now going *Out with Romany*. Then the interval of silence would follow and the programme would start *in medias res*, with a fade into a conversation between Muriel and Doris in the countryside or Romany talking to Raq. This fading in technique was also used at the end of the programme, where the sound would be faded during a conversation in order to suggest that the walk continued even though we were not able to hear it. Along with the fading out, the programme did not give a cast and hence the anonymity of the voices helped to maintain the illusion of reality.

Bramwell Evens also included topicalities, for example, a reference to the Coronation of 1937 and to a broadcast by Churchill during WWII in order to increase the realism of the series. All of these techniques of suggesting 'the real' were obviously effective because Eunice Evens's biography of Romany reports that throughout the programme's run her husband received many letters convinced that the broadcast took place out of doors.[44] Listeners also requested to stay with Romany on Fletcher's farm and asked whether their children could go along with Romany on his next walk. As such the revelation that the series did not take place out of doors seems so shocking because the programme worked so hard to establish the illusion of an outside broadcast.

I now want to finish by saying something more about the construction of 'the child' in the series. What can *Out with Romany* tell us about the figure of the child in children's broadcasting?

Constructing the child: the performance of childhood

Josie Dolan's recent work on *Children's Hour* points out that when the programme started it was not necessarily inevitable that adults would broadcast to and on behalf of children.[45] Child performers were of course a well-known feature of the stage and early cinema. But it was their very association with these mass communication technologies which contributed to certain judgements being made. Dolan's essay goes on to trace the way it was decided that children were mainly unsuitable for broadcasting.[46] Hence, although there were child broadcasters on *Children's Hour*, their broadcasting was circumscribed. *Children's Hour* thus became a broadcasting service *for* children rather than a children's broadcasting service.

Although *Out with Romany* appealed to adults as well as children, apart from one experiment in broadcasting at a later time the show stayed in its tea-time slot and hence was directed towards a child and – perhaps to a lesser extent – family audience.

Its specific address to a child, rather than a wider audience, was often made explicit in the introduction. Nan McDonald typically announced the programme with the words, 'I sometimes think this walk should be called "What Boys and Girls can see in the countryside each week if they've the right kind of eyes and ears" '.[47] This announcement suggests that the programme was constructing a certain sort of child, one with the right kind of eyes and ears. Such 'boys and girls' would presumably be those who had internalized the programme's regulatory structures. Such a comment is also reminiscent of earlier *Children's Hour* policy documents which urged children to acquire the skills of 'proper listening'. Given such an 'address' it also seems reasonable to think that Muriel and Doris were meant to be children 'accompanying Romany'.

In the series Muriel and Doris are certainly placed in discursive positions conventionally associated with 'the child'. Muriel is frequently portrayed as nervous: for example, she runs from a sawfly in one episode convinced that it is a wasp. Doris, on the other hand, is portrayed as more daring and inquisitive. Their pre-1939 introductory banter also configures them as 'child like'. In one episode Doris described Muriel's red coat as making her look like Little Red Riding Hood. So though the text *never* claims they *are* 'children' it discursively constructs them in such terms. Feeding in to this construction is a pastoral discourse in which going *Out with Romany* is explicitly suggested to be a way of escaping the grime and smoke of Manchester. This discourse could also be seen as reinforcing the child subject position in the way that it presents Muriel and Doris as innocents in the countryside – foolishly chasing ducks, running from insects, and self-deprecatingly describing themselves as 'two ignoramuses'. Romany's interactions with the two girls also add to their positioning as children. In some episodes he initiates a competition between the two on natural history matters and with a scoring system based on tennis seems to 'juvenalize' them.

But what makes the construction of Muriel and Doris harder to pin down is the fluidity of their positions. They do not stay in one discursive position but shift throughout the course of the series. Hence, their identities are, for example, called into question on the few occasions when they are accompanied by the child 'June'. June was played by Bramwell Evens's own daughter, 'Romany June'. In occasional episodes, she played the child June when she was 14 years old. In one episode in 1937 Doris underlines her difference from June by noting, 'I wish I was only 12 just fun and frolick'. The distinction between June and Muriel and Doris was also made at the points when she calls Muriel and Doris 'Aunties', or when Doris lightly berates June for spoiling her clothes.

Despite these textual positions, voices on radio can, however, be rather deceptive. Hence just as Doris Gambell's soprano voice sounded 'child-like' with just a little of the bass taken out, Eunice Evens tells us that the June episodes were difficult, because although only fourteen years old, June Bramwell Even's voice over the air sounded older than Muriel and Doris's.[48] Also problematic was apparently some of the banter between Muriel and Doris, especially one episode where they mentioned the need to powder their noses! According to a radio documentary made about the programme, such comments prompted complaints that 'children don't wear make-up'.[49] To make matters more confusing, in odd scripts between 1936 to 1938 Romany himself even refers to Muriel and Doris as 'Aunties', hence using their *Children's Hour* names and maintaining their identity as adult radio presenters. In this matter, it is instructive to consider Eunice Evens' suggestion that although Herbert Farjeon and possibly thousands of others in the south of England thought Muriel and Doris were children, Northern listeners, who had heard the stories for 6 years longer, were quite likely to have recognized them as Auntie Muriel and Auntie Doris.[50] This suggests there may have been different protocols of listening in different regions.

Finally, I would like to return to Farjeon's comments about the broadcasts and the point where he believed that what he was hearing were child actors 'performing' childhood. He wrote that the 'performance of these children is perfection'. As I noted earlier, this of course suggests that childhood, even when performed by children, is not something which is 'natural' but constructed. More often than not, children's voices on radio were performed by adult women actors. Farjeon's comments seem to anticipate Judith Butler's ideas about identity as performative.[51] Although, as I have noted, Muriel and Doris occupied a variety of different subject positions throughout the broadcasts, they were predominantly constructed as children. Hence in *Out with Romany* we hear adults performing childhood for child listeners. This could be seen as inculcating a version of childhood which children then in turn re-inscribe in their own performing of childhood. This 'performing' of childhood is then taken as an authentic expression of biological immaturity.

Notes

1. I wish to thank Jeff Walden and his colleagues at the BBC Written Archives Centre, Caversham, for guiding me to the files on *Children's Hour* and the *Out with Romany* broadcasts, archivist Monica Thapar, also at Caversham, for giving guidance on copyright issues, including permission to quote from BBC materials, and the Reverend Roly Bain, grandson of George Bramwell Evens, for permission to quote from Romany's scripts and other materials.
2. In addition to these figures, there were countless other broadcasters who were only heard in the regional *Children's Hour* programmes (in the 'North' region, for example, Richard Sharp on 'fishing and camping' and Michael Bratby on bird watching; or in Wales, William Aspden's 'Around the Countryside' series, or in the 'West', A. W. Ling on farming and A.M.C. Nicholls broadcasting as 'The Birdwatcher'). R. Samuel in his essay, 'The Voice of Britain', in *Island Stories: Unravelling Britain, Theatres of Memory*, Volume II, (eds) A. Light, S. Alexander and G. Steadman (London: Verso, 1998, pp. 172–97), notes that the countryside was one of the 'good causes' which the 'BBC embraced in the 1930s' (p. 184). He sees *Out with Romany* along with BBC Schools broadcasts as helping to popularize the 'idea of Nature Walks'. Interestingly, Samuel sees *Out with Romany* as doing this in 'a less didactic, or more theatrical vein' than the School Broadcasts (p. 185). He describes *Out with Romany* as 'a series of country walks conducted

by one who had been brought up as a gypsy, which employed a battery of sound effects – not least the "Wuf, Wuf" of Romany's make-believe dog, Raq – to sustain the illusion that the programme was being recorded, not in the BBC Manchester studios, but in the wild solitudes of the Pennines' (p. 185). This description, while it emphasizes the eschewing of overt didacticism and the 'theatrical' and artificial nature of the series, issues that I discuss in this chapter, is liable to the critique from admirers of the show that Bramwell Evens' dog Raq did exist and did occasionally make an appearance in the studio. For information about the recording of the programme see the interview with BBC Sound Engineer, Jack Hollinshead, 'My Part in "Out with Romany"' in the *Romany Magazine* – new series: no. 6, 2001, pp. 4–8.

3. Bramwell Evens produced eleven 'Romany' books during his lifetime. After he died his family maintained the franchise by producing further titles about Romany.

4. See K. Lesnik-Oberstein, 'Children's Literature and the Environment', in R. Kerridge and N. Sammells (eds), *Writing the Environment: Ecocriticism and Literature* (London: Zed Books, 1998, pp. 208–17), where she notes that

    There can be few ideas in Western culture as intimately connected and intertwined as 'nature' and the 'child'. The Child as the natural, the natural in the adult as the child, the child of nature, the child in nature, the nature of the child; these concepts permeate the processes of self-definition of adults and adult society. Both the child and nature are central to cultural characterizations of selfhood and otherness, identity and consciousness. (p. 208)

5. H. Farjeon, *The Listener*, 10 June 1943.

6. Farjeon, *The Listener*, 12 August 1943.

7. Early *Children's Hour* policy documents maintained that adult presenters needed to have a sympathy for children.

8. Farjeon, *The Listener*, 12 August 1943 no. 6, 2001, 4–8.

9. *Radio Times*, 20 August 1943.

10. The letter was signed, 'A Listener', Brighton 3 September 1943.

11. H. Farjeon, *The Listener*, 16 September 1943 no. 6, 2001, 4–8.

12. Farjeon, *The Listener*, 16 September 1943.

13. See F. Fedler's book, *Media Hoaxes* (Ames: Iowa State University Press, 1989) for a discussion of these issues in an American context.

14. Farjeon, *The Listener*, 16 September 1943.

15. R. W. Reid, *Radio Times*, 29 October 1943.

16. Reid, *Radio Times*, 29 October 1943.

17. See the interview with Hollinshead.

18. Letter to *Radio Times*, 19 November 1943.

19. N. MacDonald, *Radio Times* 26 November 1943.

20. *Radio Times* reported his death and wrote that,

    There must be many young men and women in their twenties, now possibly serving with the Forces or pulling their full weight in factories, who owe their present delight in the English countryside in great part to their memories of 'Romany' and his vivid way in his broadcasts and his books of directing young eyes towards all its wonder and beauty. ... No radio rambles along the country lanes can ever have again quite the same exhilarating flavour. (Anonymous, *Radio Times* 3 December 1943)

21. P. Scannell and D. Cardiff, 'Serving the Nation: Public Service Broadcasting before the War', in B. Waites, T. Bennett and G. Martin (eds), *Popular Culture; Past and Present* (Beckenham: Croom Helm, 1982), pp. 161–91, p. 161.

22. J. Reith, *Broadcast over Britain* (London: Hodder and Stoughton, 1924), p. 34.

23. P. Golding and G. Murdock (eds), *The Political Economy of the Media*, volume 2 (Cheltenham: Edward Elgar, 1997), p. 256.

24. *BBC Handbook*, 1928, p. 148.

25. *BBC Handbook*, 1928, p. 148.

26. D. McCulloch, 'Entertaining The Young Listener', *BBC Quarterly*, vol. 1-2, April 1946 to January 1948, p. 230.

27. John Reith in his book, *Into the Wind* (London: Hodder and Stoughton, 1949) noted, 'If radio was to become "valuable as an index to the community's outlook and personality" ... it was of first importance that the service should be trusted; it must not abuse the confidential footing it had obtained on every man's hearth rug, though opinion might vary as to what constituted abuse' (p. 135).

28. Memo from Children's Hour Organiser, Derek McCulloch (23rd July, 1937) entitled, 'Children's Hour From North, Feature Programme – Roman Wall', BBC WAC R11/28, Children's Hour File General Memos, 1932–9.

29. See E. Evens, *Through the Years with Romany* (London: University of London Press, 1946), pp. 134–5.

30. J.-J. Rousseau, *Emile*, trans. Barbara Foxley (London: J. M. Dent & Sons, 1989), p. 84.

31. Evens, *Through the Years with Romany*, p. 135.

32. Evens, *Through the Years with Romany*, p. 73.

33. Evens, *Through the Years with Romany*, pp. 141–2.

34. J. Rose, *The Case of Peter Pan or the Impossibility of Children's Fiction* (London: Palgrave Macmillan, 1984, revised edition 1994), p. 46.

35. Rose, *The Case of Peter Pan*, p. 47.

36. Rose, *The Case of Peter Pan*, p. 47.

37. Eunice Evens notes in her biography of Romany that she can find no essential connection/affinity between gypsies and nature. See Evens, *Through the Years with Romany*, pp. 173–4.

38. D. Matless, *Landscape and Englishness* (London: Reaktion Books, 1998).

39. The use of dialect in *Out with Romany* is significant in the sense that it represented Northern dialects on radio even before the wartime employment of Wilfred Pickles, the Yorkshire born actor and one time *Children's Hour* presenter who briefly broadcast the national news during the Second World War. Pickles is remembered for his signing off, 'Goodnight to you all – and to all Northerners, wherever you may be, good neet.' At the same time, as much as dialects were used in the programme, Romany often corrected those who used dialects and mispronounced or confused words. For instance, the occasional character of the farmer's wife, Mrs Fletcher, often used dialectal words such as 'clemmed' for cold. At the same time, Romany who spoke with a soft northern accent himself, and used dialectal idioms such as 'go inside for a warm' often corrected Mrs Fletcher's malapropisms.

Hence in one episode she confused the word 'incandescent' with 'indecent mantles'. Such moments, when Romany corrected her, suggest an ambivalence towards words and dialect.

40. Evens, *Through the Years with Romany*, p. 147.
41. S. Connor, *Dumbstruck. A Cultural History of Ventriloquism* (Oxford: Oxford University Press, 2000), p. 22.
42. A. Crisell, *Understanding Radio* (London: Routledge, 1986), p. 56.
43. Announcement in *Out with Romany*, 22 April 1937.
44. Evens, *Through the Years with Romany*, pp. 135–6.
45. J. Dolan, 'Aunties and Uncles: The BBC's Children's Hour and Liminal Concerns in the 1920s', *Historical Journal of Film, Radio and Television*, 23: 4, 2003, 329–39.
46. Dolan, 'Aunties and Uncles', 331.
47. Introduction for *Out with Romany*, 17 November, 1938.
48. Evens, *Through the Years with Romany*, p. 151.
49. The radio documentary, 'Remembering Romany' (narrated by Dilys Breese) was broadcast on 21 November 1973 (BBC Sound Archive). More recently, the myth that Muriel and Doris were children is still being maintained. Sean Street's *A Concise History of British Radio 1922–2002* (Tiverton: Kelly Press, 2002) includes an entry on the programme which runs, 'Out with Romany – The Rev. G. Bramwell Evens, a Methodist minister of Gypsy stock, "Romany" conducted studio-bound "walks in the countryside" with two children from 1933' (p. 56).
50. Evens, *Through the Years with Romany*.
51. J. Butler, *Gender Trouble: Feminism and the Subversion of Identity* (London: Routledge, 1990).

11
Vital Victims: Senses of Children in the Urban

Jenny Bavidge

In a set of brightly-coloured pictures, Shelley Rotner's simple photographic text for pre-school children, *Senses in the City*, set in New York, encourages its readers to 'See the murals,' but also to 'Taste a giant warm pretzel,' 'Touch the elevator buttons,' 'Hear the sirens.'[1] Rotner's book is part of a series which includes more traditional, pastorally-inflected titles such as *Senses on the Farm* and *Senses at the Seashore* and such optimistic valorization of children's physical interaction with the city is fairly rare. This chapter discusses the presence of children in urban environments with a particular emphasis on the tensions inherent in linking children and embodied urban experience. Anxieties around the image of the child in the city are often articulated through ideas about sensual experience: either a lack of connection to natural objects is seen as damaging to children's moral or physical well-being, or the city 'touches' them in threatening ways. The very inclusion of children in any given urban image changes its meaning and reception. This chapter suggests that such images are so ubiquitous and intertextual that they are not only necessarily interdisciplinary but they demonstrate quite clearly how the construction of childhood or child experiences underpins our accounts of urban life; here, they will be discussed with reference to visual texts that attempt to place the child in the city through a variety of generic and discursive strategies. The chapter will go on to focus on one particularly emotive and fertile image, that of a child holding (and often losing) a balloon in a city street. This image is one which is passed on, reworked and recontextualized, just as the image of Little Red Riding Hood disappearing into the woods has so consistently been in children's literature and culture, for example. Interdisciplinary approaches can point out how such images are mobilized in different moments and for different purposes, but share the characteristic of serving as a shorthand (as the image of the child always does) for a whole set of concerns and discourses. Because the child/balloon image so often stands as a metonym for something unrepresentable (a moment of trauma, violence or loss) in some of its manifestations, or as something nostalgically ineffable in others, it also expresses many of the associations we commonly make between the child and the city.

Looking to visual images sharpens questions of how, where and why children appear in urban representations. The image of the child in the urban highlights ideas around visibility and occupation; children's geographers have consistently noted how children's presence in place is marked by discourses of belonging and not-belonging, presence and absence. In film too, as Vicky Lebeau has argued, the discussion of images of children in cinema has circulated around the difficulties of rendering childhood experience on screen, as 'something' that is simultaneously insistent and unrepresentable. Lebeau shows how the child (in images of suffering and sexuality in particular) has occupied a particular place in the institution of cinema and how 'from its inception, cinema has laid claim to the child' in part to define the very nature of an object of spectacle and the gaze.[2] Of course, many films depict children in cities in a variety of genres. My intention here is to note examples of how images from film, television and advertising made for and about children, negotiate the problematic of the child's physical presence in the urban.

The haptic city

Images of children in cities are always striking, in that they reveal in the starkest terms the image of childhood in an adult world. The clash of an idealized pastoral world of childhood with the stratifications and miseries of urban life is a standard theme in both realist and fantastic children's fiction and film.[3] Sometimes the emphasis is placed upon social or economic ills, sometimes upon the poverty of consumer culture, but often the distinction is between different kinds of sensual worlds.

Nicholas Fyfe has written of how the Western city street has moved from a more fully sensorial experience to one where sight (of rigidly organized consumer spectacles) is privileged. 'Sensually, the Western street is a place for gazing rather then communicating...marked by deprivation in all sensory capacities, contemporary Western streets are marked by their non-sensuality.'[4] Perhaps this is one reason why children are routinely depicted as 'out of place' in urban settings, in that they are so closely associated with a freedom of movement and intercourse with the material world. Because, as Paul Rodaway has suggested, the haptic touch is one which is particularly associated with childhood (playful, explorative, indiscriminate) it is also (and particularly in the context of public spaces) forbidden. 'Don't touch!' is one of the earliest interdictions, associated with the outside world as well as the body.[5] In particular, children are excluded from discussions of the sensual, or conversely are presumed to have access to a more immediate but rather indefinable sensual experience of their environment, glimpsed from the point of view of adult nostalgia.[6] Furthermore, their presence in representations of urban life comes to seem less a depiction of any actual state of being and more a stand in for a concept or (more likely) as an image of a something lost or threatened: innocence, instinctiveness, contact with nature, or vitality itself.[7] But to look at representations of children in the urban as guarantors of, or embodied expressions of, such vitality, presumes the kind of transparency of meaning that this volume is interested in further unpicking. The child is either 'vital' or a victim; child and city are constructed as incompatible categories, any meeting between the two is fraught with tension and complication. The fruitful way forward is to get into the heart of these knotted meanings, not to reveal their origin or truth, but to see how such images expand, repeat, reflect, reproduce and regenerate. The victim is vital to the discourse of the city conceived as a desensitized zone and to the understanding of what constitutes urban selfhood.

This polarization of the vital victim is reflected in scholarly and critical theorizations of urban life too. In a footnote to her essay on the aesthetics and ethics of urban walking in the eighteenth century, Clare Brant notes that 'though discussions of walking as an urban experience now consider gender...few (any?) consider it from other than an adult, able-bodied perspective.'[8] David Serlin (2006) has written convincingly of the ways in which modalities of urban subjectivity have been figured in ways which exclude disabled bodies. In recent years, the ubiquitous flâneur has been the paradigmatic figure of urban exploration and observation, figured in terms of 'the modern subject who takes the functions of his or her body for granted.'[9] Even when interrogated and expanded to include women, Serlin argues, 'the category of the flâneur or the flâneuse as an agent of modern experience already presumes that the codes of urban modernity – what really counts as urban and/or modern – are organized around narratives of normative able-bodiedness.'[10] Equally, ways of understanding or explaining urban life based on aspects of physical urban experience (flâneurie, response to and involvement in spectacle, or play with consumer identities for example) are often examined in terms of erotic and economic freedoms, which are in part defined *against* the figure of the child, especially the child as 'natural' object. Focus on these excluded bodies then, not only brings to light a whole set of urban experiences that have not been previously considered, or which have only been understood in terms of lack, but, as so many other articles in this collection and *Children in Culture I* show, calls into question founding ontological categories. To analyse these through film draws another thread into the knot of the meaning of the child in the urban, as film itself has constructed its idea of an object in part through depictions of children and the category of childhood. As Emma Wilson has suggested, writing on the formal and aesthetic experiments in recent women filmmakers' representations of childhood, 'childhood itself, child experience and its representation offer particularly prescient and urgent material for thinking about the public and the private.'[11]

Images of children in the city

When Iris M. Young and other urban theorists posit the pragmatically utopian vision of the city as a 'being together of strangers',[12] we see another example of the problematic position occupied by the figure of the child in urban theory. In contemporary urban culture, children and 'strangers' are antithetical. The city is commonly depicted (and has a long history of being so) as an environment that operates to entrap and endanger children. One memorable version of this narrative forms my first example of representations of the child in the city. In an advert for Volkswagen released in 1994, to the soundtrack of Billie Holiday singing 'God Bless the Child' a little girl walks through the streets of New York, holding her father's hand. In a succession of quick edits, we see the child shrink from the noise of sirens, threatening shouts and aggressive arguments, and the amplified thud of a man forced onto the bonnet of a car by a policeman. An extreme close-up accentuates the light and cleanliness of her face as contrasted with the looming darkness around her. At one point, the camera offers us a more distant shot of the child performing an unconscious little dancing step which appears unscripted and seems to gesture towards something free and uncontained. The moment is of course immediately co-opted by the logic of the advert. The car appears, a kind of solving intermediary between flesh and stone and carries the child away – as David Sibley imagines in his reading of the advert – to some safe suburban heaven or 'commisionaired apartment building'.[13] The car is an extension of her

father's hand, protective and encircling. The VW child has all the qualities of one of Wordsworth's clear-eyed infant seers: she is a victim of
the city, is assaulted by it, aurally and visually and her uneasy presence
within it makes clear the city's malignity. The advert also attributes to
the child the ability to see through, above and beyond the degradation
of the environment she is (temporarily) lost in.

Sibley's account of this advert in his *Geographies of Exclusion* thoroughly demonstrates how this advert draws on the rhetoric of urban
threat and danger to purity, and a discourse of dirt/cleanliness which
also has racialized overtones. The advert is shot in black and white and
the contrasts are extreme, so that the child's face is almost bleached
white and the darkness of the antagonists' faces, and the city streets
they meld into, exaggerated. What I would like to foreground here is
that as well as constructing the city streets and their inhabitants as
threateningly, frighteningly 'other' as Sibley suggests, the advert draws
on a complicated matrix of representation of real and imagined space,
rendering both uncertain. The child is insulated from the city, she does
not touch it and the whole advert is based around the idea that it must
not touch her ('*They cannot touch her*', writes Travis Bickle in Martin
Scorsese's *Taxi Driver* as his idealized Betsy moves in slow-motion, pris-
tine in white, through the same New York streets). The child is grounded
and protected by the one touch that is maintained, that of her father's
hand, and so operates as a paradigmatic image of the separation of children from the urban realm. Despite the coding of realism present in the
sequences (in the seemingly unscripted and instinctive movement of
the child), the advert is told in fairy-tale schemata, employing the black
and white shorthand of advertising imagery to achieve its narrative and
aesthetic effect. The ideology of the advert is stark and serves its function to promote the car in question as a sanctuary from the reaching
hands of the urban jungle. The 'hands off' message of the advert is,
however, undercut by its invitation to the spectacle of the child herself,
whose beauty (accentuated and coded by her old-fashioned, dark coloured pea-coat) is emphasized by the closeness of the shots which linger
on her curls and large eyes.

There are however many examples of texts, literary and visual, that
encourage a more hands-on approach to city living, representative
of pro-urban, liberal attitudes which encourage participation in the
urban realm in sanctioned and non-sanctioned ways. A particular set
of images arises from what David Serlin has called 'an urban inner-city
aesthetic' promoted in the 1970s by American television programmes
such as *Sesame Street* or *Schoolhouse Rock*. These productions had a stated

intention of producing positive images of children's urban communities and practices, to celebrate the street, the stoop and the yard as a 'children's garden of soul'.[14] Indicative of this attitude is another New York text, *The Fur Coat Club*, a children's film made by the Learning Corporation of America, and directed by Joan Micklin Silver in 1973 (also screened in the UK by the BBC). The film follows two nine year old New York girls who have invented a game where they compete to touch as many fur coats as they can without being caught. The girls roam with unproblematic freedom in and around Central Park and their game prompts a mischievously tactile relationship to the city. The film's moments of peril occur when the girls find themselves trapped in a fur shop where they foil the plans of a burglar and are rewarded by the owner of the shop with two very desirable fur muffs, that, sick of the sight of the stuff after their adventure, they hand over to their little sisters. They film closes as they try out a new city game, eavesdropping on park-bench smoochers via a walkie-talkie.

So, we have a film made for children which tells an urban story about moving around the city, touching what you're interested in, using its materials and persons for your own amusement, behaving badly and breaking the rules. There is no dramatic come-uppance and adults appear only in strictly confined roles as dupes, villains and prize-givers. It's a film which imagines a child's geography of the city mapped by touch, but also running, jumping, playing and desiring. A Wordsworthian reading of the film might describe children so tragically alienated from their own environment that their instinct for pleasure in touch has been directed from the natural to the unnatural and manmade. Instead of living animals, or living earth, they desire and touch dead fur. 'Perhaps we should read the film via Susan Buck-Morss' description of Walter Benjamin's critique of the switching of real and artificial in the modern city: 'for children (like Benjamin) born into urban environments [an artificial landscape of buildings and consumer items] appeared to be nature itself'.[15] The VW ad is all about removing the child from the scene of that disorder while *The Fur Coat Club* is about a daring raid on the objects of the adult world.

However, the film is more interested in pointing out how the girls use expectations of good behaviour as a chance to get they want: they pretend to be nice girls admiring a baby for example, but only to get at the mother's coat. Their senses are not valorized as belonging to some more lofty dimension of being. Neither are their bodies themselves used as sensual objects, as the VW child's arguably is and their experiments with make-up and adult accessories are played for comic effect. The children break out of the bounds of their circumscribed play spaces and their game brings them into contact with different areas and persons in the city. A fur coat in a park for example, turns out to belong to a very tall, and for a moment, scary looking soul man, who gives a groovy high-five and grins through his gold teeth. Susan Soloman has written on the architecture of children's playspaces in her *American Playgrounds* and her main point is just what we might expect – she argues that children's play spaces are increasingly gated, fenced and separated from the space around them. They do not answer to the sites they are in, they do not encourage sensuous connection with the environment in which they are placed, but serve to remove children from any contact with the actual materials of their environment: 'Use is set and determined, leaving scant prospect for improvisation.'[16] Playgrounds in their strict demarcation of appropriate users and function have thus become stratified and been removed from the fluid rhythms of the city which might see their use change through the day as the space is occupied by different ages and types of user. The playground has been removed from the context identified by Colin Ward in his 1970s study of British children's street culture, *The Child in the City*, where the barriers between child and adult world, public and play space were much more porous. Understandings of 'play' as a resistive or creative response to the city have become more associated with adult practices such as parkour or flashmobbing (in what Stevens calls the 'ludic city').[17] In texts such as Ward's photographic essay children are documented as they take possession of derelict or overlooked corners of the city to make them their own. These territorial appropriations are of course a popular theme in children's literature, with a child making secret gardens in a small space, a window box perhaps or corner of wasteland. Children's sensorial relationship with an urban environment is often represented through depictions of their relationship with such small or insignificant objects in the city world, whether that is a fur coat, a scrap of garden or a balloon. Such objects are charged with all the associations discussed above, and also occupy a number of positions in relation to the child: sometimes they are directly metaphorical of the child-body (representing both vitality or victimhood) and sometimes comment on the status of the child in the city. In all cases they are vital objects in the construction of narratives of the urban child. I will discuss one such image in greater detail: that of the balloon.

Balloons

Although the image of a great crowd of multi-coloured balloons rising up from an urban street has become a signifier for optimism and hope frequently conjured in public events or advertising, the image of lone child with a single balloon has a much stronger association with vulnerability and threat. In his famous discussion of Fritz Lang's *M* (1931), Christian Metz shows how the central image of a child kidnapped from a city street is expressed metonymically and diegetically through the image of a lost balloon. The image is both paradigmatic, in that the balloon stands in for the child, and syntagmatic, in that the two objects (child and balloon) have been linked in the narrative.[18] I want to argue here that in the bank of images through which child and city are imagined, the haptic quality of how the city touches the child, or how the child touches the city, are crucially important. For this reason, objects such as balloons and balls operating as part of the *mise-en-scène* or as narrative signifiers, are also negotiations of often uncomfortable meetings between child and city. I'd argue that the image of a child with a balloon (often a red balloon, though not always) on a city street has become ubiquitous and, in common with other metaphors of child experience, protean and viral in quality. From around 2002, the British graffiti artist Banksy, for example, has given us multiple versions of his stencilled image of a girl with a heart-shaped red balloon (Figure 11.1). Sometimes the child is able to keep her grip on the balloon, in other images, it drifts away. In later images, in which the child wears a gas mask, the balloon is torn and deflated. Along with his rats and kissing policemen, the child with balloon is part of Banksy's self-conscious gallery of urban images, themselves graffittied and reproduced as they appear and disappear on the city's fabric.

Figure 11.1   Girl with balloon by Banksy

Bansky's use of this image taps into a shared collective understanding of what this particular image means, which can be easily unpacked. One reading of the use of balloons in the visual iconography of urban childhood is obvious: the balloon, like childhood, can only last for a short period. However, it also suggests the body and physicality of the child itself: it moves in contradistinction to the solid mass of city architecture; it is colourful; it tugs away from its possessor and has the mischievous ability to alarm with its erratic freedom. The many stories written about balloons for children, or the several films which feature balloons which I will go on to discuss, combine these features and circulate around ideas of self-absorbed freedom and pleasure (often with the balloon as an animated imaginary friend with a life of its own), however, even the gentlest stories are suggestive of loss.[19] The easy and whimsical association of the balloon with the joys of childhood is undercut with some of its other properties. The balloon is both manmade (rubber) and natural (breath or gas) and has a thin, easily breakable skin. It is an uncanny object, both living and dead, charged with an animating breath and hovering between states of solidity and vacuity. When the balloon bursts what is left is an abject rag, wounded and lifeless, as depicted in Piero Manzoni's *Artist's Breath* (1960), in which a red balloon lies 'dead', bereft and slowly decomposing.

As a result of this ambivalent state, there is a correspondingly tense and uncanny quality to the structure of balloon stories, exacerbated by their proximity to the child. Any balloon narrative is kept afloat by the continual globophobic threat of the moment of its bursting. So in city stories, in particular, the balloon is a constant reminder of the danger of being touched by the city. The city's sharp edges of unforgiving stone and concrete and its lurking antagonists, all threaten the balloon's buoyancy and existence. In urban stories, the balloon operates as a founding image in several visual texts aimed at both children and adults. It operates as a metonym for the child's body (*M*), and also as an object of temptation which leads to death or shame (*The Yellow Balloon*). It is frequently used to represent the moment of loss or disappearance of a child (*M*, *Ransom*, *Heavy Rain*) to the point of cliché. Even in more utopian images of urban childhood, its connection to children is fraught with anxieties about loss or threat (*Le Ballon Rouge*, *The Flight of the Red Balloon*, *The White Balloon*).

Perhaps the most famous example of the balloon as signifier of a certain construction of the child in the city is *M*. The opening sequence of the film features the victim Elsie on her way home from school, cut with scenes which show her warmly and then anxiously awaited by her mother. She is followed by a shadowy figure, whistling 'In the Hall of the Mountain King' who buys her a balloon from a blind vendor, who will later identify the killer from the tell-tale whistle. The balloon will reappear later in the climactic court scene, bobbing upwards to elicit a confession from Beckert, the killer, who stutters Elsie's name on seeing it. In the opening sequence however, it is the balloon and Elsie's ball, rolling away, which tell the story of her fate: the abandoned balloon with its 'painted face and miniature arms' is shown tangled in overhead wires.[20] In her discussion of the imagery of *M*, Lebeau cites the image of a lone rolling ball as 'the classic signifier of the death of a child'. These edits create, as Lebeau points out, the image 'in the mind's eye of the child letting go'.[21]

The lost balloon of *M* bounces back in frequent children-in-urban-peril moves. The *mise-en-scène* of the kidnapping scene in New York-set thriller *Ransom* (Ron Howard, 1996) is full of balloons; they appear gathered in a multi-coloured giant twist arching over Central Park where children mingle, safely-moored to grown-ups, or wander holding their own balloons. In case the audience misses the visual nudge, the kidnapped child (the son of a macho millionaire played by Mel Gibson) has two gigantic, remote-controlled, orange balloons, which soar away over the city in the climactic moment of the discovery of the kidnapping. B-movie *Stolen* (Anders Anderson, 2008) raises the ante by having the balloon seller himself be the villain (dressed as a clown, for extra emphasis) and also employs the motif of the lost red balloon tangled in trees. The image has most recently emigrated to video games, where the cinematically-inspired and immersive digital landscape of *Heavy Rain* (David Cage, 2010) includes a red balloon (bought from a clown) bobbing over the scene of a child's fatal accident. The balloon offers the audience of such 'lost child' narratives a look-away moment. As Emma Wilson suggests in her *Cinema's Missing Children* (2003), the missing child as 'the lost object of desire, origin and vanishing point' has become a significant figure in contemporary cinema.[22] The repeated appearance of this figure and the objects that serve as symbols for it call up familiar questions of, simultaneously, presence and absence in relation to the child, very obviously in narratives about trauma or violence, but also in more benign city stories.[23]

In a film for children, we might expect the balloon to remain safely within the bounds of buoyancy, but even the most nostalgically remembered of balloon films, *Le Ballon Rouge* (Albert Lamorisse, 1956) offers a different kind of metonym. A red balloon follows a boy through the streets of Paris until it is stolen and destroyed by a gang of other boys.

A host of 'the balloons of Paris' (whimsically thanked for their coop-
eration in the film's opening titles) fly from their owners' hands from
all over the city and descend to rescue the boy and fly him over the
rooftops of the city, a scene which has been repeatedly recreated and
referenced in visual culture ever since. The film's theme of loss and the
nostalgic reactions it creates in adult viewers are echoed by the film's
mise-en-scène which preserves a picturesque quarter of Paris, now long
demolished. The balloon's shiny red surface also reflects the buildings
around it, seeming to underline the boy and balloon's entrapment in
the city. Bert Cardullo reads the film as an unproblematic evocation of
childhood, where the balloon is 'a symbol of shining dreams, of mys-
terious yearnings, and the poverty of those who have lost them'. In
this reading, the adult world is 'weighed down' by its post-war cares
and cannot share in the child's companionship or exultation.[24] Barbara
Korte and Claudia Sternberg have argued that the film should be put
in the context of more realist works which also explore children's diffi-
dent occupation of city spaces. They link *Le Ballon Rouge* with the 1950s
British documentary-style *Jemima and Johnny* (Lionel Ngakane, 1964),
which (also wordlessly) tells the story of two young black sisters nego-
tiating the streets of 1960s London. 'Both films,' they suggest, 'explore
an urban centre by way of following children around who have not yet
internalised their societies' rules and regulations, nor share the socially
restrictive perspective of the adult population'.[25]

This more politicized or 'childist' reading of the film points to the
way in which the balloon operates – a little as the fur does in *The Fur
Coat Club* – as an invitation to reach out and touch the fabric of the
city. However, the balloon in *Le Ballon Rouge* appears magically, as if
from another more colourful world. In other stories, the balloon is
something which, although of no value or interest to adults, has to be
bought and so encourages the child character into making a bargain
with the potentially threatening adult world. Interestingly, both the
Iranian *The White Balloon* (Jafar Panhani, 1995) and *The Yellow Balloon*
(J. Lee Thompson, 1955) centre around a moment of crisis when money,
entrusted to the child for the purchase of a much desired object, is lost
down a drain. This crisis in the circulation of capital and consumer
object allows for adult interference and threat to enter the scene and the
children of both films find their desired object (a goldfish in the case of
The White Balloon) enmeshes them into the dubious economics of city
life. The possessor of the balloon in *The White Balloon* is a young balloon seller, an Afghan refugee, homeless on the streets of Tehran. The
balloon he holds links him to the Iranian children he helps, but also

marks out his vulnerability and uncertain destiny. In *The Yellow Balloon* the possession of the titular balloon is shot through with violence: Frankie begins the film observing the street from the safety of his bedroom and is tempted into increasingly dangerous adult spaces by the first temptation of a yellow balloon. The jaunty sequence where Frankie steals Ronnie's balloon and runs away with it, ends with Ronnie's fatal fall in a bombed-out house, as the balloon drifts slowly down to his broken body. The villain of the piece witnesses the accident and blackmails Frankie into criminality; his first act is to buy the guilt-stricken Frankie a new red balloon, one he no longer wants, signifying the beginning of a loss of innocence. The desired and then ruined balloons of the film suggest, as in *M*, a metonymic and syntagmatic link between the object and child-body. As Christine Geharty points out in her discussion of the child character in this period of British film, Frankie's vulnerability is closely allied with the symbolic balloon: 'when he walks through the streets, his head bobs like the balloon he desires.'[26]

Such associations seem to be forgotten when Lamorisse's romantic image of the optimistic and uplifting red balloon is recycled in *The Flight of the Red Balloon* (Hsiao-hsien Hou, 2008), which reworks the story of *Le Ballon Rouge* to explore family dynamics and adult concerns in contemporary, multicultural Paris. An advert produced to promote Milton Keynes replaces 1950s Paris with 1970s Milton Keynes and features a boy enjoying the pastoral pleasures of the town before joining a massed crowd of children (and a clown, on stilts) who all let their red balloons fly upwards, as a voiceover suggests 'Wouldn't it be nice, if all cities were like Milton Keynes?' Elsewhere, images of colourful balloons and bouncing balls are standard images in the situationist-lite versions of the 'flash-mobbing'-style scenarios frequently employed in the language of contemporary urban advertising. Such images unproblematically reproduce the more anxious and contested imagery of children and children's objects in the city discussed above as signifiers of play, capitalizing on a version of childish wonder and excitement to promote (adult) consumer experience. For example, Fuji Xerox advertises itself in an advert titled 'Balloon' (Kosai Sekine, 2009), a 'lost red balloon' narrative featuring playful young men on a see-saw; in the 2007 advert for Ford cars, 'Desire' (Philippe André, 2007), the *Ballon Rouge*-style balloons that spill upwards from the city have come to lift away old models to make room for the shiny new Mondeo. What is curious about these adverts is how the 'child category' is invoked again and again within such adverts with their invitations to adult playfulness and consumerist pleasures. That the image of coloured balloons in the city has a shadow side is either forgotten or elided, or effectively coded into the adverts, in that children are excluded in favour of these playful grown-ups.

The representation of embodied and haptic experiences of the child in the city is therefore always pathologized or idealized, and the associations made between the two are used to underscore wider representations and constructions of the city in adult culture. Again and again, a presumed child-identity is invoked to prompt anxieties, to call up an ineffable something which has been lost and which could be recovered. Emma Wilson, in her studies of films that tell stories about the loss of children, notices that 'the theme of the missing child is interesting precisely in its conjuring of an absence.'[27] The fact that so many of the narratives I have discussed focus on the loss or disappearance of a child or a child-object would seem to proclaim an interest in something that is definitely *there* in order to be lost, as it must be to serve its purpose as a guarantor of the meanings the figure contains. However, aside from the terror, sorrow, melodrama or nostalgia the particular generic identity of such individual narratives produce, the subject seems also to recur as a way of talking about the intangibility of the child/childhood itself. The secondary theme I have tried to identify here, of the problematics of the child's embodied presence and physical touch of and by the city intensifies this idea. The repeated appearance of the theme and its narrative insistence suggests an underlying concern with the problem of absence and presence itself, and foregrounds the metonymical or symbolic devices by which narrative cinema, advertising or any other form of representation call forth their subjects and the discourses that travel with them. The child's supposed relationship to objects is invoked in order to explain understandings of what the city environment *is* and what it can do to us. In the examples I have chosen, the place accorded to children and objects associated with them operates on a faultline between vitality and victimhood which serves primarily to produce constructs of the city itself. Child and object become interchangeable in these moments and their meaning is shown to be always on the move, calling up our desire to know and assert a category against the adult environment of the city, but showing us how such an identity is created and inflated by that very desire.[28]

Notes

1. S. Rotner, *Senses in the City* (New York: Millbrook Press, 2008).
2. V. Lebeau, *Childhood and Cinema* (London: Reaktion, 2008), p. 7.
3. See discussions of various generic examples in K. V. Graham, 'Exodus from the City: Peter Dickinson's *Eva*', *The Lion and the Unicorn*, 23: 1, 2002, 79–85;

C. Mills, 'The Ambivalent Urban Idyll: *The Saturdays* and *Betsy and Tacy Go Downtown', Children's Literature in Education*, 29: 4, 2002, 211–21; J. Bavidge, 'Stories in Space: The Geographies of Children's Literature', *Children's Geographies*, 4: 3, 2006, 319–30; D. L. Russell, ' "The City Spreads Its Wings": The Urban Experience in Poetry', *Children's Literature in Education*, 29: 1, 1998, 31–42.

4. N. R. Fyfe, *Images of the Street: Planning, Identity, and Control in Public Space* (London: Routledge, 1998), p. 214.

5. P. Rodaway, *Sensuous Geographies: Body, Sense and Place* (London and New York: Routledge, 1994), p. 148.

6. See O. Jones, 'Naturally Not! Childhood, the Urban and Romanticism', *Human Ecology Review*, 9: 2, 2002, 17–30.

7. And see Owain Jones on the importance of this word 'vitality' to the Deleuzean concept of childhood as read by Francois Zourabichvili, in O. Jones, ' "Endlessly Revisited and Forever Gone": On Memory, Reverie and Emotional Imagination in Doing Children's Geographies. An "Addendum" to ' "To Go Back up the Side Hill": Memories, Imaginations and Reveries of Childhood" by Chris Philo', *Children's Geographies*, 1: 1, 2003, 25–36.

8. C. Brant, 'Seduced by the City: Gay's *Trivia* and Hogarth', *The Literary London Journal*, 6: 1, 2007, at: www.literary.london.org

9. D. Serlin, 'Disabling the Flâneur', *Journal of Visual Culture*, 5: 2, August 2006, 193–208, 198.

10. D. Serlin, 'Disabling the Flâneur', 199.

11. E. Wilson, 'Miniature Lives, Intrusion and Innocence: Women Filming Children', *French Cultural Studies*, 18: 2, June 2007, 169–83, 169.

12. I. M. Young, *Justice and the Politics of Difference* (Princeton, NJ: Princeton University Press, 1990), p. 237.

13. D. Sibley, *Geographies of Exclusion* (London and New York: Routledge, 2005), p. 62.

14. D. Serlin, 'From Sesame Street to Schoolhouse Rock: Urban Pedagogy and Soul Iconography in the 1970s', in M. Guillory and R. C. Green (eds), *Soul: Black Power, Politics, and Pleasure* (New York: New York University Press, 2005), pp. 105–20. As an aside, the *Sesame Street* franchise has recently aired a series in conjunction with the BBC, *The Sesame Tree*, which firmly (re) places a pastoral landscape for the characters.

15. S. Buck-Morss, 'Benjamin's Passagen-Werk: Redeeming Mass Culture for the Revolution', *New German Critique*, 29, *The Origins of Mass Culture: The Case of Imperial Germany (1871–1918)*, Spring-Summer, 1983, pp. 211–40, p. 213.

16. S. Soloman, *American Playgrounds: Revitalizing Community Space* (Lebanon, NH: University Press of New England, 2005), p. 1.

17. Q. Stevens, *The Ludic City: Exploring the Potential of Public Spaces* (London and New York: Routledge, 2007).

18. C. Metz, *The Imaginary Signifier: Psychoanalysis and the Cinema* (1977; repr. Indianan University Press: Bloomington, 1982), p. 190.

19. There are too many examples to list in full, but see for example, M. Inkpen, *The Blue Balloon*, (London: Hodder, 1989); K. Sakai, *Emily's Balloon* (Chronicle Books, 2006); J P. Weitzman and R. P. Glasser, *You Can't Take a Balloon into the Metropolitan Museum* (New York: E. P. Dutton, 2000).

20. R. White and E. Buscombe, *British Institute Film Classics*, vol. 1, (London: British Film Institute, 2003), p. 140.
21. Lebeau, *Childhood and Cinema*, p. 125.
22. E. Wilson, *Cinema's Missing Children* (London and New York: Wallflower Press, 2002), p. 15.
23. Such questions are key to the expanding area of studies of the child in cinema. Karen Lury's *The Child in Film; Tear, Fears and Fairy Tales* (London and New York: I. B. Tauris, 2010) discusses, for example, the 'impropriety' of the performance of child actors, whose performances are commonly read as of a different order from those of adult actors (understood either as unconscious 'captured actuality' and therefore nor 'proper' acting, or are *too* conscious in which case such performances are 'freakish', produced by a child who 'must possess adult-like qualities which allow it to act in a child-like rather than child-ish manner... In neither of these versions of the child on screen does the performance of the child actually offer or establish what it is to "be" a child, only what we think or perceive that children may be "like"' (pp. 10–11). See on this also J. Kelleher, 'Face to Face with Terror: Children in Film', in K. Lesnik-Oberstein (ed.), *Children in Culture: Approaches to Childhood* (Houndmills: Macmillan and New York: St Martin's Press, 1998), pp. 29–55.
24. B. Cardullo, *In Search of Cinema: Writings on International Film Art* (Ithaca, N.Y.: McGill Queen's University Press, 2004), p. 33.
25. B. Korte and C. Sternberg, *Bidding for the Mainstream?: Black and Asian British Film Since the 1990s*, (Amsterdam and New York: Rodopi, 2004), p. 52.
26. C. Geharty, *British Cinema in the Fifties: Gender, Genre and the 'New Look'* (London: Routledge, 2000), p. 142.
27. Wilson, *Cinema's Missing Children*, p. 158.
28. I am grateful to Elly Bavidge, Matt Beeke and Cherry Smyth for their discussions and suggestions for this chapter.

Selected Bibliography

Arac, J., *Huckleberry Finn As Idol and Target: The Function of Criticism in Our Time* (Madison, WI and London: University of Wisconsin Press, 1997).

Ariès, P., *Centuries of Childhood: A Social History of Family Life*, trans. R. Baldick (New York: Vintage Books, 1962 [1959]).

Barker, M., *Comics: Ideology, Power and the Critics* (Manchester and New York: Manchester University Press, 1989).

Bavidge, J., 'Stories in Space: The Geographies of Children's Literature', *Children's Geographies*, 4: 3, 2006, 319–30.

Baxter, J., *The Archaeology of Childhood* (Walnut Creek: AltaMira Press, 2005).

Beisaw, A. and J. Gibb (eds), *The Archaeology of Institutional Life* (Tuscaloosa: University of Alabama Press, 2009).

Bignell, J., 'Writing the Child in Media Theory', in K. Lesnik-Oberstein (ed.), 'Children in Literature', Special issue of the *Yearbook of English Studies*, 32 (Leeds: MHRA, 2002), pp. 127–39.

Bignell, J., 'Familiar Aliens: *Teletubbies* and Postmodern Childhood', *Screen*, 46: 3, 2005, 373–88.

Boler, M., *Feeling Power: Emotions and Education* (New York: Routledge, 1999).

Bruhm, S. and N. Hurley (eds), *Curiouser: On the Queerness of Children* (Minneapolis: University of Minnesota Press, 2004).

Burke, K., *Language as Symbolic Action: Essays on Life, Literature, and Method* (Berkeley, Los Angeles and London: University of California Press, 1966).

Burman, E., *Deconstructing Developmental Psychology* (London: Routledge: 1994, 2nd edn, 2008).

Burman, E., *Developments: Child, Image, Nation* (London: Routledge, 2008).

Burman, E., 'Beyond "Emotional Literacy" in Feminist and Educational Research', *British Educational Research Journal*, 35: 1, 2009, 137–55.

Butler, J., *Gender Trouble: Feminism and the Subversion of Identity* (New York: Routledge, 1990).

Canella, G. and L. Soto (eds), *Childhoods: A Handbook* (New York: Peter Lang Publishing, 2010).

Casella, E. C. and S. M. Croucher, *The Alderley Sandhills Project: An Archaeology of Community Life in (Post)-Industrial England* (Manchester: Manchester University Press, 2010).

Castañeda, C., *Figurations: Child, Bodies, Worlds* (Durham, NC: Duke University Press, 2002).

Cocks, N., *Student Centred: Education, Freedom and the Idea of Audience* (Ashby-de-la-Zouch: Inkermen/Axis Series, 2009).

Davis-Floyd, R. and J. Dumit (eds), *Cyborg Babies. From Techno-Sex to Techno-Tots* (New York and London: Routledge, 1998).

de Man, P., *Allegories of Reading: Figural Language in Rousseau, Nietzsche, Rilke, and Proust* (New Haven, CT and London: Yale University Press, 1979).

Derrida, J., *Of Grammatology*, trans. G. C. Spivak (Baltimore: Johns Hopkins University Press, 1997 (corrected edn) [1967]).

Dolan, J., 'Aunties and Uncles: The BBC's Children's Hour and Liminal Concerns in the 1920s', *Historical Journal of Film, Radio and Television*, 23: 4, 2003, 329–39.

Dolan, J., 'The Voice That Cannot Be Heard: Radio/ Broadcasting and "The Archive"', *International Studies in Broadcast and Audio Media*, 1: 1, 2003, 63–72.

Ecclestone, K. and D. Hayes, *The Dangerous Rise of Therapeutic Education* (London: Routledge, 2009).

Felman, S. (ed.), *Literature and Psychoanalysis. The Question of Reading: Otherwise* (Baltimore: Johns Hopkins University Press, 1982 [1977]).

Freud, S., 'Beyond the Pleasure Principle', in S. Freud, *The Standard Edition of the Complete Psychological Works of Sigmund Freud*, trans. and general ed. J. Strachey, vol. 18 (London: The Hogarth Press, 1955 [1920]), pp. 7–65.

Harris, N., 'Pupil Bullying, Mental Health and the Law in England', in N. Harris and P. Meredith (eds), *Education and Health: International Perspectives on Law and Policy* (Aldershot: Ashgate, 2005), pp. 31–58.

Higonnet, A., *Pictures of Innocence: The History and Crisis of Ideal Childhood* (London: Thames and Hudson, 1998).

Holland, P., *Picturing Childhood: The Myth of the Child in Popular Imagery* (London: I. B. Tauris, 2004).

Hultqvist, K. and G. Dahlberg (eds), *Governing the Child in the New Millennium* (New York and London: RoutledgeFalmer, 2001).

Hutcheon, L., *Irony's Edge: The Theory and Politics of Irony* (London and New York: Routledge, 1994).

James, A. and A. Prout (eds), *Constructing and Reconstructing Childhood: Contemporary Issues in the Sociological Study of Childhood* (London: The Falmer Press, 2nd edn, 1997 [1990]).

James, A., C. Jenks, and A. Prout, *Theorizing Childhood* (Cambridge: Polity Press, 1998).

Jenks, C. (ed.), *The Sociology of Childhood: Essential Readings* (London: Batsford Academic and Educational, 1982).

Jenks, C., *Childhood*, series: Key Ideas, series ed. P. Hamilton (London: Routledge, 1996).

Jones, O., '"Endlessly Revisited and Forever Gone": On Memory, Reverie and Emotional Imagination in Doing Children's Geographies. An "Addendum" to "To Go Back up the Side Hill": Memories, Imaginations and Reveries of Childhood" by Chris Philo', *Children's Geographies*, 1: 1, 2003, 25–36.

Kelleher, J., 'Face to Face with Terror: Children in Film', in K. Lesnik-Oberstein (ed.), *Children in Culture: Approaches to Childhood* (Houndmills: Palgrave Macmillan and New York: St Martin's Press, 1998), pp. 29–55.

Kincaid, J., *Child-Loving: The Erotic Child and Victorian Culture* (London: Routledge, 1992).

Lebeau, V., *Childhood and Cinema* (London: Reaktion, 2008).

Lemish, D., *Children and Television: A Global Perspective* (Oxford: Blackwell, 2007).

Lesnik-Oberstein, K., *Children's Literature: Criticism and the Fictional Child* (Oxford: Clarendon Press, 1994).

Lesnik-Oberstein. K. (ed.), *Children in Culture: Approaches to Childhood* (Houndmills: Palgrave Macmillan, 1998).

Lesnik-Oberstein, K., 'The Psychopathology of Everyday Children's Literature Criticism', *Cultural Critique*, 45, 2000, 222–42.

Lesnik-Oberstein, K. (ed.), 'Children in Literature', Special issue of the *Yearbook of English Studies*, 32 (Leeds: MHRA, 2002).

Lesnik-Oberstein, K. (ed.), *Children's Literature: New Approaches* (Houndmills: Palgrave Macmillan, 2004).

Lesnik-Oberstein, K., *On Having an Own Child: Reproductive Technologies and the Cultural Construction of Childhood* (London: Karnac, 2008).

Matless, D., *Landscape and Englishness* (London: Reaktion Books, 1998).

Munt, S., *Queer Attachments: The Cultural Politics of Shame* (Aldershot: Ashgate, 2007).

Pilcher, J. and S. Wagg (eds), *Thatcher's Children? Politics, Childhood and Society in the 1980s and 1990s* (London: The Falmer Press, 1996).

Qvortrup, J. (ed.), *Studies in Modern Childhood: Society, Agency, Culture* (Houndmills: Palgrave Macmillan, 2005).

Qvortrup, J., W. A. Corsaro, and M. Honig (eds), *The Palgrave Handbook of Childhood Studies* (Houndmills: Palgrave Macmillan, 2009).

Rose, J., *The Case of Peter Pan or the Impossibility of Children's Fiction* (London: Palgrave Macmillan, 1984).

Rose, J., *Sexuality in the Field of Vision* (London: Verso, 1986).

Rousseau, J.-J., *Emile*, trans. B. Foxley (London: J. M. Dent & Sons, 1989).

Sofaer Derevenski, J. (ed), *Children and Material Culture* (London: Routledge, 2000).

Stainton Rogers R. and W. Stainton-Rogers, *Stories of Childhood: Shifting Agendas of Child Concern* (Hemel Hempstead: Harvester Wheatsheaf, 1992).

Steedman, C., *Strange Dislocations: Childhood and the Idea of Human Interiority, 1780–1930* (Cambridge, MA: Harvard University Press, 1995).

Steedman, C., C. Urwin, and V. Walkerdine (eds), *Language, Gender and Childhood* (London: Routledge & Kegan Paul, 1985).

Walkerdine,V., *Schoolgirl Fictions* (London: Verso, 1990).

Walkerdine, V., *Daddy's Girl: Young Girls and Popular Culture* (London: Palgrave Macmillan, 1997).

Walkerdine, V., *Counting Girls Out: Girls and Mathematics* (Abingdon: FalmerRoutledge, 1998 [new edition]).

Walsh, S., *Kipling's Children's Literature: Language, Identity and Constructions of Childhood* (Farnham: Ashgate, 2010).

Warwick, I., R. Goodrich, P. Aggleton, and E. Chase, 'Homophobic Bullying and Schools – Responding to the Challenge', *Youth and Policy*, 91, 2006, 59–73.

Weare, K. and G. Gray, *What Works in Developing Children's Emotional and Social Competence and Wellbeing?*, Research Report no. 456 (London: DfES, 2003).

Zelizer, V., *Pricing the Priceless Child: The Changing Social Value of Children* (New York: Basic Books, 1985, republished with a new preface by Princeton University Press, 1994).

Index